# Contingent Employment in Europe and the United States

# Contingent Employment in Europe and the United States

*Edited by*

Ola Bergström

*Assistant Professor in Business Administration, School of Economics and Commercial Law, Göteborg University, Sweden*

*and*

Donald Storrie

*Senior Lecturer in Economics and Social Policy and Director, Centre for European Labour Market Studies (CELMS), School of Economics and Commercial Law, Göteborg University, Sweden*

**Edward Elgar**

Cheltenham, UK • Northampton, MA, USA

Published by
Edward Elgar Publishing Limited
Glensanda House
Montpellier Parade
Cheltenham
Glos GL50 1UA
UK

Edward Elgar Publishing, Inc.
136 West Street
Suite 202
Northampton
Massachusetts 01060
USA

A catalogue record for this book
is available from the British Library

**Library of Congress Cataloguing in Publication Data**

Contingent employment in Europe and the United States/edited by Ola
Bergström and Donald Storrie.
p. cm.
Includes bibliographical references.
1. Contracting out—Europe. 2. Temporary employees—Europe. 3. Labor market—Europe. 4. Contracting out—United States. 5. Temporary employees—United States. 6. Labor market—United States. I. Bergström, Ola II. Storrie, Donald W.

HD2365.C657 2003
331.5′42′094—dc21 2003044096

ISBN 1 84376 033 9

Printed and bound in Great Britain by MPG Books Ltd, Bodmin, Cornwall

# Contents

# Figures

# Tables

# Contributors

**Ola Bergström** is an assistant professor in business administration at the School of Economics and Commercial Law, Gothenburg University, Sweden.

**Surhan Cam** is a research officer at the Employment Studies Research Centre, Bristol Business School, UK.

**Rebecca Ellis** is Professor of Human Resource Management at California Polytechnic State University, San Luis Obispo, USA.

**Doug Glasgow** is a lecturer in business and employment law at California Polytechnic State University, San Luis Obispo, USA.

**Kay McGlashan** is an assistant professor of human resource management at Southwest Texas State University, USA.

**Bas Koene** is an assistant professor in the Department of Business and Organization of Rotterdam School of Economics, Erasmus University, Rotterdam, the Netherlands.

**Jaap Paauwe** is Professor of Business and Organization at the Rotterdam School of Economics, Erasmus University, Rotterdam, the Netherlands and research fellow of the Erasmus Research Institute for Management (ERIM).

**Manuel Pérez Pérez** is Professor of Labour Law at Seville University, Spain.

**Thomas Peuntner** was formerly a scientific assistant in the Human Resource Department of the Faculty of Management, University of Mannheim, Germany. Since November 2001 he has been assistant to the Head of Human Resources of the BASF Group, Ludwigshafen, Germany.

**Ferrie Pot** is a researcher at the Dutch court of audit, The Hague, the Netherlands.

**John Purcell** is Professor of Human Resource Management at the University of Bath, UK.

**Donald Storrie** is Senior Lecturer in economics and social policy and Director of the Centre for European Labour Market Studies (CELMS) at the School of Economics and Commercial Law, Gothenburg University, Sweden.

**Stephanie Tailby** is principal lecturer in Industrial Relations at Bristol Business School, UK.

# Preface

This volume is concerned with labour market developments in advanced economies in the 21st century, in particular as regards the use of contingent employment. Contingent employment is here defined as an *employment relationship that, from the point of view of the user, can be terminated with minimal costs within a predetermined period of time.* The aim of this volume is to comment on the increasing use of contingent employment in several advanced economies and to assess the impact of labour market regulation and institutional frameworks. We also wish to help policy makers at the European, national and regional levels to understand these developments and to assist them in policy formation and the design of more effective legislation. Furthermore, our aim is to support labour market actors, such as trade unions and employers' associations, in their policy making. The comparative analysis in this volume is based on data collected by an international group of researchers in an EU-financed project, 'New Understanding of European Work Organization' (NUEWO). We gratefully acknowledge SALTSA, RALF, Malmstensfonden and the European Union (5th framework, Improving the Socio-economic Knowledge Base) for the financial support for this project. This volume is the first attempt to draw conclusions from the national reports from this project.

O.B.
D.S.

# 1. Introduction

**Ola Bergström**

The increasing use of contingent employment has caused extensive writing and debate among academics and practitioners in recent years. The concept 'contingent employment' stems from the US term, 'contingent work'. We have chosen to use this term not only because of the lack of agreement in the European literature, but also because it gives an opportunity to take a broader perspective of the phenomenon. 'Contingent employment' is here used as a unifying concept for all types of employment contracts or work arrangements *that, from the point of view of the user, could be terminated with minimal costs within a predetermined period of time*. This includes employees working on limited duration contracts (LDCs) or working through temporary work agencies (TWAs).[1]

Commentators have argued that these work arrangements should increase the flexibility of labour markets and enable firms to adjust to changes in the business environment (de Roos *et al.*, 1998; Philpott, 1999). As a result, they predict that organizations will adopt new work practices or organizational forms, such as core–periphery structures (Atkinson, 1984). Commentators also claim that temporary work agencies will facilitate entry in the labour market for the unemployed and create better opportunities for job growth and employment (de Roos *et al.*, 1998; Levine, 1999). Temporary work agencies are also said to favour job matching for both employers and job seekers (de Roos *et al.*, 1998). Likewise, many claim that these employment relationships have several inherent problems. Most contingent workers have lower wages compared to permanent workers, they experience income insecurity, worse working conditions and get fewer training opportunities. Above all, contingent workers tend to have more difficulties in influencing their working conditions and it is difficult for them to get support from trade unions.

Of course, the use of contingent labour is not a new phenomenon, but the way in which these people are being used, and the magnitude of their use, are new (Gannon, 1996). It is only within the last decade that the incidence and growth of contingent employment has spread to new sectors and occupations in most advanced economies. Governments are adjusting their legal frameworks in order to respond to this development (Purcell and

Purcell, 1998). In Europe the interest in contingent employment is further intensified by the European Commission's initiation of negotiations between social partners for EU-level agreements on fixed-term contracts (Vigneau, 1999) and temporary work agencies (EIRO, 2000).[2] Moreover, although the interest in temporary work agencies is growing in the media, popular press and academic literature and the temporary work industry is expanding, temporary work agencies were not legally accepted prior to 1992 in several European countries (Storrie, 2002). In short, because researchers have had little time to study the implications of contingent employment, most discussions of how the use of contingent labour affects the function of labour markets are, at best, still speculative. Therefore it is not easy to come to any clear conclusions about whether these employment relationships should be facilitated or inhibited.

## PREVIOUS STUDIES

There is an emerging academic literature on the implications of labour market regulations on the use of contingent employment. Most of the discussions, in both the academic and the popular literature, however, suffer from three main problems that make it difficult to reach easy conclusions. First, authors refer to similar phenomena with a wide range of terms. For example, terms for contingent employment relations include temporary work, temp work (Klein, 1999), flexible work, fixed-term contracts (Clauwaert, 1998), non-standard work (Blanpain and Biagi, 1999), alternative work arrangements (Barker and Christensen, 1998), atypical forms of work (Bielenski and Köhler, 1999), precarious work (Benavides and Benach, 1999), insecure work (Heery and Salmon, 2000) or market-based employment relationships (Cappelli, 1999).

Second, independent of scope or approach many studies suffer from what may be referred to as a 'national myopia'. The explanations provided are dependent on the specific national labour market policies and their regulatory frameworks.[3] Furthermore, as comparative studies of contingent labour have shown, there are considerable differences between countries in terms of regulation on the use of contingent employment (OECD, 1993; 1996; 1999). The national differences mean that the results of national studies are difficult to translate into policy recommendations in other countries. Comparative studies offer a valuable opportunity to discover the role played by laws, collective bargaining structures and labour market institutions that differ across countries in affecting contingent employment. Moreover, as Leonard (1996) points out, the apparent national differences are sometimes artefacts of differences in measurement across nations.

The legal differences make statistical comparisons difficult. National statistics mirror categories given by national laws. This means that single country studies use different types of data, time periods and definitions. It is not uncommon for comparability to be lost because of the limited availability of statistics in certain areas or time periods. Given the important differences in definitions and regulations of contingent employment across OECD countries, cross-country comparisons of the incidence of contingent employment are hazardous (OECD, 1996). Thus the lack of commonly agreed definitions is an important problem. Another problem with comparative studies is that they are often shallow. They entail the difficulty that the depth of analysis of country studies must be maintained, while at the same time the multiple dimensions of the varying country of employment systems should be made more explicit (Rogowski and Schömann, 1996). Owing to the historical evolution of systems of employment, some functional equivalents in one country may not be considered valid equivalents in another country, and hence detailed country studies will have little to offer for comparative evaluations.

The problem of shallowness of comparative studies often leads to studies that are limited in terms of the number of countries studied. A problem with these limited studies is that they may give a somewhat biased comparison, favouring one system, social context or regulatory framework rather than the other. This type of *home-blindness* tendency to evaluate others on the basis of one's own system may only be corrected by more general theoretical reasoning. As Gannon and Nollen (1997) point out, developing a theoretical framework would give opportunity to compare national differences not favouring one or the other national policy or approach.

Third, the impact of labour market regulation on contingent employment is not clear. On the surface there seems to be a relationship between the use of contingent employment and the strength of regulation of contingent employment (OECD, 1999). But the particular dynamics and interrelationships between different types of regulation are not well known. For example, what is the impact of employment protection regulation and the various forms of regulations of different forms of contingent employment (TWAs and LDCs)? Is there a causal relationship between legislation and the use of contingent employment or are there intermediate factors affecting how labour law is used and interpreted? Furthermore, some forms of deregulation may, because of the surrounding institutional environment, have effects that run counter to the aim of flexibilization and job stimulation. What is the impact of the institutional framework, the enforcement of the laws and the risks associated with violating the law? Moreover, regulations may reinforce rather than solve problems that they aim to prevent.

It may be argued that policy makers are mistaken if they assume that an extra dose of deregulation will automatically translate into an extra dose of flexibility. They are equally mistaken if they assume that a given deregulatory practice that works in one country can be made to work similarly in another. As Esping-Andersen (2000) notes, deregulatory policies may, paradoxically, have the perverse effect of strengthening other rigidities. It is difficult to know with certainty what needs to be reformed or deregulated.

In order to answer these questions a comparison of the use of contingent employment and the legal framework in several countries is needed. The comparison of national legal frameworks needs to be complemented by qualitative analyses of the institutional framework of each particular country. This means considering other forms of regulatory institutions affecting the employment relationship, such as codetermination, collective bargaining and social security systems guaranteeing a steady income stream against risks (Schmid, 1994). Moreover, a myriad of individual habits, values and preferences, group routines and norms have to be taken into account. Habitual, routine and imitative behaviour is, according to Schmid (1994), the reason why even identical formal rules of the game might be played quite differently and different formal rules might end with the same results. To the extent that these norms and values affect individual expectations of the continuation of the employment relationship they may also have an impact on the way regulatory regimes are played out in practice. Thus the use of contingent employment may be influenced by other institutional arrangements than statutory law.

In order to address these issues, this volume will focus on the following questions:

- *What are the driving forces for the use of contingent employment?*
- *How are contingent employment relationships regulated?*
- *How are institutional frameworks affecting the use of contingent employment?*

## A COMPARATIVE APPROACH

We have chosen to compare the development of contingent employment in five European countries (Sweden, the Netherlands, the UK, Spain and Germany). The European countries are also compared with the development in the USA. The selection of countries for investigation is based on the fact that there are important differences in labour market traditions, legislation, industry structure and trade union membership, possibly affecting the use of contingent labour. We aimed at covering the different regulatory regimes of labour market regulation: the Continental countries, the Anglophone countries, the Scandinavian countries and the Netherlands (Storrie, 2002). We also wanted to compare developments and consequences of contingent employment in Europe to those in the USA, where contingent employment has been least regulated. Furthermore, the countries studied cover what Ronen and Shenkar (1985) refer to as the various cultural clusters in the European continent: the Germanic cluster, the Anglo cluster, the Latin European cluster and the Nordic cluster. This does not mean that the results may be generalized to other countries in these respective cultural clusters or regulatory regimes, rather that the results represent some of the divergence and variation that exist within the European Union. This study could thus function as a background and inspiration for both broader comparative studies and also more detailed analyses.

This study relies on an interdisciplinary and international group of researchers from six countries: Spain, Sweden, Germany, the UK, the Netherlands and the USA. The researchers cooperate in a project, 'New Understanding of European Work Organization' (NUEWO), financed within the EU: Key Action Improving the Socio-economic Knowledge Base. Each participant is expert in his or her respective fields of study, varying from sociology, law and economics to human resource management and business administration. Thus the study is an example of both cross-disciplinary and cross-country research. The analysis was conducted in meetings where comparisons of the national data took place.

## NATURE OF THE EVIDENCE

Although it is possible to draw conclusions about the impact of labour market regulation on the use of contingent employment, it is difficult to interpret the data with clarity. Several researchers have in recent years collected indications of the changing nature of employment relations. There are a great number of statistical sources but their use in providing good estimates for the development of contingent employment is limited (McLean Parks *et al.*, 1998). This is partly due to the difficulty of creating satisfactory definitions of contingent work (see, for example, Polivka, 1996a). There are no official definitions of contingent and non-standard employment (Rosenberg and Lapidus, 1999). An additional problem is created in attempting to draw comparisons between the labour market characteristics of different countries owing to the variation in employment definitions, terminology and varied regulations that exist (International Labour Office, 1989; Schömann *et al.*, 1998). There are many employment arrangements that might be considered temporary and their relative importance can differ across institutional and policy settings (OECD, 1996). The nature of the alternative work arrangements (temp, independent contractor and so on) and differences related to labour market traditions and industry variation may cause difficulties in drawing generalizations across types of contingent work (McLean Parks *et al.*, 1998).

Maybe the most comprehensive studies of contingent employment have been conducted by the US Bureau of Labor Statistics (BLS).[4] The result of the BLS researchers' efforts to find more 'effective measures' of contingent employment was, what could be called, a 'bottom up' definition of contingent workers: *individuals who do not perceive themselves as having an explicit or implicit contract for continuing employment.* Based on this definition, a special survey of contingent and alternative arrangements was conducted as a supplement to the 1995 Current Population Survey (CPS), a survey of households that is a primary source of information on the American workforce. Since then similar studies have been made every second year. These efforts have certainly raised the awareness and the level of discussion regarding contingent employment in the US context.

In Europe, similar efforts are non-existent. Instead most studies of contingent employment in Europe use national Labour Force Survey data, allowing measurement and analysis of the distribution of various forms of temporary work. This type of data is based on self-reports and basically asks individuals what type of contractual relationship they have (limited duration contract, self-employment and so on). There are individual surveys, for example Burchell *et al.* (1999), which use a similar approach to that of the US BLS surveys; however, they are limited in scope and not as extensive and systematic as the US studies. Lacking similar statistics in most European countries, we have tried to find an estimate of contingent employment in the European context. Alternatively, contingent employment may be defined as *an employment relationship that could be terminated with minimal costs within a predetermined time from the point of view of the employer*. This definition includes all types of contractual relationships that both parties may regard as limited in time: limited duration contracts, temporary agency work and self-employment. Compared to the BLS definition of contingent work, this definition is broader (Blank, 1998) and more relevant when comparing developments in the European labour markets, in particular in terms of evaluating the impact of labour market regulation. Thus, in order to be able to compare the development in Europe with that of the USA, we use the term 'contingent employment' for what in the US context is generally referred to as 'alternative work arrangements'.

The study started by investigating the developments and trends in the use of contingent employment in each country. Data collection was structured according to a common general framework applied in each country. Data were collected from national labour force surveys in the respective countries.

The goal was to compare developments over a 10-year period (1990–2000). Data included general employment trends, unemployment, the use of contingent employment, distribution in various industries and types of contracts, and the composition of the contingent workforce by gender, age, education and ethnicity. We also collected data from previous studies investigating employers' use of contingent employment in terms of reasons for use and consequences for individuals, such as health, security and training.

Comparing the data, we sorted out the variables that appeared to be relevant to explain the use of contingent employment. We compared data concerning unemployment and the use of contingent employment in six countries over the 10-year period, 1990–2000. This means that, when data were available, we were able to compare the development of the use of contingent employment with that of unemployment and changes in regulation and the institutional frameworks, which makes our study different from other studies in the same field. The most complete study – OECD (1999) – compares a great number of countries and it also compares the impact of regulation at two points in time, late 1980s and late 1990s. Furthermore, the evolution of the institutional framework and legislation of each country was described. The comparison of regulatory frameworks was made on three dimensions: statutory laws regulating the employment relationship, the enforcement of the laws and the consequences for the employer if the law is enforced. It should be noted that we did not conduct formal testing of the relationship between the identified variables. Given the type of data available in this context, such an analysis would probably oversimplify the highly complex relationships between regulation, institutional frameworks and the use of contingent employment. Instead our analysis should be regarded as a tentative first step in developing questions and hypotheses for further analysis to be conducted at a later stage.

## A CONCEPTUAL FRAMEWORK

The study is based on a common conceptual framework for contingent employment. Three significant actors closely related to the concept of contingent employment were identified: the employee, the user and the intermediary. In this section these concepts will be defined in more detail.

### The Employee

The employee is the individual who conducts work under conditions that are regulated in a way that may be defined as contingent employment. The contingent employment relationship is a work relationship in which the employee works for a user of contingent employment for a limited time, after which the user has no responsibilities towards the employee anymore. Contingent employment relationships can take various forms. Not all those who regard themselves as temporary workers are in fact, in legal terms, occupying temporary jobs (Casey *et al.*, 1989). Similarly, not all people who hold temporary jobs regard themselves as temporary workers. In many cases there are social relations between employer and employee, implying that the individual expects another contract when the temporary contract has expired. Thus one needs to consider the individual's subjective definition of the character of the employment relationship (McLean Parks *et al.*, 1998). Furthermore, different types of contractual relationships can be distinguished. Contingent workers can be employed by the user of their labour on a temporary contract basis, they can also work through an agency or other type of intermediary, or they can be self-employed (Purcell and Purcell, 1998, p. 44). In the following we will use the abbreviation LDC for limited duration contracts, TAW for workers mediated or employed by temporary work agencies and TWA when we refer to the agencies themselves. However, when we refer to studies where other concepts are used we will use the concepts of the original studies.

### The User

The term 'user' refers to the actor in the contingent employment relationship who is the user of contingent labour. The user is the actor with a demand for work to be conducted. The term refers to all 'users' of contingent labour, regardless of ownership (private or public) or purpose (non-profit organization or profit-maximizing firm). Users are the buyers of contingent labour but they do not always exclusively hold the employers' responsibility. This rests with the employee when he or she is self-employed, or with an intermediary if the employee is hired through an agency or a consultancy firm. However, the employee is working under the user's supervision and guidance, as opposed to being in a subcontracting relationship (Blanpain, 1993). Thus the term 'employer' is problematic and inadequate to describe the function of the user of contingent labour. It is important to distinguish between the user as an employer and the purposes and interests connected with this role, and the user as an actor engaging in a market relationship, that is, as an agent in the labour market.

### The Intermediary

The introduction of intermediaries in the labour market means that the employment relationship takes the form of a three-party relationship (see

Figure 1.1). There is no common agreement on what to call this intermediate actor. In Convention 181 (Convention on Private Employment Agencies), the International Labour Organisation (ILO) defines intermediaries as 'Services consisting of employing workers with a view to making them available to a third party . . . which assigns them their tasks and supervises the execution of these tasks.' This definition is also put forward by the International Confederation of Temporary Work Businesses (CIETT) (de Roos *et al.*, 1998). Blanpain (1993) uses the term 'temporary work firm'. We use the term *temporary work agency (TWA)*, which we define as an *intermediary in the labour market that provides both the individual and the user with the services of matching supply and demand of labour and risk diversification.*

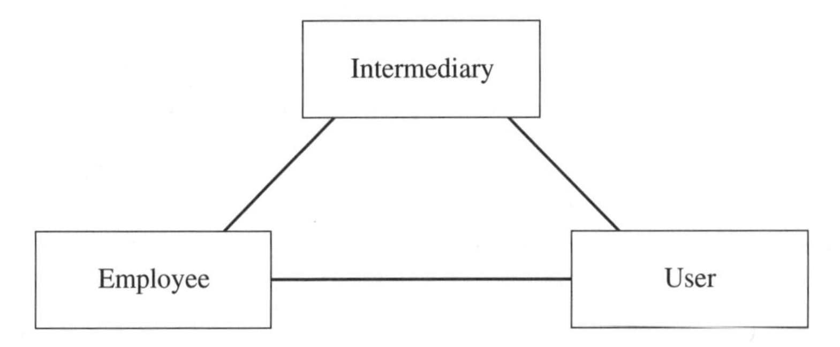


*Figure 1.1 The main actors of contingent employment*

This definition highlights the fact that the temporary work agency provides the service of job matching and risk diversification to both parties in the contingent employment relationship. Furthermore, it distinguishes TWAs from placement agencies, which provide the service of matching seller and buyer, but not of engaging in any employment relationship with the individual. It also distinguishes them from subcontractors, where the employers and employees may regard their relationship as permanent, while selling services to the user on a permanent or temporary basis (Nesheim, 1997). It should be noted that intermediaries are not always included in contingent employment relations (as in the case of a direct LDC between employee and user). In fact, in most cases they are not. However, we regard TWAs as important catalysts in the development of the labour market. In their role as labour market intermediaries they may help to solve some of the negative consequences of contingent employment, for example by providing opportunities for risk diversification. These possible functions in the labour market will be discussed further in Chapter 2.

## THE STRUCTURE OF THIS BOOK

To create a better understanding of the implications of labour market regulations for the use of contingent employment, we will begin by discussing the nature of contingent employment and the different forms of regulation that apply to its use. In Chapters 3 to 8 we go on to compare the use of contingent employment and the institutional framework in five European countries and the United States. By 'institutional frameworks' we mean not only the statutory regulations affecting the use of contingent employment, but also the national industrial relations context, collective bargaining procedures and other labour market institutions.

This highlights two characteristics of the use of contingent employment, which are summarized and discussed in Chapter 9. First, the use of contingent employment varies considerably among the different countries studied, but there are some features common to all countries in the study. Second, the statutory regulations of contingent employment in the European countries are rarely designed on the basis of the nature of contingent employment. Instead they are a result of institutional blockage, favouring insiders rather than outsiders. Regulatory frameworks are only partially reformed. In this instance it is valuable to compare this with the US case. We find that, despite the various efforts to control and limit the use of contingent employment in the countries studied, the problematic features of contingent employment still exist. We argue that temporary work agencies limit some of the problems of limited duration contracts and that they have a particular function in the labour market that may be facilitated. However, we find that the efforts by various European countries to limit and control the use of TWAs are contradictory and that they are most often not taking into account the difference between regarding a TWA as a form of employment and regarding it as an industry with specific functions in the labour market that should be treated like any other industry. This distinction, we believe, is important in identifying labour market policies in trying to limit or facilitate the use of temporary work agencies in any labour market context.

## NOTES

1. In this definition we do not include part-time work or self-employment, since these contracts and employment relationships are not necessarily limited in time. Both part-time employment and self-employment are increasing in most advanced labour markets and their character is similar to other forms of contingent employment in our definition. However, in this study we do not discuss these forms of employment explicitly.
2. As we are writing, the European Commission has distributed a Proposal for a Directive

of the European Parliament and the Council on working conditions for temporary workers, owing to the failure of the previously initiated negotiations between the social partners.
3. According to Rogowski and Schömann (1996), there are several advantages of country-specific evaluations. However, an evaluation of parts of a legal system that treats law only as an external reference without its own dynamics adopts a static view of law and thereby overlooks the fact that legislation is itself not stable, but is continuously changed by amendments, collective agreements or judicial interpretations (ibid.). Thus a combination of national studies and comparative analysis would be preferable.
4. Dissatisfaction with the statistics of the national labour force survey to measure recent developments in the US labour market, in particular the permanence of the employment relationship, led the BLS to sponsor a substantial effort to develop estimates to measure the permanence of employment relationships in the US labour market in 1995. The major criticism against previous estimates was that data on part-time jobs, self-employment or jobs in certain industries did not automatically qualify as 'contingent', since they were not necessarily jobs which lacked permanence (Cohany *et al.*, 1998). Previous studies were also criticized because the categories used were not mutually exclusive, so that double and even triple countings of the same people could occur. Furthermore, Cohany *et al.* claimed that some jobs that were clearly temporary did not fit into any of those categories, such as when workers are hired directly by a firm to fill a temporary position.

## REFERENCES

Atkinson, J. (1984) 'Manpower Strategies for Flexible Organizations', *Personnel Management*, August.

Barker, K. and K. Christensen (eds) (1998) *Contingent Work: American Employment Relations in Transition*, Ithaca, NY: ILR/Cornell University Press.

Benavides, F.G. and J. Benach (1999) *Precarious Employment and Health-Related Outcomes in the European Union*, Dublin: European Foundation for the Improvement of Living and Working Conditions.

Bielenski, H. and E. Köhler (1999) 'Atypical forms of work in the European Union: Experiences at the Establishment level', in I.U. Zeytinoglu (ed.), *Changing Work Relationships in Industrialized Economies*, Amsterdam: John Benjamins Publishing Company.

Blank, R.M. (1998) 'Contingent Work in a Changing Labour Market', in R.B. Freeman and P. Gottschalk (eds), *Generating Jobs, How to Increase Demand for Less-Skilled Workers*, New York: Russell Sage Foundation.

Blanpain, R. (1993) *Temporary Work and Labour Law of the European Community and Member States*, Deventer: Kluwer Law and Taxation Publishers.

Blanpain, R. and M. Biagi (1999) *Non-Standard Work and Industrial Relations*, London: Kluwer Law International.

Burchell, B.J., D. Day, M. Hudon, D. Ladipo, R. Mankelow, J.P. Nolan, H. Reed, I.C. Wichert and F. Wilkinson (1999) *Job Insecurity and Work Intensification: Flexibility and the changing boundaries of work*, Cambridge: Joseph Rowntree Foundation.

Cappelli, P. (1999) *The New Deal at Work, Managing the Market-driven Workforce*, Boston: Harvard Business School Press.

Casey, B., R. Dragendorf, W. Heering and G. John (1989) 'Temporary employment in Great Britain and the Federal Republic of Germany', *International Labour Review*, 128(4).

Clauwaert, S. (1998) *Survey of Fixed Term Contracts*, Brussels: European Trade Union Institute.

Cohany, S.R., S.F. Hipple, T.J. Nardone, A.E. Polivka and J.C. Stewart (1998) 'Counting the Workers: Results of a First Survey', in K. Barker and K. Christensen (eds), *Contingent Work: American Employment Relations in Transition*, Ithaca, NY: ILR/Cornell University Press.

de Roos, H.J., E.M. Zoetmulder, M. Huybregts and H. Haveman (1998) *Temporary Work Businesses in the Countries of the European Union*, Diemen: Bakkenist Management Consultants.

EIRO (2000) *A Review of Developments in European Industrial Relations*, European Industrial Relations Observatory, Annual Review, Dublin: European Foundation for the Improvement of Living and Working Conditions.

Esping-Andersen, G. (2000) 'Who is Harmed by Labour Market Regulations? Quantitative Evidence', in G. Esping-Andersen and M. Regini (eds), *Why Deregulate Labour Markets?*, Oxford: Oxford University Press.

Gannon, M. (1996) 'Managing Without a Complete, Full-time Workforce', in P.C. Flood, M.J. Gannon and J. Paauwe (eds), *Managing Without Traditional Methods, International Innovations, Human Resource Management*, New York: Addison-Wesley.

Gannon, M. and S. Nollen (1997) 'Contingent Labour: Understanding the Changing Employment Relationship', in J. Wallace, T. Dalzell and B. Delany (eds), *Continuity and Change in the Employment Relationship*, Vol. 1 of the Proceedings of the 5th European IIRA Conference, Dublin, Dublin: Oak Tree Press.

Heery, E. and J. Salmon (2000) *The Insecure Workforce*, London: Routledge.

International Labour Office (1989) *Conditions of Work Digest: Part-time Work*, vol. 8, Geneva: International Labour Organisation.

Klein, N. (1999) *No Logo*, New York: Picador.

Leonard, J.S. (1996) 'Institutional Influences on Job and Labour Turnover', in R. Schettkatt (ed.), *The Flow Analysis of Labour Markets*, London: Routledge.

Levine, L. (1999) *Temporary Workers as Members of the Contingent Labour Force*, CRS Report for Congress, 16 February.

McLean Parks, J., D.L. Kidder and D.G. Gallagher (1998) 'Fitting square pegs into round holes: Mapping the domain of contingent work arrangements onto the psychological contract', *Journal of Organizational Behavior*, 19, 697–730.

Nesheim, T. (1997) *Mot externalisering av arbeid? Analyser av tilknytningsformer for arbeid*, SNF-rapport 35/97, Bergen.

OECD (1993) *Employment Outlook*, Paris: Organization for Economic Co-operation and Development.

OECD (1996) *Employment Outlook*, Paris: Organization for Economic Co-operation and Development.

OECD (1999) *Employment Outlook*, Paris: Organization for Economic Co-operation and Development.

Philpott, J. (1999) 'Temporary Jobs, Constant Opportunity? Flexibility, Fairness and the Role of Employment Agencies', *Economic Report*, 14(3), Employment Policy Institute, London.

Polivka, A.E. (1996a) 'Contingent and Alternative Work Arrangements, Defined', *Monthly Labor Review*, 119, 3–9.

Polivka, A.E. (1996b) 'A profile of contingent workers', *Monthly Labor Review*, 119, 10–21.

Purcell, K. and J. Purcell (1998) 'In-sourcing, outsourcing and the growth of the contingent labour as evidence of flexible employment strategies', *European Journal of Work and Organizational Psychology*, 7(1), 39–59.

Rogowski, R. and G. Schömann (1996) 'Legal Regulation and Flexibility of Employment Contracts', in G. Schmid, J. O'Reilly and K. Schömann (eds), *International Handbook of Labour Market Policy and Evaluation*, Cheltenham, UK and Lyme, US: Edward Elgar, pp. 623–51.

Ronen, S. and O. Shenkar (1985) 'Clustering Countries on Attitudinal Dimensions: A Review and Synthesis', *Academy of Management Journal*, September, 435–54.

Rosenberg, S. and J. Lapidus (1999) 'Contingent and Non-Standard Work in the United States: Towards a More Poorly Compensated, Insecure Workforce', in A. Felstead and N. Jewson (eds), *Global Trends in Flexible Labour*, London: Macmillan Business.

Schmid, G. (ed.) (1994) *Labour Market Institutions in Europe, A Socioeconomic Evaluation of Performance*, New York: M.E. Sharpe.

Schömann, K., R. Rogowski and T. Kruppe (1998) *Labour Market Efficiency in the European Union, Employment Protection and Fixed-Term Contracts*, London: Routledge.

Storrie, D. (2002) *Temporary Agency Work in the European Union*, Dublin: European Foundation for the Improvement of Living and Working Conditions.

Vigneau, C. (1999) 'The principle of equal treatment of temporary and permanent workers', in C. Vigneau, K. Ahlberg, B. Bercusson and N. Bruun (eds), *Fixed-term Work in the EU, A European Agreement Against Discrimination and Abuse*, Stockholm: National Institute for Working Life.

# 2. Beyond atypicality

**Ola Bergström**[1]

There is no such thing as a common form of contingent employment. Legal definitions vary among countries. The phenomenon is labelled differently, depending on the perspective from which it is regarded: from the point of view of employers, workers, trade unions, governments and so on. Moreover, in academic literature the phenomenon is characterized in different ways according to the disciplinary perspective of the author. However, the most common element regarding contingent employment is that it is often referred to as different, atypical, alternative or non-standard. This chapter takes the view that contingent employment has its own character that should be understood in its own terms. Classifying contingent workers as atypical may be accurate considering the incidence in the labour market, but the classification of workers as atypical also has social consequences. Contingent workers are often regarded as having less value and in practice they are often provided with worse working conditions, salaries and benefits. They also have fewer opportunities to influence, affect working conditions and have their voice heard. Thus the classification of workers as atypical has effects on the way contingent workers are treated in workplaces, among co-workers, by trade unions and in labour law. Therefore there is a need to look for new ways of conceptualizing contingent employment beyond atypicality.

Contingent employment relationships are different from traditional employment relationships in at least two ways. First, contingent employment relationships mean that both parties regard their relationship as temporary. There may be implicit expectations among the parties of a long-term relationship, but in principle there are no formal grounds for a continuing relationship. Second, contingent employment relationships imply that risks and responsibilities are distributed among the participating parties in different ways from what is generally the case in standard open-ended employment relationships. This may vary according to the type of contingent labour; that is, whether it is limited duration contract or temporary agency work. In limited duration contracts the employer has much of the managerial responsibility. In the case of temporary agency work the responsibility and risk are shared among the three parties. In short, in contingent employment relationships, managerial work is organized through a horizontal division of labour – managerial responsibilities are distributed among the parties in the employment relationship.

These two features imply that contingent employment may have a certain function in the labour market, distinct from other forms of employment. It also means that contingent workers are exposed to problems different from those of other workers. Furthermore, these features mean that contingent employment relationships are difficult to control and regulate. This chapter will discuss the nature of contingent employment. First, it will outline the problems and conflicts associated with contingent employment often referred to in the literature. Second, it will describe the various forms of regulation used to limit the undesirable effects of contingent employment for workers and discuss the impact and the applicability of the different forms of regulation to the inherent conflicts in the contingent employment relationship. Third, it will review the most common arguments concerning the function of contingent employment in the labour market and suggest an alternative approach to conceptualizing that function which may be regarded as more suitable for both employers and workers. The chapter concludes by discussing the consequences of taking contingent employment beyond atypicality.

## CONTINGENT EMPLOYMENT: A NEXUS OF CONFLICTS

Given the widespread belief that contingent employment will somehow alter organizational forms and practices, research on the topic is surprisingly scarce. There are examples of studies exploring both positive and negative effects, with a slight dominance towards the former. Commentators claim that the use of flexible work arrangements is to the benefit of the organizations and is a strategic response to changes in the organizational environment (Atkinson, 1984; Wright and Snell, 1998). Rarely do these authors investigate whether organizations are really more flexible, cost-effective or competitive. The main idea of this literature can be reduced to three broad claims: the use of contingent employment will (1) increase firm flexibility and cost-effectiveness, (2) deteriorate quality of products and worker commitment, and (3) destroy hierarchies and create market-based employment relationships. A further discussion of these claims and the evidence available to support them can be found in Bergström (2001a).

Several studies show that contingent employment has spread into new occupational groups and sectors where the situation is less difficult for workers (Purcell and Purcell, 1998). However, there is no doubt that the most important consequences of contingent employment are on the individual level and it is also on this level that the problems are most difficult to deal with. It is no coincidence that it is the individual level that has attracted most research. The focus in this section is on the various negative effects of contingent employment and the conflicts that are (re-)emerging as an effect of the use of contingent employment. The emphasis is on how workers relate to their employer (the user of their labour), to their permanent co-workers and to other contingent workers.

**Wages and Benefits**

There is a widespread belief that contingent workers earn less than permanent workers (Gannon, 1996). However, there are few studies that are able to give straight answers on this point. Some scholars argue that contingent employment paves the way for increases in the earnings of workers (Sarfati and Korbin, 1988). Others believe that such a system would undermine employees' earnings (Rex, 1988). Summers (1997), for example, argues that the most serious problem of contingent employment from the employee point of view is discrimination in wages and benefits provided by the employer. Experiences from the American labour market suggest that the few benefits normally afforded to permanent employees by firms, such as medical insurance, paid holidays and paid sick leave, are not offered to contingent workers. Furthermore, the absence of unions gives the employer the bargaining power to dictate the terms of the contract, particularly for the unskilled and unemployed. However, this argument is limited to the conditions in the American labour market where employment benefits are not generally applied to all employees.

The lower wages of contingent workers may have important social consequences. Contingent employment may exacerbate insider bargaining power in wage formation and segmentation in labour markets by creating a pool of marginal labour (Bentolila and Dolado, 1994). Contingent employment is regarded as an unstable and insecure form of employment tending to reduce workers' bargaining position in relation to the employer. Thus the temporary nature of the contingent employment relationship affects the bargaining power of workers and as a result they get lower wages. It should be noted that contingent contracts in most countries are overrepresented in some segments of the labour market (women, young people, foreign workers and ethnic groups) and that they are often at a disadvantage because of lower wages, abuse by employers in relation to dismissal, working hours and so on, and little or no social security protection with respect to unemployment, retirement and invalidity (for example, Meulders and Tytgat, 1989). Thébaud-Mony (2001) claims that the increase of unskilled contingent work in France, in particular industrial cleaning where ethnic community men and women are working, is an example of a modern form of slave labour.

Working as a contingent worker means not only earning less; such workers also endure a higher level of income insecurity (Belous, 1997). Switching between jobs often means that there are periods of unemployment. The individual is pressed to get another job in order to secure a stable income. This means that contingent workers experience greater levels of insecurity and also, as in the case of Sweden, may have difficulties with other things, such as getting bankloans and renting apartments (Aronsson *et al.*, 2000; Clauwaert, 1998). Belous (1997) argues that nations with more advanced social welfare systems may be in a better position to obtain the benefits from contingent employment practices, and that the USA may be at a competitive disadvantage. However, as Greiner (2000) points out, social insurance systems installed to protect workers with atypical jobs from income fluctuations may also help these employment patterns to arise and develop. From this point of view the welfare systems may lead employers to encourage contingent employment at the expense of standard forms of employment. Thus previous studies support the view that the wage level and income stability of contingent workers are generally low, but measures to protect these workers from income insecurity may contribute to making contingent employment a permanent condition.

**Health and Safety**

In a recent study of 'precarious' employment and health-related outcomes in the European Union (Benavides and Benach, 1999), it was found that workers in precarious employment were more likely to report dissatisfaction but less likely to report stress in comparison to workers with open-ended contracts. The findings suggest that different types of employment have an independent effect on the health-related outcomes studied regardless of working conditions. However, the authors emphasize that these results should be considered with caution, because of the relatively small size of some of the categories analysed. The European survey of working conditions also points to a statistically established link between insecure employment and more arduous working conditions: 57 per cent of temporary workers work in painful and tiring positions (compared to 42 per cent of permanent workers); 38 per cent are exposed to intense noise (against 29 per cent); 66 per cent perform repetitive movements (against 55 per cent) (Letourneux, 1998).

There are other results shedding light upon the relationship between contingent employment and health and safety issues. Contingent workers, because of their limited knowledge of the work site's practices and familiarity with its people and equipment, are also exposed to *higher personal risk of work-related accidents*, injuries and deaths than non-contingent workers (Rebitzer, 1998; Rousseau and Libuser, 1997). Demands on hygiene and safety may imply that employees need to be familiar with the workplace in order to be able to meet the requirements. In most countries there are rules concerning employer responsibility for work environment issues. However, they are difficult to enforce. In contingent employment relationships, questions regarding responsibility are in practice open to interpretation. This is why, for example, contingent employment relationships are regarded as a problem for trade unions in Sweden (Bergström, 2001b).

There are several reasons for this. According to Rebitzer, organizations do not provide contractors with adequate training and have tried to limit their liability for contract employee roles in accidents (Barker and Christensen, 1998, p. 16). Since temporary employees in many cases, in particular in the USA, do not have access to insurance systems and the like, there is also a risk that they miss opportunities to benefit from corporate health care programmes, social security and retirement income (Mangum *et al.*, 1985; Summers, 1997). Thus contingent employment may have important implications for the health and safety at work for the individual employee.

## Working Conditions and Psychological Well-being

A controversial issue in the context of contingent employment is the particular work conditions provided for workers and the effects on worker psychological well-being and family life. Sociologists (and psychologists) have extensively researched these issues since at least Jahoda *et al.* (1933) and, later, in Warr (1987) as important elements of sociopsychological well-being. The impact of flexible work patterns on sociopsychological well-being has been graphically described more recently in Sennet (1999). Maybe the best overview of the relationship between job insecurity and psychological well-being is provided by Nolan *et al.* (2000).

There are several aspects of the contingent employment relationship that may affect workers' psychological well-being. Perhaps the most distinguishing feature of contingent employment in this context is the fact that the worker may have to continually change workplaces (Isaksson and Bellaagh, 1999). This may have important consequences for the social life of the agency worker. Issues such as having workmates (both during and after working hours), working together for common goals, observing the fruit of one's labour materialize, experiencing support and receiving feedback from one's workmates, may be difficult for agency workers to realize. There is some evidence that individuals working as temporary employees are disengaged from *social relations* with other employees and, thus, are regarded as second-class or peripheral to permanent workers (Arvidsson, 1997; Rousseau, 1995; Rogers, 1995; Henson, 1996).

Furthermore, it has been argued that contingent employment leads to higher levels of stress, feelings of insecurity and less motivation for workers. Flexible work practices have allowed employers to rationalize working time but also forced a division between permanent and contingent workers who may have opposing interests in speeded-up working (Thébaud-Mony, 2001). The job insecurity assumed to be linked to contingent employment may not only affect the individual's psychological well-being – it may also have effects on issues in the individual's family life, such as marital functioning and parenting (Nolan *et al.*, 2000). However, the results are not clear. There have been mixed results when comparing contingent workers and permanent workers along attitudinal lines (McLean Parks *et al.*, 1998). Pearce (1993), for instance, found no difference in organizational commitment or cooperativeness between employees and independent contractors in a large US aerospace company. The level of 'voluntariness' in being in a contingent arrangement may have an impact on contingent employee attitudes such as job involvement and satisfaction (Krausz *et al.*, 1995; Ellingson *et al.*, 1998). As summarized in McLean Parks *et al.* (1998), Lee and Johnson (1991) found in a study of US National Park Service workers that voluntary temporary workers had higher levels of job satisfaction and organizational commitment than permanent and involuntary temporary workers. In the USA, Krausz *et al.* (1995) found that voluntary TWA employees had higher satisfaction levels than permanent employees or involuntary temps. Purcell *et al.* (2000) claim that coerced flexibility is unlikely to lead to organizational suppleness and, indeed, is probably impossible to achieve, whereas mutually agreed flexibility almost certainly reflects good organizational health and high trust relations. Thus the question of the voluntariness of working contingently may be crucial for individuals' attitude towards the working conditions of contingent employment (Ellingson *et al.*, 1998).

## Training Opportunities

Another problem with contingent employment is the level of training provided for this group of workers. It is often argued that contingent workers do not get access to the same training as permanent workers and as a result they risk being caught in an employment relationship where they have fewer possibilities for development. It is assumed that employers are much less likely to invest in training of these workers since they do not have expectations of a long-term relationship (Belous, 1997). This deskilling hypothesis is widespread and often studied. However, there is sometimes a problem in distinguishing between the low level of education, the interest in training among these workers and their access to training.

It is obvious that there may be problems in ensuring an adequate level of training of contingent workers. As the worker will only be at the user firm for a limited duration, one should hardly expect much training from the user firm. Here there may be an important difference between agency workers and other forms of contingent employment. It may be assumed that temporary agency workers would be provided with training by the temporary work agency. However, the levels of training for agency workers vary across Europe (CIETT, 2000). Here the problem can be framed in terms of human capital theory and in particular related to problems of the firm in securing a return on investment in general human capital (Gannon and Nollen, 1997; Autor, 2001b). As the function of TWA firms is to provide several user firms with labour, it is obvious that the skills provided are not firm-specific. Indeed, the concept of agency work is based on transferable skills traded in an occupational labour market. According to human capital theory, firms will not be prepared to pay fully for investment in non-firm-specific human capital as the investing firm cannot ensure a return on their investment since the worker is free to leave for another firm (Gannon and Nollen, 1997). The key element is that training investment is recovered only if the trained worker stays on the job or in the company long enough to pay it back (Gannon, 1996). The likelihood of temporary agency workers leaving the agency is higher than for most forms of employment and their assignments at user firms will provide ample opportunities for poaching.[2]

The lack of training provided for contingent workers is related to the responsibility distributed among the three parties in the contingent employment relationship. This is evident when the question of who should finance the training of the worker is discussed. In principle, there appear to be three solutions to the problem of financing training: the worker finances training; it is financed by the state or some other appropriate body; or TWAs are compensated for their investment in training if the worker leaves the TWA firm. While these three alternatives may, at first glance, appear unlikely, there is in fact some evidence that all three forms are used (Storrie, 2002).

### Influence and Representation

The temporary nature of the contingent employment relationship also implies that it is more difficult for contingent workers to influence working conditions and achieve equal treatment. Temporary workers are more difficult to organize and may have different objectives from permanent workers, making collective bargaining more complex and less legitimate for all members (Gjelsvik, 1998). Temporary workers do not have the time to develop channels and contacts to express themselves in the workplace. It is more difficult for temporary employees to express criticism and they also find that they are not heard when they do so (Aronsson and Göransson, 1998). Responsibility for expression of their interests is less determinable, as well as who has the responsibility to negotiate their rights. Contingent workers have little if any recourse if they are adversely affected by problems such as discrimination by race, gender, age or other prohibited categories, or sexual harassment or wrongful discharge (Gannon, 1996). The low membership of temporary workers in trade unions further actualizes this problem. There may also be conflicts regarding what particular trade union should represent the individual employee when he or she is crossing vocational borders.

Thus the temporary nature of contingent employment relations may counteract and limit the possibility of achieving equal treatment for contingent workers. Furthermore, the increasing use of contingent labour can represent a potent threat to both the security of existing (permanent) employees and the power of their unions (Heery and Abbot, 2000). How trade unions should respond to this threat is a controversial issue. On the one hand, trade unions could rebuild the security of existing permanent members, by excluding contingent workers from employment and perhaps also from union membership (ibid.). On the other hand, they could extend membership to contingent workers and try to influence the regulation of labour markets (ibid.). Thus the nature of the contingent employment relationship means that the problem of influence and representation for contingent workers remains.

## Discussion: Conflicts and Equal Treatment

Even if there are contingent workers who are well off in the labour market, most contingent workers are subject to worse conditions than their comparable counterparts. Previous studies suggest that they often have lower wages and benefits. Their health and safety protection is worse than that of other workers and they have less opportunity to influence their working conditions. Furthermore, they are often treated differently from permanent workers and they do not get the same opportunities for training and development. These problems are exacerbated by the fact that women, young people and ethnic minorities are often overrepresented in these types of employment relationships. This means that the growth of contingent employment highlights several intricate conflicts and problems in the labour market. It is argued that this trend has left many contingent workers in a worse situation than permanent ones, mainly because contingent employment is inconsistent with a means of calculating employment and social rights based on the standard employment relationship of indefinite duration (Vigneau, 1999).

It should be noted that the inferior working conditions combined with limited duration contracts (LDCs) occur, despite the fact that the principle of equal treatment is guaranteed by law in most of the EU member states (Clauwaert, 1998). There are directives for member states to ensure that LDC workers are afforded, as regards safety and health at work, the same level of protection as that of other workers in the user undertaking: that is, workers with open-ended contracts. This may involve issues such as access to personal protective equipment, provision of information, training, medical surveillance and so on. However, the principle of equal treatment is not easily applied to LDCs.[3] This may also be valid for temporary agency workers to the extent that they are not employed permanently with the agency.

Equal treatment requires the prohibition of all direct or indirect discrimination based on the temporary nature of the employment contract, but the principle of equal treatment is of a limited duration. The termination of the employment contract puts an end to its relevance. Once he or she is no longer an employee, the temporary worker falls into another category and his or her rights become completely different. As Vigneau *et al.* (1999) put it, the temporary nature of the employment contract constitutes its 'fundamental weakness' and the main difference between temporary and permanent workers. Thus, to achieve equal treatment for temporary workers certain conditions must prevail, which makes it very difficult to enforce the rights in practice.

## REGULATING CONTINGENT EMPLOYMENT

Contingent employment is a nexus of possible conflicting interests between employers and workers, unemployed and those who have employment, contingent workers and permanent workers. These conflicts have led to the initiation of several different types of regulation with the aim of limiting its undesirable effects. Often regulations have been a means of correcting unequal power of contingent workers, although many have been used to enhance the advantage of employers and insiders or to produce more stable labour supply. Some regulations have been intended to promote the use of contingent employment, in order to support employment and flexibility in the labour market, some to reduce exploitation of contingent workers and insecurity of permanent workers.

However, there are also those who argue that the problems of contingent employment may not be best dealt with by regulating the employment relationships. Instead they argue that labour markets should be deregulated as much as possible. From this point of view, any asymmetries or negative effects should be dealt with either by the employer's sense of social responsibility or by market forces. On the other hand, it may be argued that there is no such thing as a deregulated labour market. As Standing (1999) argues, no society could exist without modes of regulation and a regulatory framework. The relevant question is therefore how labour markets are regulated rather than whether they should be or not.

This section will describe various forms of regulation used to limit the undesirable effects of contingent employment, and will also discuss the impact and the applicability of the different forms of regulation on the inherent conflicts in the contingent employment relationship.

## Statutory Regulations

Statutory regulations are what many regard as the only form of regulation in the labour market. There are rules, procedures and institutions established by laws or decrees designed to set parameters of acceptable behaviour. They may be pro-collective or pro-individualistic, in that laws may give incentives to collective institutions or may set out to limit or control them. There are at least three different types of statutory regulation that may affect the use of contingent employment: regulation of open-ended contracts, limited duration contracts and temporary agency work.

### Regulation of open-ended contracts

The most common form of regulation is to presume that employment contracts are open-ended unless the employer explicitly states otherwise. There are also several regulations concerning how employment contracts should be agreed upon. Regulation of the standard employment contract also includes administrative procedures for individual notice and dismissal, required notice and severance pay, prescriptions under which individual dismissal is fair or unfair and compensation and remedies following unjustified dismissal (OECD, 1999). For example, dismissal is only allowed if the employer has a just cause, notice should be in written form and employers should pay the employee a salary for a certain number of months after contract termination. Furthermore, most countries have regulations defining the procedures and responsibilities if the law is violated.

The regulation of open-ended contracts affects not only the dismissal of workers holding such contracts but also the employer's willingness to hire new workers. In theory, strong regulation would lead employers to hesitate when hiring new employees on open-ended contracts. Instead, when there is uncertainty regarding both the duration of the job and the competence of the individual, employers may choose to hire on a temporary basis or a limited duration contract. Thus there may be a relationship between the regulation of open-ended contracts and the use of contingent employment.

**Regulation of LDCs**

Regulation of limited duration contracts serves the purpose of protecting the individual worker by providing minimum standards for the employment relationship. This includes measures to prevent abuse of LDCs, such as the maximum total duration of successive contracts, the number of renewals and specifications of objective reasons justifying renewal. The general idea is to prevent contingent employment from being a long-term relationship for these workers. Without such regulation, employers could circumvent notice and severance payment requirements by hiring workers on LDCs and repeatedly renewing these contracts (Houseman, 1997). There are also examples of rules aimed at preventing contingent employees from being treated in a less favourable manner than comparable permanent workers. LDC workers should enjoy the same rights as workers on open-ended contracts. The basic assumption of this type of regulation is that the standard open-ended contract is and should be the norm of all employment relationships. LDCs are regarded as an exception and any divergence from that norm should be held to a minimum.

**The regulation of temporary agency work**

There are two main ways of regulating intermediaries: product market regulation, that is the regulation of the business, and the labour law regulation of contracts and assignments. *Product market regulation* is primarily directed towards regulating by means of licensing and monitoring procedures, and some countries curtail the scope of the activities of intermediaries by, for example, prohibiting recruitment services. There may also be some occupations or sectors where TAW is not allowed owing to health and safety conditions. *Labour law regulation* is not primarily applied to the contract of employment, but rather the assignment at the user firm. Labour law regulations include the reasons for using temporary agency workers, how long they may be hired and the type of information to be shared between the social partners concerning the use of temporary agency workers.

Product market regulation may be regarded as an addition to rather than a substitute for labour law. It differs from regulating by labour law in important ways. Even if regulators claim that they leave TWAs free to operate as any other industry, opportunities to control are not completely left out. Instead of regulating the assignments and the type of employment relationships within the TWAs, there is a shift to regulating the firm and its scope of operation. Moreover, the product market regulation implies that government has an interest in regulating the conditions to establish a TWA, compete and make a profit. Thus regulations of TWA differ between regulating the assignments and the market of the TWA firm. In practice, however, these two forms of regulation are used interchangeably. This will be further developed in Chapter 9 of this volume.

## The Limits of Regulation

The aim of statutory regulations is to overcome discrimination and inequalities that would not disappear otherwise. According to Standing (1999) one must not presume that statutory regulations have a redistributive effect, even if that is the intended objective. They may help one vulnerable group relative to another, but, according to Standing, regulations may also sanction or reinforce forms of discrimination and injustice. This may apply to statutory regulation of open-ended contracts that may foster discrimination of contingent workers, in that it may legitimize different treatment of these workers in other areas than employment protection: wages, benefits, training and discrimination based on gender, race or ethnicity. Regulation of open-ended contracts may also reinforce discrimination of certain groups of workers or segmentation in the labour market (Samek Lodovici, 2000).[4] As Esping-Andersen (2000) argues concerning the impact of employment protection on unemployment, strong regulations nurture more stable employment relationships and, therefore, fewer worker flows. Deregulating labour markets may diminish the security for insiders and enhance the chances of the outsiders, and this may help redistribute who is contingent (ibid). Furthermore, Esping-Andersen claims that, if 'rigidities' do matter, they do so interactively – when they combine with other, possibly more powerful, impulses such as massive deindustrialization or the nature of industrial relations. Thus one cannot regard regulation and contingent employment in isolation. They have to be related to broader developments in the economic context, such as unemployment and economic transformation.

### Enforcement of the law

Another problem with statutory regulation is how the law is enforced. Even if there is extensive statutory regulation, we cannot assume that the regulation is always enforced in practice. Statutory regulations may be very complex, because of the numerous situations that have to be covered. They may also cause bureaucracy. A condition for achieving the aims of statutory regulations is the capacity of the legal and administrative apparatus to operate them efficiently and equitably (Standing, 1999). There may be great variations in terms of both the character of the legal framework and the enforcement of it that determine the strength of the regulation in a particular country.

In countries where employment protection may be regarded as weak, collective bargaining procedures and legislative practices may compensate for the lack of regulation in statutory law. Furthermore, employers have reasons to create their own self-imposed regulations. There is a general assumption that employers are against regulation and would rather have the flexibility to hire and fire at will. The costs associated with employment protection are sometimes regarded as a 'tax' on workforce adjustments (OECD, 1999). However, as Esping-Andersen (2000) points out, regulatory frameworks are valued not only by workers, but also by firms because they stimulate commitment, trust, cooperation and long-term horizons in the employment nexus.

In a similar vein, Pfeffer (1999) argues that in fact employers' claims for deregulation of labour markets may be a mistake. He states that almost all high-performance work practices, such as investing in training, sharing information and putting people in self-managing teams, depend on continuity of employment. Without the expectation of employment of long duration, no company will invest in training. Furthermore, without employment stability, there would not be the trust necessary to share information, and working in teams requires that the team composition be stable enough for people to be able to learn how to work with and learn from each other effectively. Moreover, employment security is virtually a requirement for having people share their knowledge and insights with each other and with the company. In addition, secure workers may be less likely to resist technological innovation and the reorganization of working practices (Esping-Andersen, 2000; OECD, 1999).

As a consequence, firms operating in a deregulated environment may initiate 'in-house' regulatory practices (Esping-Andersen, 2000). For example, employers may set up internal policies or guidelines to guarantee some degree of employment security (Guest, 2000) or provide employees with stock options or other benefits in order to retain their loyalty to the employer. In other words, deregulation may breed its opposite. What appears as weak regulation may be relatively strong on a sub-legal level.

In countries where employment protection may be regarded as strong or extensive the lack of legal enforcement may contribute to opportunism or a 'wild' use of contingent employment. What appears as strongly regulated may be very difficult to enforce in practice. Formalized regulatory environments may provoke what Esping-Andersen calls 'informal flexibilities'; that is, employers invent ways to avoid regulations. Systems that rely mainly on statutory regulations will be inclined to generate opportunism, particularly if the labour system is diversified and flexible (Standing, 1999). For example, firms may deliberately misclassify employees as contingent workers in order to evade various employment laws (Houseman, 1998). Furthermore, opportunism may breed disrespect and undermine the system's legitimacy, encouraging avoidance and evasion, with tacit connivance from others in the system, perhaps including those with responsibility to operate it.[5] Moreover, employers may try to offset some of their costs of complying with employment protection by negotiating lower wages (OECD, 1999). Thus regulation could imply both costs and benefits for employers and they may find ways to deal with their flexibility needs independently of the regulatory regime.

In sum, it is difficult to say which labour market is more flexible (the one with low employment protection or the one with a high level of use of contingent employment) without making explicit what one means by labour market flexibility. Labour markets with low levels of employment protection may have as strong a regulation as more strongly regulated regimes on the local level, where management adjusts its human resource practices in order to create stability. Similarly, in labour markets with strong employment protection, employers find ways to avoid regulation. The high level of use in these countries may be regarded as evidence that there are no problems for employers to provide the numerical flexibility that they need. Thus the impact of regulation in labour markets is difficult to predict.

**Considering the alternative**

Given these problems of statutory regulations one may argue that contingent workers would be better off if statutory employment protection was deregulated. Advocates of deregulation usually support market regulation. Market regulation is where the authorities seek to maximize reliance on market forces and use legislation and other regulatory instruments to achieve this (Standing, 1999). The advantages of market regulation are that it encourages and rewards risk taking, involves less costly administration than statutory protective regulations, fosters an atmosphere of entrepreneurship in which agents can pursue economic opportunities, and is likely to lower transaction costs of most economic activities (ibid.). It is often argued that deregulation fosters job creation and employment growth. For contingent workers and the unemployed it would mean that it is easier for them to enter the labour market and take permanent jobs.

However, market regulation or deregulation of statutory regulation does not necessarily mean more use of contingent employment. Even if it is often argued that the liberalization of regulations on temporary contracts in Spain in the mid-1980s has been the dominant factor in that country in explaining the increasing use of LDCs (OECD, 1996; Esping-Andersen, 2000) the association of deregulation with contingent employment is not strongly supported by the evidence. Several empirical studies (OECD, 1993) suggest that extensive labour market regulation is correlated with a high level of contingent employment and the other way around.

Countries that rely on market regulation do not necessarily make intensive use of contingent employment. Robinson (2000), for example, concludes that, while the USA has one of the least regulated labour markets, it also has a relatively low proportion of its workforce in flexible employment. Relatively more regulated labour markets such as those in southern Europe tend to have high levels of temporary employment (Robinson, 2000). Furthermore, there is no clear evidence that countries with deregulated labour markets have greater work flows; that is, that contingent workers take permanent jobs more easily (see, for example, Levine, 1999). Thus the relationship between statutory regulation and the level of use of contingent employment is not evident. It may be played out differently according to the institutional framework, labour market policies and collective agreements.

## Collective Bargaining

The use of contingent employment is not only regulated in law, it is also regulated by collective agreements, or what Standing (1999) calls 'voice regulation'.[6] The necessary conditions for success with collective bargaining are the sharing of accurate and relevant information, without which coordination failures are almost certain to occur, and the recognition by all sides of the importance of having a long-term relationship – the recognition that the bargainers will be facing each other over a prolonged period (ibid.). The mechanisms must be inclusive of not just the strong but also of all those on the margins, and the powers of the negotiating parties must be approximately balanced and strong. Thus the onus on collective bargaining comes down to the question: is the institutional bargaining and decision making sufficiently representative and responsive?

Conflicts are most often regulated by collective agreements; that is, they are negotiated by the social partners and formalized by protection of national legislation. Statutory regulations may be regarded as a support for the negotiating power of the trade union. Standing (1999) argues that the potential advantages of statutory regulations are that they are, in principle, predictable, transparent and equitable. Transparency helps structure labour bargains, since those entering labour relationships have reasonable information on the basis of the bargain. For example, conflicts regarding dismissal are most often resolved between the social partners and there might be agreements that go much further than what is stated in the law.

In practice it is most often the trade union representatives in the workplace who have the responsibility of putting forward the interests of the individual employee and of making sure that negotiations follow a particular pattern. In order to achieve equal treatment, contingent workers are dependent on the extent to which trade unions are willing to represent them, even if they are not members of the trade union. But there are also examples of extension procedures, which means that contingent workers are covered by collective agreements negotiated by trade unions even if they are not members or are only available at the workplace for a limited time. More specifically, this means that the trade unions fill a number of functions: information and consultation, consent on the use of contingent labour, the participation in the administration of temporary work, recognition and withdrawal of procedures, collective bargaining and also settlement of disputes (Blanpain, 1993, p. 10). Thus the conditions for the establishment of negotiations on equal treatment for contingent employees differ from those of permanent employees. This problem may be even more aggravated when it comes to temporary work agencies, since there are three parties in the employment relationship that have opinions on how the business should be operated.

**Norms and Values**

How do norms and values have an impact on the use of contingent employment? The norms and values concerning contingent employment may be found by analysing studies of the attitudes of employee representatives. In a study of attitudes of employee representatives towards fixed-term contracts in eight European countries, Bielenski (1994) found that there was great variation in the attitudes between countries. The attitude of employee representatives seemed to depend not only on the general situation in their countries but also on the practical experience in their establishments.

Trade union strategies also express norms and values concerning contingent employment. In most European countries, trade unions regard contingent employment as something different and it is opposed directly or indirectly (Clauwaert, 1998). In the Netherlands, for example, trade unions have been opposed to temporary employment because they were afraid of labour market segmentation and the weakening of the labour market position for the workers concerned (Bielenski, 1994). In the USA, temporary employee use tends to be either banned or limited in union contracts (Cappelli *et al.*, 1997). However, there are also countries where trade unions have a more positive attitude towards contingent work. For example,

UGT-P, the social democratic trade union in Spain, accepts the use of LDCs as a labour market policy measure, particularly for young persons (Clauwaert, 1998). Thus trade unions approach contingent employment in different ways, but in general they are opposed to an extensive use and argue that LDCs should remain the exception rather than becoming the rule.

Furthermore, studies of worker preferences concerning type of contract show that some, but not all, contingent workers want a permanent job if they can find one (Bielenski, 1994). However, there is a decreasing proportion of workers expressing such opinions (see, for example, Chapter 3 in this volume). How should we interpret the results of such studies? On the one hand, they may be regarded as a reflection of the interest of workers in having a permanent open-ended contract. On the other hand, they may be regarded as a reflection of the institutional norms and values of the context in which the workers are embedded. If open-ended contracts are institutionally preferred it is not surprising that workers answer in favour of open-ended contracts. Respondents know that permanent workers often have higher wages, better working conditions and less insecurity. Thus the increasing preference for contingent employment may be explained by changes in the organizational and societal context in which workers express their preferences. In particular, it may be explained by the increasing use of contingent employment in new groups of workers who are better paid and have better working conditions, for example professional groups, people with higher education and men. This is the case for all countries with an increasing acceptance of contingent employment. However, the main message of such studies is that most workers are embedded in an institutional context where standard open-ended contracts are regarded as the norm and the most preferred type of contract.

## Discussion: the Impact of the Institutional Framework

The emphasis on the regulation of contingent employment (both LDC and TWA) to limit the employers' abuse and exploitation is complemented by the institutional framework (legal practices, collective agreements and norms and values of employers, trade unions and employees). However, the institutional frameworks of the European countries do not provide the unproblematic support and protection that one would like to think. Statutory regulations may be regarded as an expression of norms rather than providing equal treatment in practice. In all countries, LDC workers in principle enjoy the same rights as workers with open-ended contracts. Nevertheless, there are many thresholds to be reached before the LDC worker can enjoy certain rights (for example, thresholds covering dismissal rights, notice periods, redundancy pay, unfair dismissal protection, vocational training, supplementary pension schemes, sick pay, holiday pay, health and safety, and so on). In practice, this often leads to the exclusion of large numbers and categories of LDC workers. This means that statutory regulations tend to contribute to the reproduction of the interests of insiders rather than of outsiders.

Furthermore, statutory regulation and institutional frameworks reproduce the conditions of existing institutions, norms and values on how to understand contingent employment for both workers and employers. They may also reproduce ideas among workers of being different, not valued and marginal. I therefore argue that the institutional frameworks reproduce the norm of atypicality. Thus statutory regulation, legal practices and collective agreements imply that workers are constituted as different. Otherness is made into a part of workers' identity, which legitimizes contingent workers being treated unequally. As long as they are regarded as atypical they will be treated as atypical, by employers, regulators and co-workers, independent of their own reasons, rationale or interest. They may not have had alternatives, but they may have had good reasons not to tie their loyalty to the employer. Garsten (1999) points out that temporary work is characterized by an experiential ambiguity: 'The attractive side of it promises freedom to transcend the institutions of regular, full-time employment and to create a personalized work biography. The other side is one of marginality – being disposable, "just-a-temp", with few resources at hand.' She argues that the position of temporary agency workers in organizations may be viewed as essentially transient and that they are often relatively detached from local, collegial ties. It may be argued that contingent workers are deemed to be in a constant state of otherness, an alien coming and going, and thus they are denied their own subjectivity, the right to express their own voice and to be heard. This may be caused by the inherent nature of the contingent employment relationship, but it may also be a consequence of the strong normative claim that employment relationships should be stable, permanent and long term. Thus the institutional framework does not change the norms and values of the statutory regulation; it rather reinforces the idea of contingent employment as atypical.[7]

In sum, despite the various efforts to regulate the use of contingent employment, the problems for workers still exist. The characteristics of contingent employment make it difficult for the regulatory framework to limit its undesirable effects. Even if there is a growing proportion of contingent workers whose working conditions are improved, most contingent workers suffer income instability, health and safety problems, and difficulties in influencing working conditions and have less access to training. It seems that contingent workers will never be treated as equal to permanent workers.

TWAs, however, support the possibility for workers to get a more stable or long-term employment contract, and there is a greater chance of training being provided for employees, since this may be regarded as a way for TWAs to satisfy the needs of their clients. Even if it is somewhat artificial, TAWs are offered a community of temps, possibilities of interacting with other people who are in the same situation and the creation of an individual and collective identity as temps (see, for example, Garsten, 2002). TWAs also install different forms of actions or procedures directed to support the particular needs and interests of TAWs. As Garsten (2002) points out, transferring between jobs, contracts and careers places a great deal of pressure on the agencies and the temps alike to learn the ropes quickly, and to be clear about expectations, competencies and job requirements. Isaksson and Bellaagh (1999) found that agency workers experienced social support from the staff at the agency, which was important for work satisfaction. Furthermore, compared to LDC workers, there may be a greater chance for temporary agency workers to be covered by collective agreements, to influence and participate in negotiations on better wages and working conditions. But this is not the case in all countries. Thus TWAs may provide some form of security and a potential to neutralize some of the problems characterizing LDCs. But not all problems are solved.

TWA employment differs from the standard open-ended contracts. It does not provide the same level of security as standard open-ended contracts. Even if TWAs claim that they take responsibility for employees, they do so on certain conditions only: for example, as in the case of Sweden, workers are only paid a guaranteed salary of 90 per cent when there are no placements. Thus there are certain conditions for taking responsibility and these are explicit and understood by both parties. The offer to take responsibility is only valid as long as the agency can provide assignments. Furthermore, the capacity, flexibility and willingness of the worker to take different jobs are crucial for the agency's ability to take responsibility. Hence the tendency for temporary work agencies to look for individuals with a particular set of skills, both professionally and socially (Garsten, 1999). Let us now look more carefully at the different functions of contingent employment and in particular the functions of temporary work agencies in the labour market.

## THE FUNCTION OF CONTINGENT EMPLOYMENT IN THE LABOUR MARKET

The question of the function of contingent employment in the labour market, and TWAs in particular, is crucial for policy making. The function of contingent employment in the labour market establishes a notion of what contingent employment actually does, the different criteria by which we could evaluate it, measure it, and how we should go about inhibiting or supporting it. Studies of contingent employment most often refer to two general functions in the labour market. These are related, first, to the flexibility of labour markets and, second, to the possibility of facilitating the entry of newcomers, the unemployed or people who have been temporarily out of the labour market because of maternity leave, education or other reasons. This section will critically examine the arguments of these two perspectives on the function of contingent employment in the labour market and discuss the differences among the different forms of contingent employment in performing these functions. Furthermore, it will suggest two alternative ways of conceptualizing the function of TWAs in the labour market. These two approaches, it will be argued, have the benefit of taking the interests of both users and workers into account.

**Labour Market Flexibility**

There are at least two perspectives arguing in favour of contingent employment as a facilitator of labour market flexibility. Perhaps the most common argument is that contingent employment facilitates employers' access to numerical flexibility. From this perspective, labour market regulations are regarded as causing rigidities that restrain firms' hiring behaviour and thereby limit their adaptation to changes in the environment, such as competition, globalization and economic cycles. The reasoning behind this argument is that, if contingent employment is allowed, in particular when it implies a lower cost and/or easier procedures of hiring and firing, economic growth might lead to employment growth through such jobs (Levine, 1999). In a slump, employers would tend to let these workers go first. During upturns, the bulk of hirings would then be in the form of contingent employment. According to Gannon and Nollen (1997), the employment of contingent labour is cyclical and responds to the peaks and valleys of the business cycle. More temporary workers are used in peak times, when the demand for labour is high, than in slack times and more involuntary part-timers are used in slack times, when the demand for labour is low, than in peak times. The incidence of contingent employment would thus increase in upturns and decrease in downturns (OECD, 1996). Thus, from this perspective, regulation of contingent employment should be avoided since it is to the benefit of employers and they are of benefit to society. As Walwei (1998) argues, contingent employment may not necessarily have a precarious character, and 'banning such employment would be absurd and unnatural'.

The second argument for labour market flexibility is concerned with the flow of people from unemployment to contingent or permanent jobs. This argument is put forward by social scientists claiming that contingent employment should be interpreted in the light of a new phase of development in capitalist economies, where globalization, competition and the use of new technology create a new situation that needs extraordinary changes and restructuring. For example, Rifkin (1995) argues that what we see is the 'end of work' where the use of new technology and automatization leads to greater productivity and less need for labour, which means that there will be a continuing problem of unemployment in the labour markets of the advanced economies. Flexible labour markets, in terms of greater use of contingent employment, are regarded as a way to share the burden of underemployment among a greater number of people (Beck, 1999; 2000). They cause unemployment to become more equally spread among the total labour force: the total pool of unemployed consists to a larger extent of short-term unemployed instead of a small group of long-term unemployed (Zijl and Budil-Nadvorníková, 2001). Thus, from this perspective, regulation would create social segregation and conflict rather than avoiding it.

**Facilitating Entry in the Labour Market**

It has been argued by some scholars that the 'flexibilization' of employment relations in general and the growth of contingent employment in particular could reduce unemployment by increasing people's job opportunities (Siebert, 1999). There are several studies that try to find out whether contingent employment, through both TWAs and LDCs, is a good way to enter the labour market or not. See, for example Atkinson *et al.* (1996), Booth *et al.* (2000), Granlund (2000), Levin (1998) and Håkansson (2001). The evidence presented by these studies is, however, unclear. Granlund (2000), for example, found in a study of TWAs in the Swedish labour market that the flow of employees from temporary work agencies to other industries is substantial. However, this is not valid for all workers. Granlund (2000) concludes that characterizing the intermediary industry as an entry stage to the rest of the labour market would be misleading.

Håkansson (2001) argues that LDCs may facilitate entry in the labour market, but only for certain groups of workers. In particular, men on probationary jobs and with a high level of education may use the temporary job as a bridge to a permanent job. Women are more likely to stay in the contingent employment relationship. These results are supported by Levin (1998) in Sweden and Booth *et al.* (2000) in the UK. However, they conclude that data are most often insufficient to make reliable comments about the exit rate of contingent employment to permanent jobs. US staffing industry spokesman Edward Lenz divides the temporary workforce into three categories: 'traditional temps', 'transitional workers' and 'longer-term workers'. It is the 'transitional workers' who are using temporary work as a bridge to permanent employment, a group that Lenz estimates at 55 per cent of the temporary workforce (Lenz, 2000). His observations are indirectly supported by a staffing industry survey which determined that 'temp-to-hire' arrangements were the fastest growing segment of the US staffing industry in the late 1990s (*Staffing Industry Review*, 1998).

It should also be noted that contingent jobs do not always lead to permanent jobs, either with the same employer or with other employers. There is a risk of contingent workers being caught in a vicious circle jumping between contingent jobs. In the long run, individuals, young people in particular, may find themselves circulating between temporary work arrangements and government labour market activities (SOU, 1997, p. 40). Thus, as Delsen (1999) argues, there is a danger of segmentation not only between incumbent workers, the insiders, and the unemployed, but also among the insiders: a segmentation of both the external and the internal labour markets.

## Discussion: Avoiding a One-sided View

Studies of contingent employment are most often based on two particular functions in the labour market. First, most studies assume that all forms of contingent employment have a potential to support numerical flexibility for employers and labour market flexibility in terms of flows of workers between types of contracts. There are also studies arguing that they provide workers with a possible stepping-stone into a permanent job or a way to enter the labour market (for example, Zijl and Budil-Nadvorníková, 2001). However, there are some important differences among the various forms of contingent employment in their ability to perform these functions. Compared to hiring through temporary work agencies, LDCs do not provide the same possibilities for employers to hire temporary workers with higher skills and workers do not have the same opportunity to try out different employers while they are entering the labour market. Even though LDCs may facilitate entry in the labour market and numerical flexibility for employers, they are not likely to be as effective as temporary agency work. Thus different forms of contingent employment may support the functions in the labour market differently.

Secondly, numerical flexibility for employers does not necessarily mean better opportunities for entry in the labour market for workers. Employers may want to hire the same workers temporarily in order to avoid training and introduction costs, with reduced opportunities for less experienced workers as a consequence. Furthermore, the 'flexible' jobs offered by employers are not necessarily best suited for the purposes of workers, either when it comes to their interests in getting a permanent job, developing their experience or finding a job they are motivated to do. Thus the two functions of contingent employment most often presented in the literature do not serve both parties equally.

However, TWAs may play an important role for both employers and workers in the employment relationship. For example, some of the negative effects of using LDCs for the user may be balanced when using TWAs. Feldman *et al.* (1994, p. 62) point out that managing a temporary workforce through a TWA takes considerable pressure away from supervisors. The agency does the recruiting and selection; the organization sets the cost of labour and benefits, rarely leaving this open to negotiation; most of the training and orientation is done outside the firm; and the employment relationship is readily terminated at will. Thus using workers from an external agent (Nollen and Axel, 1996) could reduce many types of employment and administrative costs. This kind of employment may also offer a firm a way to exploit highly specialized skills that are needed for only a short period of time, such as engineering or computer skills needed only for a single project (Wright and Snell, 1998).

Temporary work agencies may also provide solutions to some of the problems and negative consequences of LDC workers. First, in some countries, temporary work agencies produce more stable work conditions and employment security, allowing workers to be permanently employed but working contingently with the clients of the agency (see, for example, Chapter 4 in this volume). Second, temporary agency workers often have opportunities to gain experiences of working with different work tasks and making contacts with different clients, thus enabling them to upgrade their skills and not get caught in development traps. This also means not only that contingent employment facilitates entry in the labour market but that it may also be easier for workers to find a job that they are better suited for and are more willing to do. Thus TWAs may have an important function for both parties in the labour market which is not yet fully explored.

There are also particular problems related to the use of TWAs. The use of agencies means that the user firm does not have the same level of social control over employees, since promotions and pay rises are rarely given for work well done. In addition, the psychological contract between the organization and the employee engenders little commitment or effort on the part of the employee beyond the call of duty (Feldman *et al.* 1994, p. 62). Furthermore, the existence of intermediaries may further contribute to an institutionalization of a more externalized three-party employment relationship, but the consequences and effects of this development on the organizational level are not well documented. There are also problems related to this form of employment for workers. Temporary agency workers have two simultaneous jobs: working at the client company and as a representative of the temporary work agency (Rogers, 1995). Gottfried (1991) suggests that having two employers may often lead to role conflict, as multiple agency relationships create more than one 'boss' for the contingent employee. Thus TWAs seem to be a growing actor in the labour market with great influence on the employment relationship, but the consequences and effects of this development for the individual and the user of the services of TWAs are ambiguous.

## REDEFINING THE FUNCTIONS OF THE INTERMEDIARY

As a result of the discussion of the functions of contingent employment in the labour market, reasons become apparent to pay attention to two alternative approaches concerning the use of TWAs in the labour market. TWAs need to be understood in terms of their position in the labour market as intermediaries providing both the individual and the user with the services of matching supply and demand of labour and risk diversification. This section will explore these two functions in further detail.

### Job Matching

Temporary work agencies are a part of a recurrent problem in allocating labour in the labour market. Two main problems stand out. First, there is a problem for individuals to obtain realistic information about the job that they are best suited for and that they are motivated to do. Secondly, there is a problem for employers to find the right people for the jobs available.

A limitation on job matches and thus the mobility of labour is the information interchange between the parties. Good job matches require realistic information and opportunities for both parties to try each other out (Wanous, 1991). From this perspective, temporary agency work provides a potential benefit arising from the information interchange between workers (capabilities and effort) and user firms (working conditions and job characteristics) during the placement period. This occurs without any commitment whatsoever as regards a possible future employment relationship, is without cost to either party and, as it occurs in a realistic situation, it may be presumed to be a very informative exchange. This situation is, of course, similar to a probationary contract.

## Job matching and temporary work agencies

Working for a temporary work agency may be beneficial for the job search and information gathering of individuals who are looking for a job. Individuals may use temporary agency work as a way to find a job they are better suited for and that they are more motivated to do. Furthermore, temporary agency work allows workers to upgrade their skills, try out different types of jobs and companies, and discover the types of work they would ultimately like to perform (Feldman *et al.*, 1994). Temporary work may also be used as a way of providing access to employment for certain vulnerable groups (such as the young and the long-term unemployed) as in some targeted active labour market programmes (OECD, 1996).

From the employer's perspective it may be regarded as an advantage to be able to screen out good from bad job matches before they decide to hire anyone permanently. This is of course dependent on the level of competition in the labour market. If labour is scarce, employers may need to offer a permanent contract or higher salaries in order to be able to hire them at all. However, as mentioned in the discussion on flexibility above, LDCs and agency work differ as regards commitment to hire on a more permanent basis. Furthermore, hiring through an agency may contribute to the quality of the match between employer and employee. It may be argued that mismatch is less likely as the agency has already screened their assigned employee. Moreover, the transaction costs of enabling these probationary periods through the work agency are likely to be much lower than if the worker and user firm were to search for each other without the intermediary (this is one of the advantages of the outsourcing of the recruitment function of the firm) and thus agency work may be able to generate the exposure of more workers to more firms and more and better job matches. Indeed, CIETT (2000) and Storrie (2002) provide evidence that user firms are increasingly using agency work as a probationary employment.

## The effects of job matching

The job-matching function of temporary work agencies may have important macroeconomic effects. Katz and Krueger (1999) suggest a potentially important role for work agencies in their search for explanations for the non-inflationary fall in unemployment in the USA during the 1990s. They note that, while the sector is still relatively small, worker flows are appreciably higher. Using cross-state panel regressions, they present some evidence suggesting that the availability of agency workers may lessen the wage pressure that usually accompanies tight labour markets, possibly by enabling firms to fill vacancies quickly and possibly more cheaply and with better matches without having to adjust their overall wage structure. While they term their results 'highly speculative', they award work agencies a potentially major role in the decline of US unemployment from 1989 to 1998 and underline their potential to improve the functioning of the labour market by reducing frictional unemployment without increasing inflation.

It may be argued that the job-matching function may be supported by new information technologies as well. The increase in temporary agency work has coincided with widespread use of information and communication technology and indeed the Internet is full of various job sites, which are able to contain appreciably more vacancy and job seeker information at much lower cost than, for example, newspapers (Storrie, 2002). However, this technology does not appear to have increased direct contact between the firm and job seekers without going through a matching intermediary. The fact that the technology significantly lowers the cost for the job seeker to apply for jobs may lead to employers being inundated with applications. Thus, as argued in Autor (2001a), intermediaries such as recruitment and temporary work agencies (often both functions are performed within the same firm) are required to reap the benefits of the computerized matching technologies. Autor also cites evidence that Internet job site applicants suffer adverse selection. Furthermore, the role of intermediaries in establishing a reputation for providing accurate information is a much-researched issue in the economics of e-commerce. Owing to their longevity and economies of scale and scope, institutions are a more efficient means of maintaining reputation than individuals.

The implied focus in the discussion above was on the agency's reputation at the client firm. However, the issue is broader than this and the improvement of the reputation of TWAs was a prominent strategy of the temporary agency sector during the 1990s (see Storrie, 2002). Prior to deregulation, agency work was illegal in some countries and often associated with 'shady practices'. A variety of tactics has been used by the agencies to improve their reputation among not only client firms but also potential employees and trade unions. These include ethical codes of good practice, advertising campaigns and the signing of collective agreements (ibid.). Moreover, market forces, largely economies of scale and scope, have pushed out many of the smaller and probably less reputable operators. Indeed since deregulation, the sector has undergone a rapid consolidation process and, by the end of the 1990s, in 12 of the 15 EU member states, the five largest companies accounted for over 50 per cent of market share (see CIETT, 2000). These companies, often multinationals, are now recognizable and generally reputable brand names: for example, Manpower, Addeco and Randstad. This improved reputation has presumably improved the matching efficiency of TWAs in that they are able to attract better job applicants and to gain acceptance of agency workers with the personnel departments and the trade unions at the client firm. Thus TWAs may offer both parties a possibility of solving the job-matching problem in the labour market.

## Risk Diversification

Another way of understanding the function of temporary work agencies in the labour market is to regard TWAs as an intermediary that diversifies risks. This approach raises questions concerning the distribution of responsibility and risk among the agents in the three-party relationship. From the employer's perspective, the risk is related to the costs of hiring and firing the worker. Hiring decisions are always associated with a risk in relation to the need of the labour provided by the worker. From the worker's perspective, the risk is related to the income insecurity that would arise from spot market trading of labour services. As Gregg *et al.* (2000) assert, the individuals' experience of insecurity is about risk assessment. We may call it *employment risk*: the chance of losing the current job involuntarily and of securing a new job. At least three types of risks may be identified: firm-specific risks, product market risks and risks associated with the job, competence and behaviour of the individual.

Firms operating in different economic sectors are exposed to different levels of risk. Some sectors are more exposed to risk than others owing to different levels of competition, the nature of the product (whether it is a standardized or a differentiated product) or the nature of the market. Furthermore, different firms operating in the same economic sector are exposed to different levels of risk, depending on how they operate in their market, organize their operations and the type of skills that they need for the production. These dimensions determine the probability that the firm may need to reduce its workforce and thus the employment and income security of the individual employee.

Moreover, there is a risk related to the individual's skills and relationship to his or her employer. When the conditions of work require that the individual increase his or her knowledge and skills within a narrow field, specific to the operations of the company, at the expense of the possibility of developing knowledge that is applicable to other jobs and/or companies, the individual is exposed to employment risk. The confinement of the individual's competence to the workplace and the organization creates a problem both for each individual and for the company when parts of the operation need to be closed down or rationalized because of technical development or changing demand in the market. Some of the work tasks and skills are not needed any longer. The employee risks being made redundant. However, when skills are general and the individual's employability is higher, both for the existing and for other employers the unemployment risk is lower.

**Risk and temporary work agencies**

From this perspective, it may be argued that, in some circumstances, for example in times of economic transformation and uncertainty, various forms of contingent employment may better serve the needs of both the individual worker and the user. First, since contingent employment contracts most often clearly state when the employment relationship is ended, expectations of the continuation of the employment relationship are calculable (Bergström, 2001c). This is particularly true for LDCs but also true for most contracts with TWAs. For employers it means that it is easy to terminate the employment relationship whenever the labour is not needed. The employer is rid of the labour costs associated with the employment contract. For the individual the short-term employment relationship means that he or she has incentives to engage in job-search activities in order to secure a continuous income. Second, the contingent employment relationship, when it implies switching between different employers, adds to the work experience of the individual, which may increase the likelihood of getting another job. Furthermore, the switching between jobs means that the individual has a broader network of contacts, which may be valuable when it is time to change jobs. This is particularly so when the contingent job is combined with part-time employment. Individuals may create a *work portfolio* (Handy, 1990), which serves the purpose of spreading the risk of unemployment (Bergström, 2001c; Wallulis, 1998). However, when job duration is very short the time required or costs of searching for a new employment relationship may be too high. This may be taken care of by temporary work agencies that provide the employee with new job opportunities by managing the work portfolio of the employee as a stockbroker does in financial markets.

These job opportunities are found in many user firms, which may be located in different economic sectors. This diversity enhances the potential of the TWA to adopt more risk than other employers do and thus may lead to higher levels of profit and employment. However, if risk is related to a macroeconomic shock in all economic sectors (such as increases in oil prices or interest rates) there is no potential for risk spreading, and thus, in this context, no benefit in organizing labour in temporary work agencies. Thus TWAs provide a function in the labour market by providing risk diversification for both employers and employees. This means that risk related to labour is diversified and distributed among the three parties in the employment relationship.

## Discussion: Towards a New Understanding

Temporary work agencies may mediate the concern for the interests and needs for flexibility and security in the labour market. In this context, agency work seems to neutralize and to some extent avoid some of the problems of limited duration contracts. The decreasing demands on TWAs to offer long-term relationships are balanced by the TWAs' ability to spread their risks and offer a better matching between employees and employers. However, there are problems specific to agency work. The continual shifting of the workplace and the dual 'employer' responsibilities make matters such as health and safety and worker representation intrinsically difficult to deal with whatever regulation is applied. Furthermore, the provision of training is not obvious, since the financial arrangements are not clear. Moreover, the fuzziness of the three-party relationship may facilitate abuse by opportunistic employers. Thus the problems of contingent employment do not change with TWAs, they are only mediated from being left completely to the individual worker, they are shared with the agency.

TWAs may be regarded as a way to mitigate the problems of working temporarily on LDCs. This is not done by providing work for the unemployed or by offering flexibility to users, but by creating conditions to be able to spread risks for both parties. But this is not possible if they are not independent of upturns and downturns in industries, an internal portfolio of clients and workers whose knowledge and skills could be used in different work tasks, in different industries and locations. Thus TWAs may serve a function to facilitate job matching and to distribute risks for both employers and employees.

In sum, TWAs may not be understood apart from the risk diversification function that they fill in the labour market. But this function is partly dependent on the strategy of the TWAs, what sectors they operate in, the composition of clients and what types of competencies the temporary workers have. These aspects are particularly important when business cycles are fluctuating. To the extent that business cycles are fluctuating more intensively and with increasing depth and peaks, this type of function has increasing importance. Thus the question is not only whether TWAs are of benefit to employers and employees. The question is also what consequences they have for the general functioning of labour markets and therefore also as a privatized form of employment policy.

## CONCLUSION: BEYOND ATYPICALITY

What is the nature of contingent employment? A review of both theoretical and empirical studies of contingent employment reveals much diversity. Studies of contingent employment vary according to theoretical approaches, disciplinary background and interests. In one way or the other the focus has varied with the actor or interest the studies serve or represent. In more general terms, contingent employment, independently of whether it concerns the individual employee, the user or the labour market in general, is regarded and treated as something atypical. The increasing use of contingent labour is regarded as a consequence of exceptional changes in firms' ways of organizing work, at the same time as the use of contingent labour threatens traditional employment relationships in the workplace. Governments and social partners try to adapt legislation and agreements on the use of contingent employment to the norms and values of open-ended contracts. Thus contingent employment challenges traditional understanding of organizational membership, loyalty, safety, welfare and social integration.

As was mentioned earlier, there are several different ways of describing the phenomenon of contingent employment. We have chosen to use the American concept of contingent employment in order to create a distance from national concepts, categories and understandings of the phenomenon. It also means that we may create a distance from the various political, ideological and disciplinary approaches. The use of the concept of contingent employment may also help us to understand the particular nature of the three-party relationship. Maybe the most important reason for using the concept is to create an understanding of the functions of contingent employment in labour markets. Above all, it may move the debate on contingent employment beyond the notion of atypicality.

Independent of the reasons for the use of contingent labour, it may have important consequences for both employers and employees. For employers, the use of contingent labour is regarded as a way to cut labour costs and to adjust to fluctuations in product demand and changes in the organizational environment. For employees, being a contingent worker is regarded as a way to facilitate entry into the labour market or as a way to balance financial and personal demands, as with adults working temporarily while taking care of children, or with students who want extra money and work during their time off. More sceptical commentators say that contingent employment may lead to commodification, segregation and marginalization in the labour market.

Going beyond atypicality implies avoiding a one-sided view of the functions of contingent employment in the labour market. Conceptualizing the function of contingent employment as enhancing employer flexibility or the worker's chances of entering the labour market reproduces one or the other's point of view. As a consequence it is difficult to come to an agreement on how to regulate contingent employment in a way that suits both parties.

**Accepting Differences**

Above all the notion of atypicality tends to disregard the consequences of contingent employment for employees. But even when research is designed to be in the interest of workers, there is no guarantee that better conditions for workers are created. For example, studies of individual attitudes to working on 'non-standard contracts' or as 'temps', aiming at uncovering their preferences for contractual arrangements, are unavoidably bounded by the institutional norms of standard long-term employment relationships. These studies either are based on a 'national' political agenda or cannot free themselves from the norms and values that govern our conceptions of employment relations. As argued above, such norms have consequences for the way workers' answers to questions on preferable contracts may be interpreted. There is a risk that research on contingent employment only reproduces the notion of contingent employment as atypical and therefore also less valued. Instead more research should be focused on more grounded methods providing a better understanding of the variation and complexity of meanings from the point of view of the individual workers (see, for example, Garsten, 1999; Kunda *et al.*, 2002).

Thus going beyond atypicality should also include a discussion of how to collect information and statistics about contingent employment. Current national labour market statistics are inevitably a reflection of national institutional or legal frameworks. Each national statistical bureau collects statistics based on the categories provided by the respective national legal framework. This not only creates problems of comparability between countries, it also create vagueness concerning what we really talk about when we touch upon the problem. This of course creates problems for policy makers.

An alternative would be to use the definition of contingent employment that exists in the USA. Current statistics in Europe only give an indication of the incidence of various contractual forms in the different countries. The results of such studies are often taken as evidence for different assumptions of the properties of these contracts: increasing insecurity in the labour market, increasing flexibility, deskilling, marginalization and so on. However, generalization of characteristics or experiences of workers with similar types of contractual arrangements should be made with caution.[8] It cannot be assumed that contractual properties automatically imply similar experiences, ways of organizing or effects in the labour market. For all forms of employment, expectations of the continuation of the employment relationship are important for workers' experience of satisfaction, well-being and level of insecurity. The legal distinction between open-ended contracts and limited duration contracts implies a normative assessment of the worker's value. But in reality a permanent worker may be exposed to more risk and uncertainty than the least vulnerable contingent worker is.

The lack of common definitions and data collection procedures imposes severe limitations, making it difficult to come to general conclusions concerning the state of contingent employment in European labour markets and, thus, also to give policy recommendations on contingent employment on a European level. Additional efforts should therefore be made to standardize data collection on the use of contingent employment in European labour markets. The use of temporary work agencies should be given particular attention. Efforts should be focused on finding a non-national based definition and data collection procedure providing better information on the use of contingent labour in European labour markets. Perhaps the procedures of the US Bureau of Labor Statistics (BLS) will provide ideas of how this may be done in the European context. Furthermore, the current counting of the frequency of contracts should be complemented by collection of data of the individual expectation of the continuation of the employment relationship. Individual expectations may be independent of the contractual form. This is in line with the possible functions of contingent employment in the labour market, job matching and risk diversification.

The review of the literature, however, reveals several questions, to be further analysed and discussed in the following chapters. What are the trends in the use of contingent employment in the European labour markets? What are the driving forces of the use of contingent employment? What is the impact of labour market regulation? How do national regulatory regimes differ? How do national regulatory regimes deal with equal treatment of contingent workers? How are temporary work agencies regulated? How are the regulations enforced? And, finally, is there a convergence of the regulation of contingent employment among the European countries?

## NOTES

1. I would like to thank Donald Storrie, John Purcell, Jaap Paauwe, Kay McGlashan, Rebecca Ellis, Torbjörn Stjernberg, Kristina Håkansson, Tommy Isidorsson, Mette Sandoff and Svante Leijon for comments on earlier drafts of this chapter.
2. Autor (2001b) asks why temporary work agencies provide free general skills training. His answer is that training, in addition to fostering human capital, serves two complementary informational functions. One is to induce self-selection. Firms that offer training are able to attract workers of greater unobserved ability differentially. A second role is to facilitate worker screening. By tightly coupling worker training with worker skills testing, temporary-help firms use training to screen privately the ability of workers whom they train.
3. According to Vigneau *et al.* (1999), to create equal conditions at least two conditions are required. First, identical or comparable situations must not be treated differently, and

second, different situations must not be treated identically. In practice this means (1) that the worker with whom the temporary worker is to be compared must be identified (an equality rule implies the identification of a worker or a category of workers in relation to which temporary workers should not be discriminated against), and (2) that the discrimination must be based on criteria expressly established by the equality rule.

4. Samek Lodovici (2000) argues that the Italian experience highlights the risks associated with excessive regulation of employment relations: the development of an extremely segmented market, the exclusion of first-job seekers from regular employment, the low elasticity of wages to unemployment, the inefficiencies deriving from low interregional and intersectoral labour mobility and the presence of a large underground economy.
5. In Sweden, which is often referred to as a country with strong employment protection, laws are circumvented through collective agreements. Employers offer trade unions an agreement with generous re-employment programmes to help workers who are dismissed to find jobs elsewhere (Bergström, 2001c). This means that trade unions allow employers to dismiss workers by different criteria than constituted by law and can thus avoid the rigidities of the law when necessary. However, this is not done without costs for the employer.
6. According to Standing (1999), voice regulation has three potential *disadvantages*: (1) it is time-consuming, since it involves explicit bargaining; for their own legitimacy both parties may find it necessary to take postures, demonstrate disagreement and prolong negotiations; (2) there is a tendency for coordination failure, where lack of information, different information or some other factor leads to a breakdown in communication; (3) voice regulation may intensify labour market inequalities and insecurity if the institutions exclude the interests of more vulnerable groups. Standing further argues that voice regulation has some potential *advantages* over other forms of regulation. It can reduce both the excesses of market forces and the rigidities of statutory regulation. At the firm level, it can encourage dynamic efficiency and restructuring. It can incorporate the interests of all 'stakeholders', and it can reduce exploitation of vulnerable groups, thereby deterring low effort bargains, sabotage, exit through quitting and other forms of worker retribution. And it can prevent unilateral control by management from destroying the choice of technique away from provision of firm-specific training. In sum, voice regulation can provide monitoring so as to reduce opportunism.
7. It seems that the only legal and institutional framework that has a potential to limit these effects is the Dutch one (see Chapters 8 and 9 in this volume). In the Netherlands, the legal and institutional framework assumes that contingent employment is a transitory state. Workers are expected to move and their interests are supported by law.
8. Most studies of the changing nature of work in Europe actually examine (count) workers' self-reported contractual relationships. This means that the outcome is an estimate of the number of contractual relationships existing in the labour market. Although this may be an estimate of the use of contingent employment, it does not cover the 'true' permanency of the employment relationship. For example, employees holding an open-ended contract may regard their employment relationship as temporary, while another person holding a limited duration contract may regard the employment relationship as a continuing one. Thus counting self-reported contractual relationships does not necessarily give a good indication of the contingency of the employment relationship.

## REFERENCES

Aronsson, G., M. Dallner and T. Lindh (2000) 'Flexibla inkomster och fast utgifter – en studie av ekonomisk strtess och hälsa bland korttidsanställda (Flexible income and fixed expenses – Economic stress among on-call employees), *Arbete och hälsa*, 2000(20), 1–26, Arbetslivsinstitutet, Solna.

Aronsson, G. and S. Göransson (1998) *Tillfälligt anställda och arbetsmiljödialogen – en empirisk studie*, Solna: Arbetslivsinstitutet.
Arvidsson, S. (1997) 'Arbetsmiljö och arbetsvillkor för anställda inom personaluthyrningsbranschen', Working Paper No. 52, Stockholm University.
Atkinson, J. (1984) 'Manpower Strategies for Flexible Organizations', *Personnel Management*, August.
Atkinson, J., J. Rick, S. Morris and M. Williams (1996) 'Temporary Work and the Labour Market', Report No. 311, Institute for Employment Studies, University of Sussex, Brighton.
Autor, D. (2001a) 'Wiring the Labor Market', *Journal of Economic Perspectives*, 15, 25–40.
Autor, D. (2001b) 'Why do Temporary Firms Provide Free General Skills Training?', *Quarterly Journal of Economics*, 116(4), November, 1409–48.
Barker, K. and K. Christensen (eds) (1998) *Contingent Work: American Employment Relations in Transition*, Ithaca, NY: ILR/Cornell University Press.
Beck, U. (1999) *World Risk Society*, Cambridge: Polity Press.
Beck, U. (2000) *The Brave New World of Work*, Cambridge: Polity Press.
Belous, R.S. (1997) 'Coming to Terms with the Rise of the Contingent Workforce', in D. Lewin, D. Mitchell and Z. Mahmood (eds), *The Human Resource Management Handbook Part II*, London: JAI Press.
Benavides, F.G. and J. Benach (1999) *Precarious Employment and Health-Related Outcomes in the European Union*, Dublin: European Foundation for the Improvement of Living and Working Conditions.
Bentolila, S. and J.J. Dolado (1994) 'Labour Flexibility and Wages: Lessons from Spain', *Economic Policy*, 18, 53–100.
Bergström, O. (2001a) 'Does Contingent Employment Affect the Organization of work? Approaches to the study of contingent employment', SALTSA report series, National Institute of Work Life, Solna, Sweden.
Bergström, O. (2001b) 'Contingent Employment in the Swedish Food Manufacturing Industry', NUEWO working paper, Gothenburg University, Gothenburg.
Bergström, O. (2001c) 'Externalization of Employees: Thinking about going somewhere else', *International Journal of Human Resource Management*, 12:(3), May, 373–88.
Bielenski, H. (1994) *New Forms of Work and Activity, Survey of Experience at Establishment Level in Eight European Countries*, Dublin: European Foundation for the Improvement of Living and Working Conditions.
Blanpain, R. (1993) *Temporary Work and Labour Law of the European Community and Member States*, Deventer: Kluwer Law and Taxation Publishers.
Booth A., M. Francesconi and J. Frank (2000) 'Contingent Jobs: Who gets them, what are they worth and do they lead anywhere?', Institute for Social and Economic Research, Essex.
Cappelli, P., L. Bassi, H. Katz, D. Knoke, P. Osterman and M. Useem (1997) *Change at Work*, New York: Oxford University Press.
CIETT (2000), *Orchestrating the Evolution of Private Employment Agencies Towards a Stronger Society*, Brussels: International Confederation of Private Employment Agencies.
Clauwaert, S. (1998) *Survey of Fixed Term Contracts*, Brussels: European Trade Union Institute.
Delsen, L. (1999) 'Changing Work Relations in the European Union', in I. Urla

Zeytinoglu (ed.), *Changing Work Relationships in Industrialized Economies*, Amsterdam: John Benjamins Publishing Company.
Ellingson, J.E., M.L. Gruys and P.R. Sackett (1998) 'Factors related to the satisfaction and performance of temporary employees'. *Journal of Applied Psychology*, 83, 913–21.
Esping-Andersen, G. (2000) 'Who is Harmed by Labour Market Regulations? Quantitative Evidence', in G. Esping-Andersen and M. Regini (eds), *Why Deregulate Labour Markets?*, Oxford: Oxford University Press.
Feldman, D., H. Doerpinghaus and W. Turnley (1994) 'Managing Temporary Workers: A Permanent HRM Challenge', *Organizational Dynamics*, 23, 46–63.
Gannon, M. (1996) 'Managing without a Complete, Full-time Workforce', in P.C. Flood, M.J. Gannon and J. Paauwe (eds), *Managing without Traditional Methods, International Innovations, Human Resource Management*, New York: Addison-Wesley.
Gannon, M. and S. Nollen (1997), 'Contingent Labour: Understanding the Changing Employment Relationship', in J. Wallace, T. Dalzell and B. Delany (eds), *Continuity and Change in the Employment Relationship*, vol. 1 of the Proceedings of the 5th European IIRA Conference, Dublin, Dublin: Oak Tree Press.
Garsten, C. (1999) 'Betwixt and Between: Temporary Employees as Liminal Subjects in Flexible Organizations', *Organization Studies*, 20(4), 601–17.
Garsten, C. (2002) 'Flex fads: new economy, new employees', in I. Holmberg, M. Salzer-Mörling and L. Strannegård (eds), *Stuck in the Future? Tracing the 'New Economy'*, Stockholm: Bockhouse Publishing.
Gjelsvik, M. (1998) 'Employment Relations: Determinants and Consequences', Norwegian School of Economics and Business Administration, Bergen.
Gottfried, H. (1991) 'Mechanisms of control in the temporary help service industry', *Sociological Forum*, 6, 699–713.
Granlund, M. (2000) 'Personaluthyrningsföretag – en bro till arbetsmarknaden?', Mångfaldsprojektet, Stockholms Universitet.
Gregg, P., G. Knight and J. Wadsworth (2000) 'Heaven Knows I'm Miserable Now: Job Insecurity in the British Labour Market', in E. Heery and J. Salmon (eds), *The Insecure Workforce*, London: Routledge.
Greiner, D. (2000) 'Atypical Work in the European Union', in D. Pieters (ed.), *Changing Work Patterns and Social Security*, London: Kluwer Law International.
Guest, D. (2000) 'Management and the Insecure Workforce: The Search for a New Psychological Contract', in E. Heery and J. Salmon (eds), *The Insecure Workforce*, London: Routledge.
Håkansson, K. (2001) 'Språngbräda eller segmentering? – En longitudinell studie av tidsbegränsat anställda', Centrum för arbetsvetenskap, Göteborgs Universitet.
Handy, C. (1990) *The Age of Unreason*, Boston: Harvard Business School Press.
Heery, E. and B. Abbott (2000) 'Trade Unions and the Insecure Workforce', in E. Heery and J. Salmon (eds), *The Insecure Workforce*, London: Routledge.
Henson, K.D. (1996) *Just a Temp*, Philadelphia, PA: Temple University Press.
Houseman, S. (1998) 'Labour Standards and Alternative Work Arrangements', *Labour Law Journal*, 49, September.
Houseman, S.N. (1997) 'External and Internal Labour Market Flexibility in an International Comparison', in D. Lewin, D. Mitchell and Z. Mahmood (eds), *The Human Resource Management Handbook Part II*, London: JAI Press.

Isaksson, K. and K. Bellaagh (1999) 'Vem stöttar Nisse? Social stöd bland uthyrd personal', *Arbetsmarknad & Arbetsliv*, 5(4).

Jahoda, M., P. Lazarsfeld and H. Zeisel ([1933] 1975) 'Die Arbeitslosen von Marienthal. Ein soziographischer Versuch über die Wirkungen langandauernder Arbeitslosigkeit', Mit einem Anhang zur Geschichte der Soziographie Frankfurt a.M.

Katz, L.F. and A.B. Krueger (1999) 'The high-pressure U.S. labour market of the 1990s', *Brookings Papers on Economic Activity*, 1, 1–87, Washington, DC.

Krausz, M., T. Brandwein and S. Fox (1995) 'Work attitudes and emotional responses of permanent, voluntary, and involuntary temporary-help employees: an exploratory study', *Applied Psychology: An International Review*, 44, 217–32.

Kunda, G., S.R. Barley and J. Evans (2002) 'Why do contractors contract? The experience of highly skilled technical professionals in a contingent labour market', *Industrial & Labour Relations Review*, January.

Lee, T.W. and D.R. Johnson (1991) 'The effects of work schedule and employment status on the organizational commitment and job satisfaction of full versus part time employees', *Journal of Vocational Behavior*, 38, 204–24.

Lenz, E.A. (2000) 'The Staffing Services Industry: Myth and Reality', in 'Global Competition and the American Employment Landscape – As we enter the 21st Century', Proceedings of the New York University 52nd Annual Conference on Labor.

Letourneux, V. (1998) *Précarité et conditions de travail dans l'Union Européenne,* Dublin: European Foundation for the Improvement of Living and Working Conditions.

Levin, H. (1998) 'Precarious Footing: Temporary Employment as a Stepping Stone out of Unemployment', Swedish Institute for Social Research, Stockholm University.

Levine, L. (1999) 'Temporary Workers as Members of the Contingent Labour Force', CRS Report for Congress, 16 February.

Mangum, G., D. Mayall and K. Nelson (1985) 'The temporary help industry: A response to the dual internal labor market', *Industrial and Labor Relations Review*, 38, 599–611.

McLean Parks, J., D.L. Kidder and D.G. Gallagher (1998) 'Fitting square pegs into round holes: Mapping the domain of contingent work arrangements onto the psychological contract', *Journal of Organizational Behavior*, 19, 697–730.

Meulders, D. and B. Tytgat (1989) 'The Emergence of Atypical Employment in the European Community', in G. Rodgers and J. Rodgers (eds), *Precarious Jobs in Labour Market Regulation: The Growth of Atypical Employment in Western Europe*, Geneva: International Labour Organisation.

Nolan, J.P., I.C. Wichert and B.J. Burchell (2000) 'Job Insecurity, Psychological Well-being and Family Life', in E. Heery and J. Salmon (eds) *The Insecure Workforce*, London: Routledge.

Nollen, S.D. and H. Axel (1996) *Managing Contingent Workers: How to Reap the Benefits and Reduce the Risks*, New York: AMACOM.

OECD (1993) *Employment Outlook*, Paris: Organization for Economic Co-operation and Development.

OECD (1996) *Employment Outlook*, Paris: Organization for Economic Co-operation and Development,

OECD (1999) *Employment Outlook*, Paris: Organization for Economic Co-operation and Development.

Pearce, J.L. (1993) 'Toward an organizational behavior of contract laborers: their psychological involvement and effects on employee co-workers', *Academy of Management Journal*, 36, 1082–96.

Pfeffer, J. (1999) 'Labor Market Flexibility, Do Companies Really Know Best?', Research Paper No. 1592, Graduate School of Business, Stanford University, Stanford.

Purcell, K., T. Hogarth and C. Simm (2000) *Whose Flexibility? The cost and benefits of 'non-standard' working arrangements and contractual relations*, York: York Publishing Services.

Purcell, K. and J. Purcell (1998) 'In-sourcing, outsourcing and the growth of the contingent labour as evidence of flexible employment strategies', *European Journal of Work and Organizational Psychology*, 7(1), 39–59.

Rebitzer, J.B. (1998) 'Job safety and contract workers in the petrochemical industry', in K. Barker and K. Christensen (eds), *Contingent Work: American Employment Relations in Transition*, Ithaca, NY: ILR/Cornell University Press, pp. 263–80.

Rex, J. (1988) *The Ghetto and the Underclass: Essays on Race and Social Policy*, Research in Ethnic Relations series, Aldershot: Gower.

Rifkin, J. (1995) *The End of Work, the Decline of the Global Labor Force and the Dawn of the Post-Market Era*, New York: G.P. Putnam's Sons.

Robinson, P. (2000) 'Insecurity and the Flexible Workforce: Measuring the ill-defined', in E. Heery and J. Salmon (eds), *The Insecure Workforce*, London: Routledge.

Rogers, J.K. (1995) 'Just a temp: experience and structure of alienation in temporary clerical employment', *Work and Occupations*, 22, 137–66.

Rousseau, D.M. (1995) *Psychological Contracts in Organizations: Understanding Written and Unwritten Agreements*, Newbury Park, CA: Sage Publications.

Rousseau, D.M. and C. Libuser (1997) 'Contingent Workers in High Risk Environments', *California Management Review*, 39(2).

Samek Lodovici, M. (2000) 'Italy: the Long Times of Consensual Re-regulation', in G. Esping-Andersen and M. Regini (eds), *Why Deregulate Labour Markets?*, Oxford: Oxford University Press.

Sarfati, H. and C. Korbin (1988) 'Wage Cost', in H. Sarfati and C. Korbin (eds), *Labour and Market Flexibility : A Comparative Anthology*, Sydney: Gower.

Sennett, R. (1999) *Corrosion of Character: The Personal Consequences of Work in the New Capitalism*, New York: Norton.

Siebert, S. (1999) *The Effect of Labour Regulation on Recruitment*, York: Joseph Rowntree Foundation.

SOU (1997:40) 'Unga & Arbete, Delbetänkande från ungdomspolitiska kommitén', Ungdomspolitiska kommittén, Stockholm.

*Staffing Industry Review* (1998) 'Surveys Find More Employers Relying on Staffing Firms', 3(3), May/June, 88–92.

Standing, G. (1999) *Global Labour Flexibility – Seeking Distributive Justice*, London: Macmillan Press.

Storrie D. (2002) 'Temporary Agency Work in the European Union', Dublin: European Foundation for the Improvement of Living and Working Conditions.

Summers, C.W. (1997) 'Contingent employment in the United States', *Comparative Labor Law Journal*, 18, 503–22.

Thébaud-Mony, A. (2001) 'Casualisation and Flexibility: Impact on Workers' Health', *Working without limits? Re-organising work and reconsidering workers' health*, TUTB-SALTSA Conference, TUTB NEWSLETTER No. 15–16, Brussels.

Vigneau, C. (1999) 'The principle of equal treatment of temporary and permanent workers', in C. Vigneau, K. Ahlberg, B. Bercusson and N. Bruun (eds), *Fixed-term Work in the EU, A European Agreement Against Discrimination and Abuse*, Stockholm: National Institute for Working Life.

Wallulis, J. (1998) *The New Insecurity, The End of the Standard Job & Family*, Albany: State Univeristy of New York Press.

Walwei, U. (1998) 'Flexibility of Employment Relationships: Possibilities and Limits', in T.D. Donley and M. Oppenheimer (eds), *International Review of Comparative Public Policy*, vol. 10, London: JAI Press.

Wanous, J.P. (1991) *Organizational Entry: Recruitment, Selection, Orientation and Socialization of Newcomers*, New York: Addison-Wesley.

Warr, P. (1987) *Work, Unemployment and Mental Health*, Oxford: Clarendon Press.

Wright, P.M. and S.A. Snell (1998) 'Toward a Unifying Framework for Exploring Fit and Flexibility in Strategic Human Resource Management', *Academy of Management Review*, 23(4), 756–72.

Zijl, M. and H. Budil-Nadvorníková (2001) 'Atypical Labour, Flexible Labour from the Social and Employers' Point of View', SEO Amsterdam Economics, Amsterdam.

# 3. Contingent employment in the UK

**Surhan Cam, John Purcell and Stephanie Tailby**

## INTRODUCTION

This chapter analyses the general characteristics of contingent employment in the UK with particular focus on trends in the 1990s. Contingent employment is defined primarily in terms of limited duration contracts (LDCs) but, as explained later, there are difficulties with both definitions and data sources. The most important groups of contingent workers are those with fixed-term contracts (typically a duration of one year or less), casual and seasonal workers or those with very short contracts, and agency workers supplied by and often working for temporary work agencies (TWAs). Another group are those on 'on-call' or 'zero-hour' contracts. We first provide an overview of government policy and employers' responses to employment regulation since 1979. We then look at labour market trends in the 1990s with particular attention to trends in employment, unemployment, part-time and self-employment, and 'temporary work'. This section also considers the ways in which contingent employment can be defined and comments on the adequacy of available data sources.

Next we use Labour Force Survey (LFS) data to review the pattern and distribution of contingent employment. Finally, we attempt to assess the accuracy of some arguments on contingent employment with references to macrostatistical data. What emerges is a complex picture of great variety, which does not support the stereotypes often linked to 'temporary working'.

## GOVERNMENT POLICY AND ECONOMIC DEVELOPMENT

The UK's experience of economic recession in the early 1980s was relatively severe. In part this reflected the accumulated weaknesses of the economy's export-oriented manufacturing sector. But it was also a product of the incoming Conservative government's determination to impose a fresh discipline on firms and, more especially, on workers and their unions.

In office for four consecutive terms from 1979, Conservative government ministers extolled the virtues of 'free markets', individualism and private enterprise. They abandoned the Keynesian full-employment commitments of previous post-war administrations and established the control of inflation as the central objective of macroeconomic policy. Unemployment – rising rapidly in the early 1980s – was deemed to be a supply-side phenomenon. Government ministers urged that industry competitiveness and job creation demanded the weakening or removal of legal and institutional 'rigidities' in product markets and, especially, labour markets. A central declared aim was the weakening of trade union power. Towards this objective, a complex series of reforms of industrial relations legislation was enacted over the 1980s and early 1990s. Large-scale unemployment assisted by weakening the unions' ability to resist government and employers' initiatives. The contraction of manufacturing employment and the government's reforms of the public sector (the privatization of nationalized industry and the public utilities, and the 'marketization' of public services) undermined trade union membership and established structures of collective bargaining in the unions' 'traditional heartlands'. Employment growth after 1983 was concentrated in the types of workplace and industry that unions in the past had found most difficult to organize.

With the declared objective of making labour markets more 'competitive, efficient and flexible', Conservative governments also intervened to weaken the legal and administrative controls on employers' use of labour. The deregulation achieved in practice was limited and pragmatic (Dickens and Hall, 1995, p. 273). This was in part because there was relatively limited scope for a weakening of protective employment legislation in the UK. This was because much of the regulation of employment relations had been achieved under 'voluntarism' where collective bargaining at industry and workplace level established rules where unions were recognized. In the non-union sector (growing rapidly in the 1980s) there were relatively few regulations beyond protection for employees for health and safety reasons and, in some industries, 'wages councils' which established minimum rates of pay. These were abolished in the early 1990s. Some individual employment protection rights derived from or were enshrined in European Community legislation such as collective redundancy, unfair dismissal, equal pay and maternity leave rights. The pace of labour market deregulation was tempered by the UK's obligation to comply with EU legislation. In spite of the 'opt out' of the EU social chapter negotiated by John Major at Maastricht in 1991, EU treaty obligations and the rulings of the European Court of Justice continued to exert a force on the development of UK employment regulation. Despite this, a crucial change was progressively introduced. The qualifying period of service required by employees to achieve the right to claim unfair dismissal and the right to financial compensation for economic redundancy was raised from six months to two years. Since this was at a time when employers' use of certain types of 'non-standard' employment contracts was rising, a larger proportion of the employed workforce was excluded from access to statutory employment protection rights. In addition, employers had acquired the right to oblige fixed-term contract workers to waive their statutory employment protection rights.

Part-time employment and self-employment accounted for a large portion of the increase in 'non-standard' employment in the 1980s. Part-time employment had been rising since the 1950s and 1960s, although it became more significant in the sense that, in the recession of the early 1990s, it was virtually the only form of employment to show any increase. Service sector employment, where part-time working traditionally has been more common, was the only growth area in this period. The growth trend in self-employment dated from the 1970s, but the growth was relatively strong in the 1980s. Some portion of the increase must represent a worker response to unemployment and, in this period, the Conservative government offered public subsidies for individuals pioneering new 'businesses' (the enterprise allowance scheme). As measured by the LFS, temporary work declined slightly in the late 1980s (when unemployment was falling), although there were industry variations and different trajectories in the private and public sectors. The overall decline is nevertheless interesting, given the apparent inducements offered to employers to create limited duration jobs. Temporary employment did increase in the period of recovery from the recession of the early 1990s and use of fixed-term contracts and temporary agency work showed the strongest growth. The private recruitment industry expanded in this period. In part this was helped by the Deregulation and Contracting Out Act of 1994 which repealed the requirement for those wishing to trade as an employment agency/business to obtain a licence from the Secretary of State.

Assessments of the impact of the Conservative government's industrial relations reforms and reforms of employment legislation differ. Some commentators (for example, Crafts, 1988) have argued that employers have been able more easily to achieve productivity-enhancing changes in work organization and working practices. Others (for example, Nolan, 1996) have suggested that the effect has been to reinforce the UK's status within the international economy as a site for the location of low-skill, low-wage, low-value-added production processes. Conservative government ministers argued that the relatively swift fall in unemployment after the recession of the early 1990s was evidence of the success of their 'free market' approach; the UK labour market was operating more efficiently and more like the deregulated labour market of the United States. Critics, however, noted how labour market rigidities had been reinforced; the unemployed and those employed in low-skill, low-status jobs had limited access to regrading through training, and surveys suggested an all-pervasive sense of job insecurity, among workers in 'core' as well as 'peripheral' jobs. By the mid-1990s, when all of the legislative and employment policy changes introduced since 1979 were in place, the labour market was more deregulated and decentralized than at any time in the post-war period. For employees on open-ended contracts (sometimes, and mistakenly, described as 'permanent') with over two years' continuous service there was some protection (or rather compensation) for some types of dismissal and some procedural rights for handling a grievance and equal pay and discrimination rights. For employees on limited duration contracts and those with less than two years' service, many of these rights did not apply, and only a minority were covered by collective bargaining. In general less than 20 per cent of contingent workers are members of trade unions, compared with 30 per cent of permanent workers.

The UK's New Labour Party was elected to government in May 1997 in the context of economic growth, falling unemployment and rising employment. New Labour's pre-election commitments were to continue with a number of the policy objectives of the previous Conservative administration. These included the objectives of macroeconomic stability, public expenditure controls (subsequently relaxed in the run-up to the general election of 2001) and labour market flexibility. In office, New Labour's 'active' labour market policy has centred largely on education and training. Those in employment have been encouraged to invest in the updating of their skills in order to improve their 'employability'. 'New deal' measures have been deployed to assist the young and the long-term unemployed (among other 'socially excluded' groups) to make the transition from 'welfare to work'.

New Labour's commitment has been to steer a 'third way' between USA-style 'market liberalism' and the 'social market' model to which EU member states such as Sweden and Germany have adhered, until the recent past at least. Alongside labour market flexibility, 'fairness at work' has been elevated as a public policy objective. Much of the 1980s industrial relations legislation has been retained. But new collective and individual employment rights have also been enacted. Labour government ministers have presented these as the means of enhancing worker commitment, flexibility and mobility between jobs and of encouraging firms to compete on quality as well as price. Many (although not all) of the new rights have been conferred on *workers* as opposed to the narrower constituency of *employees* (see the next section). In principle, many workers on 'non-standard' employment contracts have access to these rights, although the employment status of self-employed workers remains unclear (Burchell *et al.*, 1999b). The Treasury, however, has continued its campaign to restrict the scope for 'false self-employment' and new Inland Revenue regulations have been introduced for this purpose (IR35: Personal Services Provided Through Intermediaries).

Among the key pieces of employment legislation introduced since 1997 are the following:

- *National Minimum Wage Act* (1998). This applies to workers. The Act instituted a minimum hourly rate of pay of £3.60 for those aged 22 years or over and a minimum rate of £3.20 per hour for workers aged 18 to 21 or aged 22 years or over and on accredited training. The minimum hourly rate is reviewed periodically.
- *Working Time Regulations*. These were introduced to comply with the EU Working Time Directive. They came into force in October 1998. The regulations apply to workers with 13 weeks' continuous service. They provide for a limit of an average of 48 hours a week, which a worker can be required to work (although they allow workers to 'choose' to work in excess of this limit) and, among other protections, they institute a worker's right to four weeks' paid holiday a year.
- *Employment Relations Act* (1999). Most provisions apply to workers. The Act revives (in a modified form) the statutory union recognition procedure introduced (initially by a Conservative government) in the 1970s although rescinded in the early 1980s. It provides workers with access to a range of 'family friendly' leave provisions and enhances certain other individual employment rights.
- *Part-time Workers Regulations*. Introduced to comply with the EU's part-time Work Directive, these came into force on 1 July 2000. They are intended to ensure that part-timers are not treated less favourably than comparable full-timers in their contractual terms and conditions.

In addition to the above, the length of service threshold for the right to unfair dismissal protection has been reduced from two years to one (with effect from 1 June 2000). The Employment Relations Act 1999 increased the ceiling on the maximum financial compensation that can be awarded by an employment tribunal to a successful applicant. Unfair dismissal protection in its general form remains available only to employees, but workers dismissed for pursuing their rights under the National Minimum Wage Act or under the Working Time Regulations can pursue what in effect amounts to a claim for unfair dismissal on the grounds of 'detriment'.

The National Minimum Wage (NMW) Act and Working Time Regulations apply to workers rather than exclusively to employees. The Employment Relations Act 1999 confers powers on the Secretary of State to extend similarly the coverage of other, existing statutory employment rights. It also extends the powers of the Secretary of State to amend the regulations that apply to the private recruitment industry. One of the amendments proposed subsequently has been that temporary staff hire should be conducted on an employment business basis. Agency temps are included as workers under the provisions of the NMW and Working Time Regulations and the intent of the proposed amendment is to clarify that their contractual relationship is with the employment business (rather than the client). The effect is to bring more workers, especially agency workers, within the ambit of legislative protection and clarifies the role of TWAs as employers.

The impact of these legislative changes on employers' recruitment and labour use practices is as yet unclear. Obviously the changes have to be considered alongside other developments, including the continuing fall in unemployment. Nevertheless, we can explore management strategies towards contingent labour as these evolved in the 1980s and 1990s.

The marked changes in the economic, political, legislative and social environment in Britain in the 1980s and early 1990s had a profound influence on management strategies towards employment. Managerial strategic choices simultaneously fed back into the business environment, so that fashions and fads of action became apparent. The combination of privatization and marketization in the public sector and globalization in much of the private sector meant that few organizations were untouched by these competitive or survival pressures. Their managements felt compelled to do something in the field of employment, but the response varied considerably sector by sector. To give some examples:

- In the retail industry, there was a rapid extension of opening hours to cover weekends and late night shopping. This rendered the traditional employment pattern no longer viable. There was a marked growth in the use of part-time workers, retired people, students and on-call work contracts.
- In the finance sector, the deregulation of the industry, matched with the revolution in IT systems, lowered the cost of entry and established banks and insurance companies found the old barriers to entry easily and decisively breached. The outcome was not only longer business hours dealing with the customer but radically new customer relationship management techniques based on telephone call centres and now Internet contact centres. This threw up a whole new industry and it is estimated that 2 per cent of the working population will

be employed in such centres by 2002. Many use agency staff extensively, while the agencies themselves have moved into providing and managing complete telebureaux.

- In local authorities, the requirement for competitive tendering, actively encouraged by the EC and the UK Treasury, led to the renegotiation of contracts, a rapid rise in fixed term contracting, and 'outsourcing' to new suppliers, for example in refuse disposal. This was also evident in part of the civil service through the development of 'Executive Agencies'.
- These general patterns were observed in the health service through the imposition of the so-called 'New Public Management' and decentralization to employment units, yet with recentralization to Treasury control of budgets. The outcome has been a rapid growth in short-term, on-call work contracts and, especially, fixed-term contracts.
- In universities, there has been a proliferation in short-term contracts, and in further education the growth of quasi-self-employment. That is, previous part-time employees were 'asked' to become self-employed and sometimes register with an agency.
- In manufacturing, the recession of the early 1980s especially (and to a lesser extent in the 1990s) was marked by 'restructuring' which meant substantial job losses achieved through 'downsizing', 'outsourcing' and a focus on core activities where cost reduction was paramount. In some cases this was associated with the near disappearance of whole industrial sectors and sub-sectors such as shipbuilding, large-scale steel making, and coal mining, (ironically these three industries were known as the Triple Alliance, or the heartland of organized labour, in the 1920s and 1930s).

It is hard to find a sector where marked employment change did not occur in the 1980s and early 1990s. What is interesting, as we discuss in later sections, is the way this has now plateaued.

## THE LABOUR MARKET IN THE UK

### The Labour Force

The labour force in the UK (those in employment plus the ILO unemployed) grew by 2.2 million in the second half of the 1980s but contracted in the recession of the early 1990s and remained stable between 1993 and 1995. Growth has resumed since the mid-1990s and is projected to continue, albeit at a slower rate than in the late 1980s. In spring 1999 there were

28.2 million 'economically active' people among a working age population of 35.9 million (*Social Trends* 30, 2000). This represents an economic activity rate of 78.6 per cent which was higher than the rate in 1993 but still below the peak of 80.4 per cent reached in 1990.

The population of working age (men aged 16 to 64 and women aged 16 to 59) grew rapidly in the 1980s by virtue of the 'baby boom' of the 1960s. The birth rate fell in the late 1970s, and the rate of growth of the working age population fell commensurately in the late 1990s. At the same time the trend, in particular from the late 1980s, has been for more young people to remain in full-time education after the legal school leaving age of 16 years. There were 4.4 million people aged between 16 and 24 years in the labour force in 1997 (15.3 per cent) compared with 5.9 million (22 per cent) in 1981 (*Social Trends* 30, 2000, p. 67). The proportion of young people progressing from school to further and higher education has risen since the late 1980s. However, the introduction of tuition fees from 1997 has encouraged a higher proportion of these to make themselves available for part-time work: 40 per cent of students had a part-time job in spring 1999 compared with 33 per cent in 1992 (LM&ST, 2000).

Economic activity rates among women and, in particular, among married or cohabiting women, have continued to rise (single women without dependent children have traditionally participated in paid work). In the 1950s and 1960s, when production industries supported relatively full employment among male manual workers, married women formed the 'obvious', fresh source of labour supply to support the expansion of service sector industries in Britain (Bruegel and Perrons, 1998). The association between rising female participation rates and service sector expansion has continued subsequently (see below).

In 1971, 56 per cent of women in the UK were 'economically active' (in work or seeking work). By 1999, the rate had increased to 72 per cent. Male economic activity rates have fallen from 91 per cent to 84 per cent over the period (*Social Trends* 30, 2000, p. 68). The decline has been most pronounced among older men: those aged 55 years or above. The number of men in the labour force remained relatively constant, at around 16 million, between the early 1970s and late 1990s. The proportion of the male labour force aged 55 years or above fell, however, from 21 per cent in 1971 to 13 per cent in 1997 (ibid., p. 67). Men still form a majority of the labour force (56 per cent in 1997). It is anticipated, however, that the gap between male and female economic activity rates will continue to narrow and that women will form 46 per cent of the labour force in Britain by 2011 (LM&ST, 2000, p. 28).

Inadequate public provision of childcare in the UK has been identified as one of the factors constraining women's labour market participation and the participation in particular of lone mothers. Of the latter, 32 per cent were classed as 'economically inactive' in spring 1999 compared with 25 per cent of married or cohabiting women with dependent children (*Social Trends* 30, 2000, p. 68). A new National Childcare Strategy has been launched by the Labour government, in office since 1997, alongside other, potentially more punitive, measures to encourage higher rates of labour market participation among single mothers (changes to the conditions for receipt of welfare benefits, and so on).

Labour force participation rates differ among ethnic groups. Ethnic minority men and women have lower rates of participation than whites but there are marked differences between the ethnic minority groups. Among men, Black Caribbeans, followed by Indians and Black Africans, have the highest rates of economic activity, with the lowest rates recorded among the Chinese (who show a higher level of participation in full-time education). Bangladeshi and Pakistani women are the least likely to be 'economically active' among women from ethnic minority groups.

## Unemployment

Following the downturn in activity in the international economy of the 1970s, unemployment rose sharply in most advanced industrial economies in the early 1980s. The increase was perhaps most pronounced in the UK where, in an effort to invigorate the disciplinary force of the market, the incoming Conservative government had relaxed exchange rate controls and allowed the value of sterling to rise. The latter affected export-oriented manufacturing industries in particular and precipitated a 'shake-out' of jobs. The claimant unemployment count rose from 1.3 to 2.5 million between 1979 and 1981 and reached its peak at over 3 million in 1986.[1] It fell to 1.7 million in 1990 and rose again to 2.9 million in 1993. Unemployment in the UK began to fall fairly swiftly from 1993. ILO unemployment has fallen from around 3 million in 1993 to roughly 1.7 million in February/April 2000 – its lowest level since the series began in 1984 (*Labour Market Trends*, July 2000; *Social Trends* 30, 2000, p. 66). This sustained fall in unemployment has been cited by UK government ministers as evidence of the virtues of a lightly regulated labour market.

Regional and interregional differences in unemployment levels and rates nevertheless persist in the UK. In spring 1999, the unemployment rate was 10.1 per cent in the north-east of England and 7.5 per cent in London, in comparison with a UK average of 6.2 per cent. Unemployment fell below 5 per cent in the south-east, east and south-west of England and in the east Midlands. In each of these regions, unemployment 'blackspots' nevertheless remained, in particular in inner-city areas.

Unemployment was slightly higher among men than women in spring 1999: 6.8 per cent compared with 5.3 per cent. Unemployment is significantly higher among ethnic minorities than among whites: the ILO unemployment rate for the former was twice that of the latter in 1998 (LM&ST 2000, p. 37).

## Employment

### Employees

There were approximately 27 million people in employment in Britain in spring 1999. This represents an increase of around 2 million on the previous low of 1993 and an increase of half a million on the previous peak of 1990 (LM&ST 2000). However, the employment rate (those in employment as a percentage of the working age population) remained below the all-time high of the mid-1970s (*Labour Market Trends*, January 2000, p. 35).

Employment growth in the period since 1992 has been accounted for exclusively by the growth in the number of employees. This contrasts with the previous period of employment growth, between 1983 and 1990. In this earlier period, the numbers in self-employment, defined as 'those who, in their own employment, work on their own account, whether or not they have employees', rose by almost a million to approximately 3.5 million.

### Industrial composition of employment

Over the past 20 years the industrial composition of employment has continued to shift away from manufacturing and the production industries and towards service sector industries. This shift, evident from at least the 1950s, was accentuated by the recession of the early 1980s when job losses were concentrated on full-time male manual workers in manufacturing and this sector's share of GDP, as well as employment, declined markedly. Britain – once the 'workshop of the world' – became a net importer of manufactured products. Currently, manufacturing's share of employee jobs is around 17 per cent, compared with 30 per cent in 1978.

It is relevant to point out that there has been a significant increase in the foreign ownership of companies in the UK and in manufacturing in particular. Foreign-owned companies generated an average of 31 per cent of manufacturing's net capital investment, 24 per cent of its gross value added and 17 per cent of its employment between 1990 and 1999 (Wolf, 2000).

Some three in four jobs were in the service industries in 1999. Employment growth among these industries in the period from 1992 has been especially strong in banking, finance and insurance (where deregulation and automation have combined to produce job cuts in the banks' branch networks, the entrance of new competitors and expansion of 'call centre' employment). Employment growth has been strong also in distribution, hotels and restaurants (LM&ST 2000).

**Public and private sector employment**

The public sector's share of employment has fallen over the past 20 years. This sector accounted for 28 per cent of all workforce jobs in 1981. Conservative governments in the 1980s and early 1990s, however, pursued the privatization of public utilities and former nationalized industries (coal, steel and so on) and enacted legislation to encourage local and central government to contract out services. By 1991, the public sector's share of workforce jobs had fallen to 22 per cent and in 1999 it amounted to less than 18 per cent. Public sector jobs in fact increased in 1999, for the first time in 20 years, with the increases concentrated in education and national health trusts. Since the rise in public service jobs was less substantial than that in some private service industry groups, the public sector's share of all workforce jobs continued to decline (MacGregor, 2000).

**'Temporary work'**

'Temporary work – or jobs held by someone who has been recruited to do them for a finite period' (Sly and Stillwell, 1997, p. 348) is the term most commonly used in the UK for contingent working. Difficulties with the definition and the reliability of statistical sources are explored in the next section. Another confusing term commonly used is 'non-standard work', which often includes part-time and self-employment. In this analysis part-timers and the self-employed are categorically excluded, although LFS figures do not necessarily exclude contingent employees working in part-time or self-employed jobs. For example, some three-fifths of part-time women workers do not have 'permanent' or open-ended contracts and are thus counted as contingent or temporary workers. Most self-employed people do not have employment contracts, as explored in the next section. Contingent working has shown some increase over the past 20 years. The exact extent of this increase is difficult to measure. The main data source – the household LFS – reports respondents' classification of their employment status. The series suggests that the growth in temporary work has been cyclical, although reaching a higher level at the end of each period of 'recovery' from an economic downturn.

Thus the proportion of all employees in temporary jobs remained stable, at around 5 per cent, in the mid-1980s and fell slightly in the late 1980s, when unemployment was falling. Temporary workers' share of all employees started to rise in the recession of the early 1990s and continued to rise in the early years of 'recovery', reaching 7.7 per cent in 1997. However, the rate of growth slowed from 1996 and by spring 1998 temporary workers' share of employment had fallen back to 7.3 per cent (representing 1.8 million in temporary work) (*IRS Employment Trends*, April 1999).

Temporary work can take various forms. Almost half of the total number of temporary workers identified by the spring 1998 LFS were on fixed-term contracts. 'Casual workers' comprised a fifth of the total, but had formed nearly 30 per cent of all temporary workers in spring 1992. The number of 'agency temps' – workers in non-permanent jobs attained through a temporary employment agency – showed the greatest absolute and proportionate increase in the 1990s, doubling to 13 per cent of all temporary workers in 1996 and rising to 18 per cent of the total in 1998 (ibid.).

The expansion of the use of 'agency temps' in this period is suggested also by the trebling in size of the private recruitment industry since 1992 (DTI, 1999). The industry embraces organizations engaged in a variety of activities such as 'permanent' recruitment, temporary staff hire and the provision of job vacancy information. The industry's own estimates suggest that total invoiced sales amounted to £14.1bn in 1997/8 and that 93 per cent of this total related to temporary staff hire. We explore various patterns of contingency working in detail in subsequent sections of this chapter, once measurement difficulties have been explained.

## CONTINGENT EMPLOYMENT: TRENDS AND PATTERNS

### Measuring Contingent Employment: Data Sources

Although contingent employment can be defined broadly (and assessed in relation to prevailing labour market conditions), we adhere here to the parameters set by contractual status. The principal data source used is the Labour Force Survey (LFS). This household survey series reports respondents' own definition of their employment status (as opposed to the definition that a court or employment tribunal might place on their employee status or otherwise). The data allow measurement and analysis of the distribution of various forms of contracts (fixed-term or fixed-task contract work, seasonal and casual work, agency temporary work and also on-call work contracts) and of self-employment. The LFS provides a consistent data series. Some limitations of the series have been noted which more or less apply to all such surveys used in EU countries.

Burchell *et al.* (1999a) conducted a survey of members of the British workforce. They excluded the 'genuinely self-employed' and asked other respondents whether they believed their job to be permanent and whether their work could be described by a given list of non-standard working arrangements. A majority of respondents (around 90 per cent of the 3753 surveyed) reported their jobs as permanent and a majority of these (three-quarters) said they were not working under any of the listed forms of non-standard working. But a sizeable minority (just under a fifth) of those who had described their job as permanent went on to describe their work as non-standard. A majority of these suggested they were working under a fixed-term contract. In short, Burchell *et al.*'s research suggests that the LFS may significantly underreport the scale of fixed-term contracting because many workers on these contracts believe their jobs to be permanent.

Difficulties also arise in relation to the self-employed. The employment status of the self-employed has become a focus of interest, in particular as recent UK employment legislation (enacted since the mid-1990s) has tended to use the concept of 'worker' rather than the narrower concept of 'employee' in defining the scope of new employment rights (for example, the National Minimum Wage Act 1998, and Working Time Regulations that came into force in 1999). The concept of 'worker' includes employees, engaged on a contract of employment, but also individuals who have entered into or who work under 'any other contract . . . whereby the individual undertakes to do or perform personally any work or services for another party to the contract whose status is not by virtue of the contract that of a client or customer of any profession or business carried on by the individual' (Employment Rights Act 1996, s.230 (3)). In relation to this worker concept, and other concerns, analysts have tended to group the self-employed into three categories: the 'false self-employed', 'dependent self-employed' (or 'borderline employee') and the 'genuine self-employed'. The first denotes individuals who are objectively employees but who have described themselves as self-employed, or have been obliged by their employer to describe themselves as such, in order to evade tax and national insurance obligations or in order to evade the provisions of employment protection legislation. Recent Inland Revenue regulations have been introduced in an effort to curb tax evasion through 'false self-employment' and may have had an impact on aggregate levels of self-employment in the late 1990s (Moralee, 1998). The notion of 'genuine self-employed' is an attempt to define persons running a business (as directors or partners and/or who employ other workers). 'Dependent self-employed' describes those who are engaged on a contract for services but who are akin to employees, because they contract to supply their own services and are to a great extent economically dependent on one client organization (see Burchell *et al.*, 1999a; Davies and Freedland, 2000).

The LFS only questions individuals who have identified themselves as employees about the temporary nature of their jobs. Burchell *et al.*'s research, however, has found high levels of non-standard working among the self-employed (the 'borderline employee' category) and that, in terms of vulnerability to summary dismissal, some among this group are 'chronically insecure'. In this report we have to rely on LFS data despite their limitations. The underreporting of fixed-term contract workers and some of the self-employed and contingent workers means that data reported in subsequent sections should be considered as minimal. However, as discussed earlier, this underrepresenting is common to most economies. We have no way of telling whether it is greater or lesser in the UK than elsewhere.

## The General Trend of Contingent Employment

In the UK, the share of contingent employment in total employment was just over 5 per cent in 1988 and had changed little over the 1980s. In the 1990s, however, there was a noticeable increase and, by 1996, its share in total employment had risen to 7.3 per cent. In the following years, this growth stopped and the proportion fell to 6.7 per cent in 1999 (nearly 1.8 million employees).

## Contingent Employment in the Public and Private Sectors

In 1984, 17 per cent of establishments in non-trading public services could be classified as 'high users of contingent employment' (Morgan *et al.*, 2000) with 5 per cent or more of the workforce being contingent. This proportion increased to 26 per cent in 1990. The evidence also indicates that, between 1984 and 1994, the number of contingent employees in public administration services in particular grew by 66 per cent. This was considerably higher than the 45 per cent growth of overall contingent employment for the same period.

In 1994, contingent employment was 9.5 per cent of public sector employment, compared with 4 per cent in the private sector. Public sector contingent employment increased slightly, to 10 per cent, by 1996, the last year of the Conservative government. It declined to 9.5 per cent in 1999. In the private sector contingent employment reached 5.1 per cent by 1999. (Noticeably, in the private sector 1.2 million employees worked on contingent jobs in 1999, compared to 600000 in the public sector.) The particular characteristic of the public sector is the reliance on fixed-term contract workers. Two-thirds of all contingent workers in the public sector, have fixed-term contracts, compared with just over a third in the private sector. In contrast, 81 per cent of agency workers are in the private sector, compared with 18 per cent in the public sector.

## Contingent Employment in Various Industries

Table 3.1 shows the sectoral variations in contingent employment in the period since 1994. Agriculture and Fishing has the highest proportionate use of contingent employment but, given the small size of these industries, the actual number of workers in contingent jobs is only 50000.

*Table 3.1 Contingent employment as a percentage of total employment in various sectors**

| | 1994 | 1995 | 1996 | 1997 | 1998 | 1999 |
|---|---|---|---|---|---|---|
| Agriculture & fishing | 7.4 | 8.4 | 8.5 | 8.0 | 8.2 | 9.9 |
| Energy & water | 6.4 | 8.2 | 8.2 | 7.3 | 9.1 | 6.6 |
| Manufacturing | 3.6 | 4.4 | 4.3 | 4.6 | 4.3 | 4.1 |
| Construction | 6.1 | 7.1 | 6.6 | 7.3 | 6.4 | 6.7 |
| Distribution, hotels & restaurants | 5.4 | 5.2 | 5.3 | 5.7 | 5.1 | 4.9 |
| Transport & communication | 4.5 | 5.1 | 5.5 | 6.0 | 5.9 | 5.4 |
| Banking, finance & insurance etc. | 5.8 | 7.2 | 7.3 | 7.9 | 6.8 | 6.8 |
| Public admin., education & health | 9.5 | 10.0 | 9.9 | 10.5 | 10.6 | 10.0 |
| Other services | 11.1 | 10.5 | 11.6 | 11.2 | 10.6 | 10.5 |
| All temporary employees | 6.5 | 7.1 | 7.1 | 7.5 | 7.1 | 6.9 |

*Note:* * Based on SIC (92) Standard Industrial Classification; Spring Term for each year.

*Source:* LFS.

Following the privatization of the Energy and Water industry in the late 1980s, company managers began to initiate new employment strategies which are often associated with labour cost reduction and efficiency improvements (Nichols and Davidson, 1993). Accordingly, the industry experienced a significant growth especially in the mid-1990s. In 1992, it was among the lowest users of contingent employment.

From 1992 to 1999, the share of contingent employment in the Construction industry was almost flat, averaging around 6.5 per cent. Likewise, in the Manufacturing sector, contingent employment remained stable as a proportion of total employment. However, overall employment continued to fall in this sector. Manufacturing firms pursued externalization[2] policies, outsourcing functions and their staffs to outside contractors. This could be considered an alternative strategy to the use of contingent labour.

In the private service sector, covering industries such as retail distribution, hotels and transport, and in the financial sector, including business services, there was a discernible growth in contingent employment levels at a time when the sector had been growing consistently.

The most noticeable growth in the use of contingent labour was in the finance sector in the first half of the 1990s, but it has declined since then in part because of falling unemployment levels and adaptation to company employment strategies. The precise reasons need to be explored in subsequent research.

## Contingent Employment in Various Occupations

Contingent employment is at the highest level amongst professionals when compared to other occupational categories.[3] In 1993, almost one in 10 professionals were employed in contingent jobs (Table 3.2). By 1996, this proportion had increased to almost 14 per cent, but since then, no significant change has been observed (In 1999, they constituted roughly one in every six contingent workers – 310000 – which is equal to the number of clerical contingent workers.)

Noticeably, amongst associate professionals,[4] the share of contingent employment grew more slowly from 6.7 per cent in 1993 to 7.4 per cent in 1999. One in 10 contingent employees were associate professionals in 1999.

Another occupational group with a significant use of contingent employment is personal and protective services. In 1996, it reached 9 per cent, up from 7.6 per cent in 1993. However, the growth of contingent employment amongst these workers also stopped in the second half of the 1990s. In

*Table 3.2 Contingent employment* in various occupations***

| | 1993 | 1996 | 1999 |
|---|---|---|---|
| 1 Managers and administrators | 2.0 | 2.6 | 2.4 |
| 2 Professional occupations | 10.9 | 13.9 | 13.4 |
| 3 Associate prof. & tech occupations | 6.5 | 7.0 | 7.4 |
| 4 Clerical, secretarial occupations | 5.6 | 8.0 | 7.4 |
| 5 Craft and related occupations | 4.3 | 4.2 | 4.7 |
| 6 Personal, protective occupations | 7.6 | 9.2 | 8.8 |
| 7 Sales occupations | 4.6 | 4.7 | 4.3 |
| 8 Plant and machine operatives | 4.6 | 6.3 | 5.7 |
| 9 Other occupations | 8.3 | 8.5 | 8.9 |
| All temporary employees | 5.9 | 7.1 | 6.9 |

*Notes:*
* Based on employees' definition of their own jobs in LFS surveys.
** As percentage of total employment in each occupational category; Spring Term for each year.

*Source:* LFS.

1999, it was nearly 9 per cent (or 250 000 out of 2 million personal and protective service workers).

In general, although there was an increase in contingent employment in most occupational categories from the early 1990s to the mid-1990s, the end of the decade witnessed an end to this growth or even a decline. In the late 1990s, contingent employment increased only among craft-related workers, but even here it was a modest growth from a low base.

## Contingent Employment by Different Forms

The most common type of contingent employment is fixed-term contract. Between 1992 and 1999, its share in total contingent employment increased from 47 per cent to 51 per cent (Table 3.3). In other words, over 900 000 people in Britain worked on a fixed-term contract in 1999. The second most common type of contingent employment is casual–seasonal employment, although its share declined slightly between 1992 and 1999. Roughly one-third of contingent employees were classified as casual–seasonal workers in 1992. By 1997, the share of these workers in total contingent employment declined to 26 per cent, but it increased to 27 per cent in 1999 (485 000 workers). Casual workers are hired for a short period (often a day or a week) usually with no fixed time limit for the work and in practice employment contracts are rarely issued. Seasonal workers tend to be employed in a particular period such as Christmas time in retail and holiday time in hotels (the spring LFS data probably underrecorded the number of such workers).

*Table 3.3 Contingent employment, by types**

| Year | Fixed-term contract work | Seasonal and casual | Agency temping | Unspecified | Total |
|---|---|---|---|---|---|
| 1992 | 47 | 32 | 5 | 16 | 100 |
| 1993 | 48 | 30 | 7 | 16 | 100 |
| 1994 | 48 | 27 | 8 | 16 | 100 |
| 1995 | 49 | 25 | 9 | 15 | 100 |
| 1996 | 48 | 25 | 11 | 17 | 100 |
| 1997 | 49 | 26 | 12 | 15 | 100 |
| 1998 | 50 | 25 | 11 | 14 | 100 |
| 1999 | 51 | 27 | 12 | 10 | 100 |

*Note:* * Percentage of total contingent workforce, not seasonally adjusted; Spring Term for each year, but for 1997/8 winter quarter.

*Source:* *Labour Market Trends*, September 1997; LFS Quarterly Supplements, 1998/1999.

Another important type of contingent employment is agency temping. Although its share in total employment is lower than other specified categories, it was in a significant upward trend until the second half of the 1990s. In 1992, its share was less than 5 per cent in total contingent employment. By 1997, it had increased to 12 per cent.

**On-call Work**

On-call work is a special form of contingent employment. On-call work contracts do not specify particular hours: the person may be required at any time or at specified times. These contracts maximize flexibility for employers and sometimes suit some people who want occasional earnings. In the UK, they are referred as 'zero-hours' contracts.

On-call work contracts have the potential to be abused. It is noted that employees, for example, could be asked to 'clock off' and so lose pay in quiet periods but without being able to leave the premises. Being 'on call' also creates difficulties in claiming state benefit, even though no work was being done or money earned (DTI, 1998).

In 1997, on-call work was 0.5 per cent of total employment. Amongst females, this proportion was 0.6 per cent as compared with 0.49 per cent males. General contingent employment declined from 7.3 per cent to 6.7 per cent of total employment between 1997 and 1999; on-call work, however, increased by 0.2 per cent in this period, reaching 0.7 per cent of total employment. In 1999, it was recorded as 0.77 per cent amongst women against 0.67 per cent for males. That year nearly 200000 people worked under on-call work contracts, which is roughly 10 per cent of all contingent employees (LFS, 1997; 1999, spring quarter).

**Gender, Age, Ethnic and Educational Characteristics**

There is a visible gender difference in contingent employment, with higher levels for females than for males, but the gap is narrowing because of the faster growth of contingent employment amongst men than women. In 1988, although contingent employment was only 3.6 per cent amongst men, this proportion was over 7 per cent for women. By 1995, contingent employment amongst males had increased to 6.2 per cent, and the annual average remained at this level for the remainder of the 1990s. Female contingent employment was recorded as 7.6 per cent in 1999. Roughly half of the 1.8 million contingent employees in 1999 were women.

The gender variation in contingent employment was less than 2 percentage points in 1999. Female contingent employment was almost twice as much as males' in the late 1980s.

The biggest proportion of male contingent employment appears to be amongst those aged 65 years and over. Arguably, the most important reason for this is that retired people tend to earn money from contingent jobs (the state pension is paid from 65 for men and 60 for women). The data suggest that 22 per cent of males in employment in this age group worked as contingent employees in 1999 (Table 3.4). Contingent employment is also at a significant level amongst the females aged 60 years and over, but less than half of the proportion for '65 and over males', at 10 per cent. It is important to note that only 6 per cent of all British contingent employees were of pensionable age in 1999.

Contingent employment is more pertinent for young people. The highest rate of female contingent employment is among 16–17-year-olds, at nearly 20 per cent. Noticeably, this age group has a high level of contingent employment for males as well. Table 3.4 shows that 17 per cent of males aged 16–17 are contingent employees. Another age group which has a high level of contingent employment is 18–24-year-olds, with 14.5 per cent of women and 12.5 per cent of men contingent employees. In 1999, nearly 29 per cent of the British contingent employees were aged from 16 to 24 years.

Contingent employment was roughly 4.5 per cent amongst the men aged from 25 to 34 and from 35 to 49. It averaged 7 per cent for the women in these age groups. In 1999, half of the British contingent employees were aged from 25 to 49 years.

Contingent employment varies by ethnic group. In 1994, for example,

*Table 3.4 Contingent employment and age structure (%)*

| | Contingent employment ratio in various age groups, by sex | | | Share in total contingent employment | | |
|---|---|---|---|---|---|---|
| Age groups | Male | Female | Overall Average | Male | Female | Total |
| All 16+ | 6.0 | 8.0 | 6.9 | 46.2 | 53.7 | 100 |
| 16–17 | 17.0 | 19.5 | 18.2 | 2.9 | 3.5 | 6.4 |
| 18–24 | 12.5 | 14.5 | 13.4 | 10.8 | 11.5 | 22.3 |
| 25–34 | 4.5 | 7.0 | 5.6 | 9.8 | 11.9 | 21.7 |
| 35–49 | 4.4 | 7.0 | 5.6 | 11.0 | 17.5 | 28.5 |
| 50–64* (50–59)** | 4.6 | 5.5 | 4.9 | 8.6 | 6.8 | 15.4 |
| 65+* (60+)** | 22.0 | 10.0 | 14.2 | 3.4 | 2.6 | 6.0 |

*Notes:*
*Males.
**Females.

*Source:* Labour Force Survey, November 1999.

contingent employment was roughly 5.3 per cent amongst white males. The proportion was very similar for Asian males, at 5.7 per cent. The proportion of contingent employment amongst Black Caribbean men was not much different, at 6.5 per cent, yet no less than 12 per cent of non-Caribbean Black men were contingent employees, as were 14 per cent of Chinese men.

Contingent employment was at its lowest level among white females, at 7.5 per cent in 1994. The lowest level of non-white female contingent employment was amongst Caribbean Black women (9 per cent). It was 11 per cent amongst Chinese females and 15 per cent amongst non-Caribbean Black females.

## ANALYSING TRENDS IN CONTINGENT EMPLOYMENT

The purpose of this section is to assess the extent to which the growth of contingent labour has distinctive characteristics, in particular by disadvantaging employees in the labour market, as has sometimes been suggested. We look at training, access to permanent jobs, job security, the link with unemployment, why people take contingent jobs and the link with childcare. We also examine why employers use temporary workers.

### Skilling or Deskilling?

There were two contradictory arguments over the implications of contingent employment for the skill levels of workers. Some scholars argue that contingent employment may work as a process in which employers can choose suitable workers for training programmes. In this sense, contingent employment may work as a mechanism to encourage companies to invest in training schemes in the process of obtaining skilled workers for permanent jobs. The other approach, human capital theory, argues that employers would prefer not to spend money on the training of contingent employees (see Gannon, 1996; Booth *et al.* 2000). Through a probability analysis of a household panel survey, Booth *et al.* found that the chance of employees on fixed-term contracts having access to a training programme is considerably lower than that of permanent workers (−12 per cent for males and −7 per cent for females). For casual–seasonal workers, access to training was even less likely (−20 per cent for males and −15 per cent for females).

It should be noted that, although contingent employment appears to be a disadvantaged model in terms of training, the extent to which it undermines such workers' chances of moving into a permanent job is not established. In general, according to British Household Panel Survey (BHPS) data, 28 per cent of male and 34 per cent of female casual/seasonal workers had become permanent workers between 1991 and 1997 (Booth *et al.*, 2000). For workers on fixed-term contracts, the transition rate to permanency is 38 per cent for men and 36 per cent for women. At the least the argument that contingent workers form a disadvantaged 'underclass' is not proven.

**Is it Good for Unemployment, or Not?**

It has been argued by some scholars that the 'flexibilization' of employment relations in general and the growth of contingent employment in particular would reduce unemployment by increasing people's job opportunities along with declining labour cost and growing investment prospects (Siebert, 1999). The data from the LFS suggest that a significant proportion of contingent employees come to the labour market from unemployment. In 1997, for example, 37 per cent of contingent workers indicated that they had been unemployed before finding a contingent job (LFS, spring 1997). In this sense, the experience of contingent employment can be seen as a transitional experience linked to the efficient operation of the labour market. A minority of contingent workers move on to get permanent jobs. Unfortunately, the data are insufficient to make reliable comments about the exit rate of contingent workers to permanent jobs. The only available figures come from the BHPS. Through the analysis of these surveys, Booth *et al.* (2000) found that the exit rate from contingent jobs to permanent ones was 28 per cent amongst male seasonal–casual workers between 1991 and 1997. The proportion was 34 per cent for their female counterparts. For workers on fixed-term contracts, the transition rate to permanency is significantly higher for men (38 per cent) and almost the same for women (36 per cent). However, using macroeconomic data and testing for any correlation between unemployment and the level of contingent employment does not reveal such a significant relationship. That is, there is no firm evidence to suggest that contingent employment has become an alternative to unemployment.

**Trap or Voluntary Act?**

It is sometimes argued that workers are left with no choice other than opting for contingent employment (Turnbull, 1986; Oliver and Wilkinson, 1988). That is, they would take a permanent job if they could find one. There was some evidence to suggest this in the early 1990s, but recently, as the UK labour market has improved, the proportion of contingent workers wanting a permanent job has fallen. In 1992, 37 per cent of contingent employees indicated that they wanted a permanent job but could not find one. This increased to 43 per cent in 1993, but stayed at this level until 1995. In the second half of the 1990s, the proportion of those who could not find a permanent job began to decline. In 1999, their proportion was no higher than it had been in 1992, at 37 per cent.

There is an important gender difference. In 1992, 31 per cent of female contingent employees and 42 per cent of male contingent employees indicated that they were working in a contingent job because they could not find a permanent job. By 1995, these proportions had increased to 37 per cent and 50 per cent, declining to 31 per cent and 40 per cent, respectively, in 1999.

Reversing the analysis, the LFS also shows that the proportion of contingent workers who do not want a permanent job (26 per cent) was at its lowest level in 1993, in the middle of the 1990s recession. Since then the number of contingent workers not wanting a permanent job has consistently risen, reaching one-third in 1999. As might be expected, the figure is higher for men than for women, although the gap is closing.

## Opportunity for the Women who have Dependent Children?

It has been argued that contingent employment would be suitable especially for women with dependent children, on the grounds that companies can avoid employing these women permanently because of their child-rearing responsibilities (Feldman *et al.*, 1994). The statistics suggest that, in 1994, there was a higher proportion of contingent employment amongst women who have dependent children. In that year the proportion of contingent employment amongst women who do not have dependent children was less than 6 per cent. The ratio of contingent employment amongst those with dependent children, on the other hand, was nearly 9 per cent. However, by 1999, there was no difference between women with and without dependent children, with 8.2 per cent of both groups working in contingent employment (Dex and McCulloch, 1995).

## Education Levels of Contingent Employees

It is sometimes argued that the core–periphery model would lead to low-skilled contingent workers competing unfavourably with high-skilled, better trained, 'core' workers. We have already shown that contingent labour has fewer opportunities for training. Table 3.5 shows clearly that seasonal and casual workers are much less likely to have a high vocational qualification than permanent employees. However, the position is markedly different for fixed-term workers. They are much more likely to have high-level vocational standards compared with any other group. This confirms the bifurcation of contingent employment in the UK. On the one hand, there are low-paid, low-skill, poorly educated workers. On the other hand, around half of contingent workers with fixed-term contracts work in professional occupations where pay (but not benefits) is higher than average and there are high levels of human capital.

*Table 3.5 Highest qualification held by employees*

| | Permanent employees | Contingent employees* | Fixed-term contract | Seasonal work | Casual work |
|---|---|---|---|---|---|
| Numbers (thousands) | 22070 | 1576 | 771 | 63 | 298 |
| NVQ level 4 or above (%) | 27 | 36 | 49 | ** | 16 |
| NVQ level 3 (%) | 19 | 18 | 15 | 25 | 21 |
| NVQ level 2 (%) | 23 | 21 | 17 | 23 | 31 |
| Below NVQ level 2 (%) | 20 | 17 | 14 | 18 | 19 |
| No qualifications (%) | 11 | 8 | 5 | 22 | 14 |

*Notes:*
* Includes unspecified contingent employees.
**Sample sizes too small for a reliable estimate.

*Source:* Labour Force Survey, spring 2000.

## Why do Employers use Contingent Labour?

One of the most contentious areas of analysis in the contingent labour debate is whether employers have or are moving to an employment strategy based on a distinction between core, permanent workers and a periphery of relatively insecure employee contractors (see Purcell and Purcell, 1998). Detailed case study research is the best way to uncover the complexity of employment strategies, but national surveys of employers which use temporary workers can provide some pointers.

The most frequent reason given for employing contingent workers is to provide cover for workload peaks. The authoritative Workplace Employees Relations Survey (WERS 98) showed that 34 per cent of employers use fixed-term contract workers, and 38 per cent use agency workers to match staffing peaks in demand (Table 3.6). In addition between 11 and 15 per cent use contingent workers because of a freeze on permanent staff members. This might suggest that around half of employers are reducing or controlling the growth of the permanent workforce, filling the gap with contingent workers.

*Table 3.6 Reasons of employers for use of contingent workers**

| | Agency workers | Fixed-term contract |
|---|---|---|
| Matching staff to peaks in demand | 38 | 34 |
| As a trail for a permanent job | — | 22 |
| Short-term cover for staff absence/vacancies | 59 | — |
| Cover for maternity leave or long/annual leave | 16 | 10 |
| Unable to fill vacancies | 19 | — |
| Obtain specialist skills | 12 | 17 |
| Freeze on permanent staff numbers | 11 | 15 |
| Other/unspecified | 4 | 18 |

*Note:* * As percentage of the employers who use both or either form of contingent employment; an employer may give more than one reason.

*Source:* WERS (1998).

What is most revealing in the WERS data is the reasons given for using fixed-term contract workers, and how these differ from agency workers. Just over one-fifth of employers use fixed-term contracts as a recruitment screen, while 17 per cent look for specialist skills. The data can only suggest reasons for using contingent workers, but they do hint at some of the underlying reasons. A freeze on permanent staff numbers implies, for example, head office instructions perhaps linked to cost-cutting measures. Failure to fill vacancies says a great deal about skill shortages in the UK economy. Cover for maternity leave or staff absences implies a distinction between internal and external labour markets, in part brought about by legislation protecting employees' job rights.

## CONCLUDING REMARKS

Looking at trends in contingent employment in the UK in the 1990s, it could be argued that there have been two clear phases, although whether these constitute a maturing of the contingent labour market or the effect of cyclical change is not possible to determine yet. In the first phase, the combination of the weakening of labour market institutions, especially unions and labour law, marketization pressures in the public sector and deregulation and competition in many markets was associated with high levels of unemployment. In these conditions, contingent labour grew fairly rapidly, aided by a rapid expansion in temporary work agencies, which also benefited from deregulation. Trends in contingent work arrangements outstripped the capacity of labour law to provide unambiguous contracts for many of these workers. There was much confusion over the distinction between 'contract of service' and 'contract of employment'. In this period, many contingent workers took these jobs because they could not find permanent employment.

This growth petered out in the mid-1990s and the contingent labour market appeared to move into a second, and still current, phase. Higher levels of economic growth and declining unemployment came at times when a new government and further European legislation both began to clarify employment law and bring more contingent workers into the ambit of legal protection. A good example of this is the decision in 2001 of the European Court of Justice that a qualifying period of 13 weeks' employment before protections and rights under the Working Time Directive apply to UK workers was unlawful. Thus, even very short-term contract workers, typically found in film production and the media, now have access to paid holidays. The number of permanent jobs has begun to grow and there is a marked decline in self-employment. In part as a result of tightening of regulations by the tax authorities and changing the status of dependent self-employed to workers, an increasing number of contingent workers are not looking for permanent jobs. Fixed-term contract workers, especially among professionals, now constitute a majority of contingent workers even before the underrecording of this category is taken into account.

Financially, for men at least, earnings, although not fringe benefits, are comparable to those of permanent employees. The disadvantaged position of low-skill casual and seasonal staff remains, but the idea that contingent workers form a distinctive group in the labour market which are disadvantaged, insecure and exploited has to be seriously questioned now. There is some evidence that the expansion of contingent working is transitionary between job loss, or entering the labour market for the first time, and finding a permanent position, especially for fixed-term contract professionals (although people's perception of what is a 'permanent' job has changed markedly in the last decade).

The full impact of recent changes in labour law and changes to the legal position and role of temporary work agencies has yet to work through the economy. The labour market remained buoyant in 2001, and this too affected both the supply of and demand for contingent workers. In these circumstances it is unlikely that there will be significant changes in the UK economy as a whole in the use of contingent employment, currently running at around 7 per cent of employment. There are, as we have shown, marked differences between sectors and it is at this level that the evolving experience of the use of contingent work arrangements can best be observed.

# NOTES

1. This was the measure commonly used at the time for unemployment based on a count of those claiming unemployment benefits. More recently, unemployment has been measured using the internationally recognized ILO definition.
2. 'Externalization' is a generic word which is often used to refer to a growing trend amongst employers to use the human and material resources of other companies or agencies in order to reduce production/labour cost (see Pfeffer and Baron, 1988; Purcell and Purcell, 1998).
3. Occupational categories are based on the 'Standard Occupational Classification' of 1990 (SOC). In this classification, those like public service administrative professionals, social workers, probation officers, clergy, scientific researchers, software specialists, IT strategists and planners, and health and education professionals are cited amongst the major professional categories (Elias *et al.*, 2000).
4. In SOC 1990, associated professionals are nurses, midwives, paramedics, medical radiographers, medical and dental technicians, IT operation technicians, IT user support technicians, youth and community workers, housing and welfare officers, newspaper and periodical editors, public relations officers, photographers and audio-visual operators (Elias *et al.*, 2000).

# REFERENCES

Booth, A., M. Francesconi and J. Frank (2000) 'Contingent Jobs: Who gets them, what are they worth and do they lead anywhere?', Institute for Social and Economic Research, Colchester: University of Essex.

Bruegel, I. and D. Perrons (1998) 'Deregulation and Women's Employment: the Diverse Experiences of Women in Britain', *Feminist Economics*, 4(1), 103–25.

Burchell, B., S. Deakin and S. Honey (1999a) *The Employment Status of Individuals in Non-Standard Employment*, March, London: DTI.

Burchell, B.J., D. Day, M. Hudson, D. Ladipo, R. Mankelow, J.P. Nolan, H. Reed, I.C. Wichert and F. Wilkinson (1999b) *Job Insecurity and Work Intensification: Flexibility and the changing boundaries of work*, York: Joseph Rowntree Foundation.

Crafts, N. (1988) 'The Assessment: British Economic Growth Over the Long Run', *Oxford Review of Economic Policy*, 4(1).

Davies, P. and M. Freedland (2000) 'Labour Markets, Welfare, and the Personal Scope of Employment Law', *Oxford Review of Economic Policy*, 16(1).

Dex, S. and A. McCulloch (1995) 'Flexible Employment in Britain', Manchester: Equal Opportunities Commission.

Dickens, L. and M. Hall (1995) 'The State: Labour Laws and Industrial Relations', in P. Edwards (ed.), *Industrial Relations, Theory & Practice in Britain*, Oxford: Blackwell.

DTI (Department of Trade and Industry) (1998) 'New Rights For Individuals' (*http://www.dti.gov.uk/er/fairness/part3.htm*).

DTI (1999) 'Regulation of the Private Recruitment Industry: A Consultative Document', Employment Relations Directorate URN:99/774, May, London: DTI.

Elias, P., A. McKnight and G. Kinshott (2000) 'Redefining Skill Revision of the Standard Occupational Classification, Skills Task Force', Research Paper, 19, Institute for Employment Research, Coventry: University of Warwick.

Feldman, D., H. Doerpinghaus and W. Turnley (1994) 'Managing Temporary Workers: A Permanent HRM Challenge', *Organizational Dynamics*, 23, 46–63.
Gannon, M. (1996) 'Managing without a Complete, Full-time Workforce', in P.C. Flood, M.J. Gannon and J. Paauwe (eds), *Managing without Traditional Methods, International Innovations, Human Resource Management*, New York: Addison-Wesley.
*IRS Employment Trends* 677 (1999) 'Diversity characterises employers' use of temporary working'.
*Labour Market Trends* (January 2000: 35) London: HMSO.
*Labour Market Trends* (July 2000) London: HMSO.
LM&ST (2000) '*Labour Market and Skill Trends*', Nottingham: DfEE Publications.
MacGregor, D. (2000) 'Jobs in the Public and Private Sectors', *Economic Trends*, June, 33–49.
Moralee, L. (1998) 'Self-employment in the 1990s', *Labour Market Trends*, March, 121–30.
Morgan, P., N. Allington and E. Heery (2000) 'Employment insecurity in the public services', in E. Heery and J. Salmon (eds), *The Insecure Workforce*, London: Routledge.
Nichols, T. and J.O. Davidson (1993) 'Privatisation and economism: an investigation amongst "producers" in two public utilities in Britain', *Sociological Review*, 41(4), 707–30.
Nolan, P. (1996) 'Industrial relations and performance since 1945', in I. Beardwell (ed.), *Contemporary Industrial Relations, A Critical Analysis*, Oxford: Oxford University Press, pp. 99–120.
Oliver, N. and B. Wilkinson (1988) *The Japanisation of British Industry: New Developments in the 1990s*, 2nd edn, Oxford: Blackwell Publishers.
Pfeffer, J. and J.N. Baron (1988) 'Taking the workers back out: Recent trends in the structuring of employment', in B.M. Staw and L.L. Cummings (eds), *Research in Organisational Behaviour*, Greenwich, CT: JAI Press.
Purcell, K. and J. Purcell (1998) 'In-sourcing, Outsourcing, and the Growth of Contingent Labour as Evidence of Flexible Employment Strategies', *European Journal of Work and Organisational Psychology*, 1(1), 39–59.
Rex, J. (1988) *The Ghetto and the Underclass: Essays on Race and Social Policy*, Research in Ethnic Relations series, Aldershot: Gower.
Siebert, S. (1999) *The Effect of Labour Regulation on Recruitment*, York: Joseph Rowntree Foundation.
Sly, F. and D. Stillwell (1997) 'Temporary workers in Great Britain', *Labour Market Trends*, September, 347–54.
*Social Trends* 30 (2000) London: HMSO.
Turnbull, P. (1986) 'The "Japanisation" of Production and Industrial Relations at Lucas Electrical', *Industrial Relations Journal*, 17(13), 193–206.
Wolf, M. (2000) 'Much ado about the UK's inward investment', *Financial Times*, 9 July.

# 4. The regulation and growth of contingent employment in Sweden

**Donald Storrie**[1]

## INTRODUCTION

The 1990s were traumatic times in the Swedish labour market. The first quarter of the decade saw massive job loss and a quadrupling of the unemployment rate. This, together with a 25 per cent depreciation of the currency, led to the perception of a country, and a model of the labour market, in crisis. However, later in the decade, the economy recovered dramatically and in the later years employment growth was as rapid as at any time since the Second World War and unemployment fell steadily, down to around 4 per cent by the end of the decade.

Institutional changes preceded the economic crisis of the early 1990s. The 1980s saw a gradual erosion of some key features of the Swedish model, and in particular centralized collective bargaining. However, these changes should not be exaggerated. Important elements of the model remain. Of most importance in the context of this chapter is that the collective bargain retained its coverage over a wider range of issues and sectors of the labour market than in perhaps any other country. Union density remained high, around 90 per cent. While the welfare state has seen appreciable cut-backs in some areas, the basic principle of a universal system of social welfare remains. Recent years have even seen some renewed coordination in collective bargaining by the social partners.

The framework for the regulation of the employment contract and industrial relations based on the laws of the 1970s also remains largely intact. However, there have been some significant changes in the regulation of contingent employment and indeed these have been greater than has been the case in nearly every other OECD country (OECD, 1999). The 1990s saw the abolition of very strict regulation of temporary agency work, which had in practice made these activities illegal, and the new law is now among the most liberal in the European Union (Storrie, 2002). The basic premise of employment protection law is that, unless otherwise stated, an employment contract is presumed to be open-ended and thus requires the observance of various procedures at termination, just cause, notice and seniority rules. Previously, the employer could hire for a limited duration in certain specified circumstances. However, the strict requirement to state a specific motivation was removed in 1997.

The 1990s saw an appreciable increase in the number of limited duration contracts. However, it is far from clear that this is due to the change in the law. On the other hand, the reform of the temporary work agency law had obviously (as it was previously an illegal activity) greater effect. The most striking feature of agency work in Sweden is the extent to which it is governed by collective agreements. These collective agreements provide a considerable degree of employment and thus also income security to the employees.

The remarkably rapid growth of limited duration contracts during the 1990s and the remarkably rapid spread of collective agreements throughout the temporary work agency sector are the striking features of contingent employment in Sweden and are the main focus of this chapter.

## THE LABOUR MARKET IN THE 1990S

In Sweden the early 1990s saw one of the most rapid deteriorations of any labour market in Europe since the Great Depression. Unemployment, which seldom rose above 2 per cent during the entire post-war period, exploded at the beginning of the decade and more than quadrupled in a period of just under two years. There was massive job loss. In 1990, there were 4.5 million jobs. By 1994 half a million of these had disappeared. Table 4.1 presents the levels and changes in the employment and unemployment rates in the last decade by age and sex.

Recently, there has been a clear improvement, particularly as regards unemployment which, by October 2000, had fallen to 4 per cent. Employment rates have not yet improved to the same extent. However, the latter years of the decade have seen a remarkable improvement and employment growth has been categorized by the National Labour Market Board as the greatest increase since the Second World War. During 1998 and 1999, employment rose by 146 thousand. However, despite the rapid recovery it should be pointed out that the basic labour market statistics clearly show a labour force at an appreciably lower rate of utilization by the end of the decade. This is most clearly observed from the fact that the employment ratio, which was 83 per cent in 1990, was still 10 percentage points lower at the end of the decade.

The structural transformation of Swedish employment is typical of that in other advanced OECD countries.[2] The long-term shift out of manufacturing continued in the 1990s. However, the previous trend of a shift into

*Table 4.1 Employment and unemployment rates, by age and sex in the 1990s*

| | Employment rate | | | | Unemployment rate | | | |
|---|---|---|---|---|---|---|---|---|
| | 1990 | 1993 | 1998 | 1999 | 1990 | 1993 | 1998 | 1999 |
| Men | 85.2 | 73.0 | 73.5 | 74.8 | 1.7 | 9.7 | 6.9 | 5.9 |
| Women | 81.1 | 72.1 | 69.4 | 70.9 | 1.6 | 5.6 | 6.0 | 5.2 |
| Total | 83.1 | 72.6 | 71.5 | 72.9 | 1.6 | 8.2 | 6.5 | 5.6 |
| Age 16–19 | 47.7 | 24.0 | 23.4 | 26.3 | 5.0 | 19.4 | 12.1 | 9.3 |
| Age 20–24 | 79.8 | 56.1 | 55.3 | 57.3 | 3.1 | 18.1 | 11.8 | 10.1 |
| Age 25–34 | 89.2 | 77.1 | 77.0 | 78.9 | 1.8 | 10.5 | 7.2 | 5.9 |
| Age 35–44 | 93.7 | 86.0 | 82.8 | 84.0 | 1.0 | 6.3 | 5.8 | 5.0 |
| Age 45–54 | 91.8 | 86.6 | 84.1 | 84.9 | 0.8 | 4.5 | 4.6 | 3.9 |
| Age 55–59 | 82.1 | 76.2 | 76.7 | 77.6 | 1.1 | 4.7 | 5.4 | 4.8 |
| Age 60–64 | 57.7 | 49.8 | 46.2 | 46.8 | 2.0 | 6.7 | 6.9 | 8.0 |

*Source:* Labour Force Survey.

the public sector ceased. Privately owned services, and in particular business services, increased their share.

Table 4.2, shows that, while the 'standard' open-ended contract has declined slightly in importance, it still accounts for 75 per cent of total employment and is thus still by far the most prevalent contractual form. The highest rate of open-ended contracts is found in Manufacturing & Mining and Public Administration. It is also by far the most common form in all other sectors, with the exception of the primary sector, where it accounts for only a quarter of total employment. The decline of open-ended contracts has occurred in every broad sector of the economy. The 4.6 percentage points drop in open-ended contracts as a share of all jobs is mainly due to a 3.4 per cent increase in contracts of limited duration. Self-employment obviously does not exist in public administration and accounts for only a very small proportion of total employment in the two other largely state-run sectors of Education & Research and Health & Care. Self-employment is most common in Personal & Cultural Services and Construction.

Temporary agency work is not captured in the labour force survey. The only estimates available are those presented by the sector organization, SPUR. This shows (see Table 4.3), a dramatic increase since the sector was made legal in 1994. Thus the most marked absolute increase of contingent employment is in limited duration contracts (LDCs) and the largest relative increase is found in temporary work agencies (TWAs). These two forms of contingent employment are the main focus of attention in this chapter.

*Table 4.2 Intensity of various forms of employment, 1987 and 1999, as percentage of total employment*

| Sector | Percentage of total employment | | | | | | | | | | | |
|---|---|---|---|---|---|---|---|---|---|---|---|---|
| | Unlimited duration | | Limited duration | | SE with employees | | SE no employees | | Family workers | | Sector's share of total employment | |
| | 1987 | 1999 | 1987 | 1999 | 1987 | 1999 | 1987 | 1999 | 1987 | 1999 | 1987 | 1999 |
| Primary sectors | 28.5 | 24.6 | 7.4 | 9.5 | 9.2 | 12.5 | 48.0 | 46.6 | 7.0 | 6.8 | 4.0 | 2.5 |
| Manufacturing & mining | 90.6 | 87.4 | 5.1 | 7.9 | 2.4 | 2.3 | 1.9 | 2.2 | 0.1 | 0.1 | 23.2 | 19.6 |
| Construction | 68.4 | 68.1 | 15.4 | 11.5 | 6.6 | 7.2 | 9.2 | 12.8 | 0.5 | 0.4 | 6.7 | 5.5 |
| Communications | 84.8 | 77.8 | 6.9 | 12.2 | 3.1 | 5.1 | 4.7 | 4.8 | 0.4 | 0.2 | 7.1 | 6.8 |
| Trade | 75.7 | 71.3 | 7.8 | 12.0 | 8.6 | 7.8 | 7.6 | 8.4 | 0.3 | 0.4 | 12.8 | 12.6 |
| Financial & business ser. | 82.4 | 72.2 | 6.8 | 11.2 | 4.5 | 6.1 | 6.1 | 10.3 | 0.2 | 0.2 | 7.8 | 12.4 |
| Education & research | 85.0 | 78.8 | 14.7 | 20.1 | 0.1 | 0.3 | 0.2 | 0.7 | 0.0 | 0.0 | 7.4 | 8.4 |
| Health & care | 79.9 | 77.3 | 19.2 | 20.9 | 0.5 | 0.7 | 0.5 | 1.1 | 0.0 | 0.0 | 18.9 | 19.1 |
| Personal & cultural ser. | 68.5 | 57.2 | 16.9 | 22.3 | 4.6 | 6.0 | 9.6 | 14.2 | 0.4 | 0.3 | 6.5 | 7.9 |
| Public administration | 90.7 | 87.9 | 9.3 | 12.0 | 0.0 | 0.0 | 0.0 | 0.1 | 0.0 | 0.0 | 5.5 | 5.1 |
| Unknown | 65.5 | 72.7 | 13.8 | 24.2 | 3.4 | 3.0 | 17.2 | 0.0 | 0.0 | 0.0 | 0.1 | 0.1 |
| Total | 79.8 | 75.2 | 10.8 | 14.2 | 3.4 | 3.9 | 5.5 | 6.4 | 0.4 | 0.3 | 100.0 | 100.0 |
| Total change in % points | −4.60 | | 3.37 | | 0.46 | | 0.89 | | −0.11 | | | |

*Source:* Labour Force Survey.

*Table 4.3 Employees in temporary work agencies*

| | TWA employees | % of total employment |
|---|---|---|
| 1994 | 5000 | 0.13 |
| 1995 | 7000 | 0.18 |
| 1996 | 10000 | 0.25 |
| 1997 | 14000 | 0.36 |
| 1998 | 18500 | 0.46 |
| 1999 | 25000 | 0.61 |
| 2000 | 33000 | 0.77 |

*Source:* SPUR, in 'Facts about the Swedish Economy', Confederation of Swedish Employers.

## THE INSTITUTIONAL AND LEGAL FRAMEWORK

The legal regulation of limited duration contracts and temporary work agencies changed in the last decade. Since 1997, there is no longer any need for the employer to provide a particular reason to employ for a limited duration. Before the reforms of the early 1990s, temporary work agencies and private employment exchanges were so strictly regulated that they could best be characterized as illegal. Now such activities are practically without regulation. The opening-up of various forms of contingent employment is a trend common to most OECD countries. While the changes in Sweden have come later than elsewhere, one could argue that the Swedish reforms have been more radical than in most other countries, particularly as regards temporary work agencies and private employment exchanges.[3]

### The Industrial Relations Background

Two cornerstones of the renowned Swedish model, centralized wage bargaining by peak organizations and tripartite involvement in the broad political process, had left the industrial relations scene by 1990. However, very seldom do systems of industrial relations change beyond recognition overnight, and important elements of the model remain. Moreover, recent years have seen some moves back towards coordination of wage bargaining within industry. Most of the legislation from the 1960s and 1970s on employment protection, work environment, co-determination and other legislation relating to trade union rights remain intact. While trade unions would appear to have less political influence in the Social Democratic party and have lost some representation in the boards of state bodies, they remain strong in the day-to-day business of industrial relations. Trade union membership is still amongst the highest in OECD countries and indeed remained stable during the 1990s.

Trade union representation and influence at the workplace is largely governed by the Co-determination Law (MBL) and the Law on the Position of a Trade Union Representative at the Workplace. MBL allows the unions to obtain information on issues relevant to them and to negotiate with the employer about impending decisions. However, the term 'co-determination' may be misleading as, in most issues, the final decision is the employer's. In most collective bargaining areas the Co-determination Law is complemented by a Development Collective, which provides more detailed content. Indeed, the primacy of the collective bargain is still a distinguishing feature of Swedish industrial relations and collective agreements still regulate almost every issue and area of the labour market. Collective agreements regulate matters that in other countries are usually regulated in statutory law; for example, industrial conflicts. One can view the Co-determination Law as being mainly designed to support the process of obtaining a collective agreement.

Employment protection is perhaps one of the most controversial of issues facing the social partners since at least 1974, when the original Employment Protection Act was passed. The law was fiercely resisted by the employers and, together with the proposal to introduce the Wage Earner Funds, lay behind their view that the labour movement had broken the social contract which the employers understood to respect their right to decide matters inside the firm. This was said to lie behind the more confrontational position taken by the employees from the 1980s, influencing the break-up of centralized bargaining and later the employers' unilateral withdrawal from their representation on public boards. The trade unions, for their part, have firmly resisted any weakening of worker protection, claiming to see the issue as purely related to fairness at work. However, it is interesting to note that the most volatile union protest against a reform of the Employment Protection Law was when the level at which a collective bargain could be made to replace the law was changed in 1997, from the central to local level, thus weakening union bargaining power. This may suggest that unions have an interest in strict employment protection not just for the rights it confers on the workers but for the strong bargaining position it gives to unions generally, (see Fahlbeck, 1984).

An important feature of Swedish unionism is that the trade unions have accepted the need for structural rationalizations and indeed the influential Rehn-Meidner Model (which was advocated by the trade union movement) called for a rapid structural transformation of the economy, out of low and into high productive activities. It is also notable that this transformation, for example, out of steel and shipbuilding, occurred more rapidly and with less worker protest (and less unemployment) than elsewhere in Europe. This can, in part, be attributed to union participation in the decision-making process, the union adherence to the production ideology and active labour market policy (see Stråth, 1986; Storrie, 1993). Moreover, it is clear that employment protection legislation in Sweden, and possibly in most other countries, was not able to prevent or even influence the major structural transformations of the 1970s and 1980s. Fahlbeck (1999) sums up the 'atmosphere' of industrial relations in Sweden as follows:

> Strong elements of trust, cooperation and mutual understanding . . . characterize the Swedish industrial relations system. Acceptance of trade unionism on the part of the employers and appreciation of the trade union contribution to the daily running of the enterprise is matched by a pragmatic acceptance on the part of the union movement of the employers' freedom to manage the business and make decisions on technological change. In most instances the relationship between an employer . . . and the union is firm and of long standing. The parties live together in something like a 'marriage of convenience' with no possibility of 'divorce' . . . Despite this rather cosy relationship there is little collusion between the parties and featherbedding is unknown. By and large the parties deal with each other at arms' length, while preserving their 'marriage of convenience'.

## The Regulation of Contracts of Limited Duration

Legislation dates back to the 1974 Employment Protection Act, which despite some minor revisions is still basically intact. The law presumes that, unless otherwise stipulated, an employment contract is until further notice. When terminating the contract the employer must provide a valid reason and advance notice. Compared to many other OECD countries, the periods of notice are lengthy but no redundancy pay is stipulated. While the grounds for collective redundancies are very liberal they are to proceed in accordance with seniority. The presumption of the open-ended contract permeates labour law. For example, if it is unclear as to what type of contract was made, the Labour Court places the burden of proof on the party claiming that the contract was *not* open-ended, that is, usually the employer.

Until 1997, the law listed eight circumstances in which the employer may use a limited duration contract (LDC). By far the most common form of LDC is hiring a replacement for an absent employee (leave replacement). The other frequently used LDC is for work that is intrinsically of a limited duration (project work) and is common in, for example, construction and research. Contracts for a probationary period and those motivated by a temporary increase in labour demand may be made for a maximum duration of six months.

Any assessment of the impact of employment protection in Sweden must consider, in addition to statutory law, both the relationship between law and collective agreement and the content of collective agreements. In both respects Sweden is rather unique. In most countries, statutory law is a floor of guaranteed minimum worker rights upon which collective agreements may build, but not erode, further protection for the employee. In Sweden, however, several paragraphs of the Employment Protection Act permit bargaining outcomes that may entail not only higher but also *lower* levels of protection.

As collective agreements cover practically the entire labour market, the potential impact of this 'negotiated flexibility' is considerable. Collective agreements may lower worker protection in existing contractual forms, for example, by permitting longer than the statutory maximum probationary period of six months. They may even allow contractual forms that are not explicitly permitted in statutory law. For example, several agreements in the trade and transport sectors permit contracts termed 'called when needed'. However, it does not seem to be the case that the regulation of LDCs in collective agreements is generally more liberal than statutory law. Indeed, Storrie (1995) found that the length of probationary periods in collective agreements for blue-collar workers in the private sector were generally shorter than the six months permitted in law and that the local unions were awarded some influence on whether the hiring should be for a limited period.

International comparisons of employment protection indicate that Sweden has a fairly restrictive legislation, but by no means does it stand out as extreme by European standards. However, these international rankings, for example in OECD (1999), have serious limitations as regards the enforcement of regulation, a point made by Bertola *et al.* (2000). The capacity of the employee to give effective voice to perceived violations of his or her legal rights is a vital factor in ensuring the observance of labour law. One would expect that the exceptionally high rate of union membership and the almost universal union presence at the workplace in Sweden would both lead to a high level of awareness of employment protection rights and provide the capabilities and resources to pursue these rights: first at the workplace, and if need be, in the Labour Court. In other words, the de facto employment protection in Sweden may be greater than suggested by only reading the letter of the law. The costs for the employer for non-observance of the law are pecuniary (fines and damages) and court judgments that transfer a limited duration to an open-ended contract.

**Changes in regulations during the 1990s**

Comparisons of the incidence and growth of limited duration contracts in various countries suggest that it is not the regulation of LDCs per se but the regulation relative to open-ended contracts that is of importance. During the 1990s there were no significant reforms of the Employment Protection

Act in Sweden concerning the termination of open-ended contracts. There have, however, been several changes to the statutory regulation of LDCs.

In January 1994, the maximum permitted duration for probationary contracts and those motivated by a temporary increase in labour demand was increased from six to 12 months. However, this was repealed in January 1995, when the Social Democratic party returned to power. Moreover, the impact of this law was minimal on actual regulation even during its brief validity as it had next to no impact on the content of collective agreements, and thus on the actual regulation at the workplace (Storrie, 1995).

The law of 1997 was of considerably more *potential* importance. It introduced the opportunity for the employer to hire for a limited duration without having to specify a particular reason. However, an employer could only use a maximum of five such contracts and a particular individual could not be employed under such a contract for more than 12 months during a three-year period. If the firm was newly established, the period could be extended to 18 months. The Bill stated that it was not the purpose of the Act to promote very short-term jobs and so the minimum permissible duration was set at one month.

The new law also addressed the difficult legal issue of repeated contracts of limited duration. While this applied only to leave replacements, these are by far the most common form of LDC in Sweden and thus the revision of the law may have had considerable potential impact. The new law stated that, if a leave replacement was employed for a total duration of three years during a five-year period then the contract becomes open-ended. This paragraph, announced in 1997, became law on 1 January 2000, presumably to enable employers to adjust, and so it probably had an effect on hiring policy long before 2000.

The most important element of the 1997 law, and certainly that which met with most heated opposition from the trade unions, was the opportunity to strike collective agreements on derogation from statutory law regarding LDCs at the local level, provided that the parties had a central agreement in other matters. As collective agreements may lead to more liberal regulation than in statutory law, the trade unions were presumably concerned that employment protection rights would be eroded by bargaining at this lower level. Prior to 1997, these agreements could only be made at the central (usually national) level.

## The Regulation of Temporary Work Agencies

Until its abolition in 1992, the law dating back to 1935 prohibited employment exchanges for profit. The first hesitant step towards the liberalization of employment exchanges and temporary work agencies was taken by the

Social Democratic government in 1992. It was repealed by the new government the following year. The current law, effective from 1 July 1993, legalized private employment exchanges and almost totally removed the regulation of temporary work agencies.

According to the current law, there is only one important restriction on the activities of private employment exchanges and work agencies, namely that it is forbidden to charge the job seeker a fee. This is strongly stated in law. In addition, the employee of the temporary work agency shall not be prevented from obtaining a job at the user firm and someone who leaves a job to work in a temporary work agency may not be placed to work for his/her ex-employer until a period of six months has elapsed. In contrast to all continental European countries, agency work is treated as any other form of activity, with no special regulation in labour or company law. There is no regulation of the assignment at the user firm nor any licensing or monitoring procedures for temporary agency firms.

The development of collective bargaining in the temporary work agency sector in Sweden is truly remarkable. Despite the fact that, previously, this activity could best be characterized as illegal, and that labour employed with such a contract is obviously among the most difficult to organize, the majority of temporary agency workers are now covered by a collective agreement with a considerable level of employment and income security.

Most agency workers are white-collar workers in the private sector (office 'temps' and so on). Even prior to the deregulation of the 1990s this sector existed, though with dubious legal status. After deregulation, it was amongst the first to conclude a collective agreement, and agreements in this sector have tended to set the agenda in other collective bargaining areas. The agreement made in July 2000 covered 15000 employees in 120 companies and was by far the most important agreement in the sector. According to union sources, the agreement covers over 80 per cent of those employed. The agreement guarantees an income corresponding to 125 hours a month and, after being employed in the company for 10 months, the guaranteed basic wage is for 142 hours per month. The two guaranteed levels have been interpreted to correspond to 75 per cent and 85 per cent of the full-time monthly wage.[4]

Regarding the employment contract, the collective agreement points out that the main principle is that the contract should be open-ended but, under certain circumstances, permits LDCs. Compared to statutory law, the collective agreement limits the use of LDCs. The employment of leave replacements (at the agency) may be of a maximum duration of six months unless the local parties agree otherwise. Furthermore, the new form of LDC introduced in 1997, that is, those that do not require objective grounds, are not permitted. On-call contracts are allowed without restrictions regarding duration or number of employees. They may be used for temporary increases in labour demand, when special competencies are required or at a newly started-up firm. However, the need for labour should be seen to be temporary. If this contractual form is abused, the local union may terminate the firm's right to utilize it.

Since September 2000, there is, in principle, one agreement covering the entire private blue-collar TWA sector. This agreement was signed by 18 unions affiliated to the blue-collar top organization, the LO. On the employee side, the negotiations were coordinated at the peak level but each union signed its own, more or less identical, collective agreement with the employer organization. The guiding principle is that agency workers shall have the same wages and working conditions as those in the user firm. The main issue was the insecurity of income due to uncertain hours of placement at the user firm. According to the parties, the guaranteed monthly wage is 85 per cent of the wage received during the previous quarter. By October 2002, the guaranteed wage is to be increased to 90 per cent for those who have been employed longer than six months. However, this does not apply to labour hired for a duration shorter than 10 days. For these persons the guaranteed wage is the average during the previous quarter for the employee at the agency. The LO's initial negotiating position was 100 per cent guaranteed wage, and the LO states that this is still their aim.

## THE GROWTH AND INCIDENCE OF CONTINGENT EMPLOYMENT

### Limited Duration Contracts

It was shown that limited duration contracts account for the major part of the decline of the open-ended employment contract in the 1990s (see p. 81). Here we present more detailed data on the growth of LDCs and with respect to economic sector, type of LDC and various socioeconomic variables.

In 1987, there were 468 000 LDCs, corresponding to 12 per cent of all contracts. From 1987, both the number and intensity of LDC contracts declined each year up to 1991. The major part of the increase in LDCs, both in number and more dramatically in intensity,[5] occurred in the period between 1991 and 1995. (See Figure 4.1.)

Labour law permits many different forms of LDCs defined in terms of the employer's motivation to employ labour for a specified duration. Figure 4.2 shows the number employed in the major categories of LDCs. A striking feature of the figure is that by far the largest type of limited duration contract is to replace an absentee. This is probably a unique feature of LDCs in Sweden, which has generous allowance for many forms of leave,

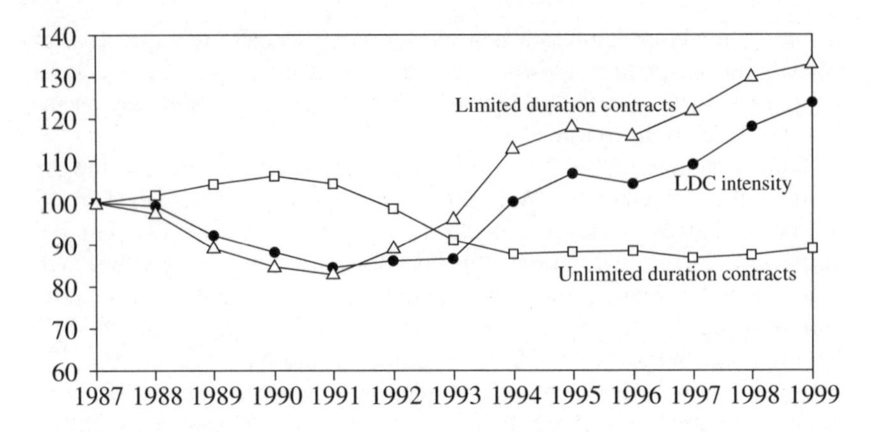


*Figure 4.1 Employment contract, 1987–99 (Index 1987 = 100)*

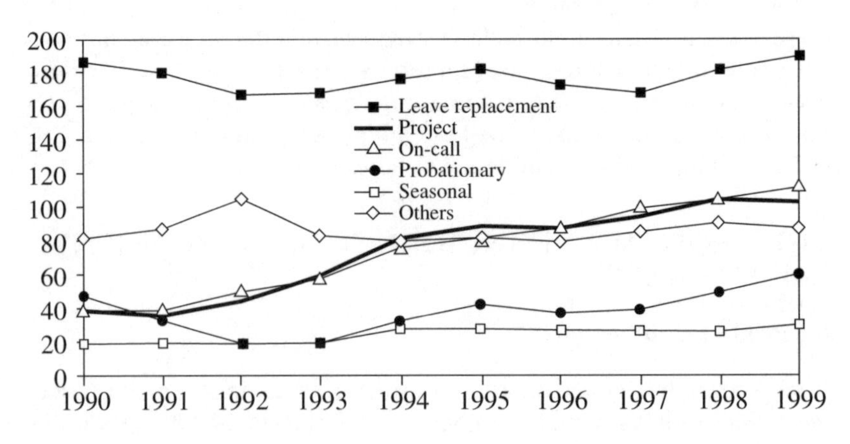


*Source:* LFS.

*Figure 4.2 Various types of limited duration contracts (thousands)*

particularly parental leave and long statutory holidays. The high level of leave replacements has remained roughly constant, at around 180000 for the duration of the decade.

On-call contracts have increased most rapidly, from 40000 to 110000. The other major category, project work, has also increased significantly, from 40000 to just over 100000. Probationary jobs declined sharply at the start of the decade but have increased rapidly in recent years. Both seasonal work and the residual category, 'others', have remained quite stable over the period. One can glean from Figure 4.2 that there has been a clear shift in the composition of LDCs over the period. This is made clearer in Table 4.4.

*Table 4.4 Various types of LDCs as percentage of all LDCs*

| | Leave replacements | Project | On-call | Probationary | Seasonal | Other |
|---|---|---|---|---|---|---|
| 1987 | 45.48 | 14.00 | 5.70 | 7.9 | 5.84 | 21.08 |
| 1988 | 46.57 | 12.29 | 8.04 | 9.41 | 5.13 | 18.56 |
| 1989 | 47.99 | 9.69 | 8.68 | 11.11 | 4.70 | 17.83 |
| 1990 | 45.15 | 9.47 | 9.47 | 11.41 | 4.61 | 19.90 |
| 1991 | 45.57 | 9.37 | 9.87 | 8.35 | 4.81 | 22.03 |
| 1992 | 41.44 | 10.92 | 12.16 | 4.71 | 4.71 | 26.05 |
| 1993 | 41.38 | 14.53 | 14.04 | 4.93 | 4.68 | 20.44 |
| 1994 | 37.37 | 17.20 | 15.92 | 6.79 | 5.73 | 16.99 |
| 1995 | 36.40 | 17.60 | 16.00 | 8.40 | 5.40 | 16.20 |
| 1996 | 35.17 | 17.59 | 18.00 | 7.57 | 5.32 | 16.36 |
| 1997 | 32.75 | 18.24 | 19.61 | 7.65 | 5.10 | 16.67 |
| 1998 | 32.73 | 18.81 | 18.81 | 8.86 | 4.52 | 16.27 |
| 1999 | 32.70 | 17.65 | 19.20 | 10.38 | 5.02 | 15.05 |

In 1987, almost half of all LDCs were leave replacements; by 1999, they made up just under one-third. In 1987, on-call contracts constituted 5 per cent of all LDCs; by 1999, they amounted to almost 20 per cent. Thus the aggregation of LDCs into a single category conceals the fact that a typical LDC in 1999 is a quite different form of contract from what it was in 1987.[6]

In the context of trying to establish whether we can observe a structural increase in the propensity to hire on a temporary basis, the declining share of leave replacements is important. The number of leave replacements is almost entirely determined by the degree of leave taken by those on open-ended contracts, as opposed to an intrinsic propensity to hire labour on an LDC because of the nature of the work to be done or other labour market conditions. They are not primarily due to an active decision of the employer regarding work organization or the possible need for numerical flexibility or the need to screen employees. They are largely outside the employer's control. The point here is that the trend rise in LDCs would be accentuated if leave replacements were excluded from the aggregate total.

While the LDC rate has increased in every broad sector of the economy, LFS data show that the major change in the distribution of LDCs, and that which accounts for the large increase during the 1990s, is the increase in the private sector. From Table 4.5, two sectors stand out. Financial and Business services exhibit both the greatest increase in LDC rate and greatest share of all LDCs, while Health and Care show the lowest growth rates in both these figures. We note, however, that the Health and Care sector still accounts for one-quarter of all LDCs in the labour market.

*Table 4.5 LDC intensity and share (of all LDCs) by economic sector, 1990 and 2000*

| | 1990 | | 2000 | | % change | |
|---|---|---|---|---|---|---|
| | Rate (%) | Share (%) | Rate (%) | Share (%) | Rate | Share |
| Primary sectors | 13.9 | 2.0 | 23.4 | 1.5 | 69.0 | −25.7 |
| Manufacturing & mining | 4.3 | 9.8 | 7.9 | 10.5 | 84.5 | 7.0 |
| Construction | 6.8 | 4.5 | 11.4 | 3.6 | 67.0 | −20.0 |
| Communications | 6.9 | 4.8 | 12.9 | 5.8 | 86.7 | 19.8 |
| Trade | 9.5 | 11.4 | 15.3 | 11.7 | 60.8 | 2.6 |
| Financial & business services | 6.7 | 5.6 | 13.5 | 11.1 | 100.9 | 98.4 |
| Education & research | 13.1 | 9.8 | 19.1 | 12.0 | 45.8 | 22.8 |
| Health & care | 17.3 | 36.8 | 18.8 | 25.0 | 8.5 | −32.2 |
| Personal & cultural services | 18.2 | 10.7 | 29.7 | 13.8 | 63.1 | 28.4 |
| Public administration | 7.7 | 4.5 | 12.1 | 4.7 | 56.9 | 5.7 |
| Unknown | 14.6 | 0.2 | 30.9 | 0.3 | 111.9 | 76.2 |
| Total | 10.1 | 100.0 | 15.2 | 100.0 | 50.5 | 0.0 |

*Source:* LFS.

Holmlund and Storrie (2002) examine the quarterly flows between the basic labour market states but with two employment states, open-ended and limited duration, during the 1990s. The flow from non-participation is the major source of inflow to temporary jobs (50 per cent), followed by the state of unemployment. The flow rates do not change significantly during the period but, as the origin states of non-participation and unemployment increased dramatically during the recession, the number of transitions to temporary jobs also increased dramatically. The data show that the increase in the stock was due to very rapid increase in the inflow between 1992 and 1995 and was not due to an increase in durations. Indeed, there is some evidence that durations shortened during the decade.

Table 4.6 shows the distinctive characteristics of workers on LDCs. They are young, female and foreign. The difference between Swedes and foreigners is even more pronounced than the difference between the sexes. The difference is greatest for the 35 to 44-year-olds, where the LDC intensity for foreigners is more than double that of Swedes.

Table 4.7 shows that on-call contracts are among the most female-dominated of the various forms of LDCs.[7] Employees in this sector have a rather low level of education. As shown below, these contracts contain many poor quality jobs. Leave replacements are the most female-dominated form of LDC and these employees have a relatively high level of education.

*Table 4.6 LDC intensity by citizenship, age and sex, 1999 (per cent)*

| Age | Men | | Women | | Total | |
|---|---|---|---|---|---|---|
| | Foreign | Swedish | Foreign | Swedish | Foreign | Swedish |
| 16–19 | 63.6 | 70.0 | 72.7 | 69.6 | 69.7 | 69.8 |
| 20–24 | 36.4 | 35.0 | 48.5 | 53.3 | 44.8 | 43.2 |
| 25–34 | 27.5 | 14.0 | 34.3 | 23.6 | 30.9 | 18.6 |
| 35–44 | 21.9 | 8.3 | 25.7 | 13.0 | 23.9 | 10.7 |
| 45–54 | 12.6 | 6.3 | 13.2 | 8.5 | 12.9 | 7.4 |
| 55–59 | 11.9 | 5.6 | 14.0 | 6.9 | 12.8 | 6.3 |
| 60–64 | 13.6 | 7.0 | 17.4 | 6.3 | 15.6 | 6.7 |
| 16–64 | 22.0 | 12.9 | 28.1 | 18.0 | 25.2 | 15.4 |

*Source:* LFS (1999).

*Table 4.7 Type of LDC by age, education level and sex (average 1987–96)*

| Type of LDC | Average age | | % with some post-high school education | | % women |
|---|---|---|---|---|---|
| | Men | Women | Men | Women | |
| Relief work | 36.7 | 32.5 | 9.3 | 13.1 | 43.3 |
| Holiday work | 20.9 | 22.8 | 9.3 | 9.6 | 51.5 |
| Project work | 34.8 | 34.0 | 25.2 | 39.5 | 37.1 |
| Work experience | 23.0 | 24.4 | 19.3 | 23.3 | 42.7 |
| Probational work | 27.6 | 28.1 | 15.4 | 13.5 | 41.0 |
| Seasonal work | 30.1 | 31.6 | 7.9 | 13.7 | 42.7 |
| On-call | 27.6 | 29.9 | 15.0 | 11.8 | 66.8 |
| Leave replacement | 29.5 | 31.0 | 27.7 | 24.4 | 74.7 |
| Others | 27.9 | 27.2 | 19.7 | 16.9 | 58.0 |

*Source:* Author's tabulation of data from the Labour Force Survey (AKU).

Project work is the most male-dominated of the contractual forms. These employees are among the oldest of LDC employees. These jobs appear to be rather good (see below) and employees in this sector have the highest level of education.

Aronsson *et al.* (2000) examine working conditions for those on limited duration contracts by type of contract. Table 4.8 summarizes their results. The table should be read as follows. Values greater than one indicate a greater probability than those on open-ended contracts (the reference category). Statistically significant results (at the 5 per cent level) are in bold type. For example, reading across the row, 'Express distaste about their work', both leave replacement and, especially, on-call workers are more likely to feel distaste compared to those on open-ended contracts. The same tendency is found for seasonal and project workers but is not statistically significant. Probationary workers exhibit less of a tendency to distaste but again this is not statistically significant.

*Table 4.8 Working conditions and contractual forms: odds ratios with reference to open-ended contracts*

| | Leave replacement | Probationary | Seasonal | Project | On call |
|---|---|---|---|---|---|
| Training during paid working time | **0.36** | **0.31** | **0.20** | **0.30** | **0.18** |
| Opportunity to learn and develop | 0.89 | 1.32 | **0.50** | 1.19 | **0.70** |
| Able to decide on work organization | 0.38 | 0.38 | **0.47** | 0.64 | **0.26** |
| Feel support from boss | 0.87 | 0.92 | 0.77 | 0.97 | 0.88 |
| Feel support from workmates | 0.91 | 0.84 | 0.75 | 1.05 | 0.59 |
| Stomach problems | **1.30** | 1.23 | 0.87 | 1.26 | 1.23 |
| Express distaste about their work | **1.34** | 0.89 | 1.47 | 1.26 | 1.52 |
| Sleep problems | 1.25 | 1.22 | 0.57 | 1.32 | 0.93 |
| Back or neck pains | 1.10 | 0.67 | 1.21 | 1.24 | **1.35** |
| Feel tired | **1.40** | 1.19 | 0.89 | **1.60** | **1.52** |
| Hesitate to comment on working conditions | **2.09** | **1.76** | 0.79 | **1.51** | **2.08** |

*Notes:*
1. Results from a multinomial logit which controls for age, sex, education level and working time. We note, however, that they have not controlled for economic sector. This is unfortunate as, for example, the majority of leave replacements are found in the health sector. The health sector often shows rather dissatisfied employees.
2. A stratified sample of 3812 from the Labour Force Survey 1997 (13% non-response); significant (5%) variables in bold type.

*Source:* Aronsson *et al.* (2000).

The results show a differentiated picture of working conditions for workers on LDCs. The two extremes are project workers who most resemble those on open-ended contracts and on-call workers. Controlling for age, sex, educational background and working time, they show that all forms of

LDC are less likely both to receive job training and to be 'able to decide on work organization'. On-call and seasonal workers are less likely to have the 'opportunity to learn and develop at work'.

On-call workers have the most marginal relationship to the workplace as they are only employed sporadically. In some countries most of the agency workers would be in this category. While it almost certainly is the case that some agency workers in Sweden are also in this category, it has been underlined above that the majority of agency workers are not, and would be in the reference category of open-ended contracts.

In earlier work, Aronsson and his colleagues have issued a survey to 750 people employed on limited duration contracts (see Aronsson, 1999; Aronsson and Göransson, 1999). Roughly one-third of the respondents who said that they refrained from expressing criticism of working conditions replied that this was due to the fact that they were on a limited duration contract. In Aronsson and Gustafsson (1999), a stratified sub-sample of employees from the Labour Force Survey are asked, 'Does the situation on the labour market make you hesitate in saying what you think about the work environment and working conditions?'. The results of logit regressions (controlling for age, sex, education and occupation) show that having an LDC (together with being in the public sector) was the most significant factor.

**Temporary Work Agencies**

It must be emphasized at the outset that there is very limited knowledge of this sector in Sweden. Temporary work agencies are not identified as a distinct sector in official government statistics (classification of industries) and the labour force survey does not ask about agency work. Thus none of the usual official statistical channels can be used to describe the sector. Neither has there been any research or public investigation that has succeeded in measuring the size of the sector. The data presented in Table 4.3, from the sector organization, SPUR, put the figure at just over 30000 or 0.8 per cent of all employment.

According to Fridén *et al.* (2000) user firms were predominantly within industry (37 per cent), service companies (excluding trade) (29 per cent), trade (6 per cent), and the public sector 10 per cent. The characteristics of the employees in the sector may be summarized as follows.

- Agency workers are generally younger than other employees. More than twice as many agency employees were younger than 30 (45 per cent) compared to all other employed.
- Some 60 per cent of agency employees were women. The corresponding figure for all employees is 47 per cent.

- Agency workers are slightly better educated than other employees in terms of post-school education. However, this is at least in part attributable to their lower age.
- Some 14 per cent of agency employees were foreign citizens.
- The Stockholm area accounts for 60 per cent of all jobs in this sector.

Fridén *et al.* (2000) studied a group employed at an agency some time during 1997 and examined their main labour market status the year before and the year after (see Table 4.9). The data show that the majority (89 per cent) had a job the year before working for an agency, and of these 57 per cent were employed in another sector the year before. A third worked at an agency during both 1996 and 1997.

*Table 4.9 Employees at temporary work agencies in 1997, by labour market status 1996 and 1998*

| | Labour market status | | |
|---|---|---|---|
| | 1996 | 1997 | 1998 |
| Employed at a TWA | 31.7% | Employed at TWA | 50.9% |
| Other employment | 57.0% | | 44.8% |
| Education | 3.5% | | 1.2% |
| Unemployed | 7.9% | | 3.2% |

*Source:* Fridén *et al.* (2000).

As roughly one-third of the employees in TWAs were employed in this sector in 1996, this means that of the workforce in 1997 roughly two-thirds were recruited in the intervening period. Fridén *et al.* (2000) present flows also for women and non-Swedish citizens. Their flow pattern is very similar to the overall total. However, foreigners were slightly more likely to have come from studies and unemployment. This result has been interpreted to suggest that agency work may be a suitable means of integrating foreigners into the labour market, and commercial agencies have been used as an instrument of active labour market policy in Sweden.

Isaksson and Bellaagh (1999) studied the degree of social support from colleagues and bosses received by these workers when working in client firms. Their study is based on a random sample of 481 office and administration workers from the employment register of a major TWA in Sweden in 1996 (53 per cent responded). On average they had been employed in the sector for 18 months, which the authors suppose to be slightly longer than is usual for agency workers. The major focus of the study is perceptions of 'social support' at their place of work. On a scale between one and five the average feeling of support was 3.5, which is slightly lower than other compatible Swedish studies. Multivariate statistical techniques were used to explain the variation of social support. The most important factor was found to be related to whether they reported experiencing problems with having two bosses. The authors then examined the determinants of general job satisfaction. They found the most important factors to be possibilities of development in their work, feelings of security and whether they were satisfied with their wage. It also appears that the lower-educated were more satisfied with their work, as were those who experienced social support. Whether they had voluntarily chosen TWA work was also statistically significant but of less importance.

While only 27 per cent reported that they preferred to work in an agency, the majority did not report deep general dissatisfaction with the agency work. They explained this largely in terms of job security and wages. As regards the social context, it should be pointed out that some stated that they had chosen this form of employment because of negative experiences of stationary work. They reported feelings of isolation from workers at both the TWA and the client company. They also reported a lack of 'feedback' on the work they performed.

This was followed up by 21 personal interviews. All of these participants had an open-ended contract, with a 75 per cent guaranteed monthly wage. However, they should not be regarded as representative as they had been employed for at least two years. Regarding social relations, most responders spoke of, on the one hand, the positive experience of meeting many people but, on the other hand, a lack of content and continuity in these social relationships. Many spoke of the vital importance of a close and continuous contact with the personnel manager of the TWA. When comparing TWA workers and stationary workers, Isaksson and Bellaagh (1999) conclude that

> the different opportunities to obtain social support are considerable . . . In a traditional open-ended contract, there is a continuity in relationships with work mates that is the basis of maybe the most important source of emotional support. This support hardly exists for the TWA workers. Their continuity consists of contact with the personnel manager at the TWA, who is expected to satisfy all expectations of various forms of social support that are needed to feel satisfaction with one's job.

## THE TWO MAIN ISSUES

There are two features of contingent labour that stood out in Sweden in the 1990s: firstly, the very rapid increase in limited duration contracts and, secondly, the fact that, despite agency work having previously been prohibited, by the end of the decade practically all agency workers were covered by a collective agreement. This occurred in a sector which might be expected to be rather difficult to organize from both an employer and an employee perspective. Both these matters merit further discussion.

## Collective Agreements Covering Temporary Agency Workers

Compared to all other countries (see Storrie, 2002), the development of collective bargaining in the temporary work agency sector in Sweden is truly remarkable. Despite the fact that this activity prior to the deregulation of the 1990s, could best be characterized as illegal and that agency work is among the most difficult to organize, the vast majority of agency workers are now covered by wide-ranging collective agreements with an appreciable degree of income security.

Before the deregulation of the sector during the 1990s, the (public) opinions of the social partners were very clear. The Employers Association (SAF) continually called for total deregulation and, at almost every step, deregulation was, at least publicly, opposed by the trade unions. However, the issue was never very controversial and did not prominently enter public debate. Since deregulation, the employers have continued to call for fuller deregulation, including the removal of the prohibition on the agency taking a fee from the job seeker. The trade unions appear, at least publicly, to have shifted their position. In the political debate they have focused mainly on the issue of authorization, though, as before, the issue does not appear to have a high priority. Since deregulation, the main effort of the trade unions has been devoted to obtaining acceptable collective agreements. It is difficult to discern strategy purely on the basis of public statements; it is conceivable that the unions were not as strongly opposed to deregulation as appeared from their initial public stance. Vocal opposition may only be part of the negotiation strategy. Indeed, it is notable that in the labour law debate at the beginning of the 1990s a number of labour law issues were under review, which appeared to be of greater importance to the unions. One issue under debate was the abolition of the trade union right of veto when outside workers are brought into the workplace. One of the most important grounds for the union to veto outside labour was if there was reason to believe that this would undermine the collective agreement. The veto has been retained and, indeed, the law was revised to state clearly that agency work was a category of outside labour falling under the veto powers. It appears obvious that the primary focus of union activity as regards agency workers was not primarily the pay and working conditions of agency workers per se but rather the potential for opportunistic employers to undermine pay and working conditions for directly employed workers at the user firm. The veto right is a very powerful tool in this context.

The explanation of the unions' role in this union 'success story' is obviously related to the general strength of unions in the country as a whole, in particular its success in organizing all forms of flexible labour. While one could argue that the vulnerable position of these workers on the labour market would suggest that they would have most to gain from union membership, this has not been the case in other countries.[8] International experience is of a fall of union membership coinciding with the increase in atypical forms of employment. It is difficult to point at any single factor that explains the divergent Swedish experience. In broad terms one could speculate that it is related to the historically well-documented phenomena of Swedish trade unions' active participation in structural change and proactive stance in the modernization of work organization.

Unions alone do not make collective agreements. From the point of view of the agency employers, a major issue after deregulation was to improve the image of the sector in order to sell their services and attract workers. In Sweden, as in other countries, the agencies have devoted considerable effort to improving their image and the sector organization, SPUR, has introduced an ethical code. However, probably the best means to gain acceptance for agency work was to come to terms with the unions by means of collective bargains. Moreover, the Swedish TWA business is the most concentrated in the European Union, with the top five companies accounting for 80 per cent of turnover (CIETT, 2000). This reflects an oft-neglected matter in Swedish industrial relations: it is not only the unions that are centralized but also, owing to a concentrated industrial structure, employers. In addition to the union explanation, both these factors, the importance of a collective agreement to the employers, in order to gain legitimacy, and the ability to organize employers, were important from the employer side.

On the issue of income security, that is, the provision of a guaranteed monthly wage, which has been the major issue in all collective bargaining in the TWA sector, the position taken by the Labour Market Board, which administers unemployment insurance, was of some importance. Since 1995, it has become clear that unemployment benefit would not be paid out to employees of temporary work agencies while not on an assignment. This made it practically impossible for the employee to obtain a satisfactory income from periods of agency wages and benefit payments. Thus the agency could not shift the costs of flexibility onto the state and, in order to attract labour, it was the agency that had to guarantee a minimum level of income. It is perhaps no coincidence that the guaranteed income for agency workers is roughly 80 per cent of a full-time monthly wage. The replacement ratio in unemployment benefit is also 80 per cent.

## The Growth of Limited Duration Contracts

LDC intensity was around 10 per cent in the 1980s. By the end of the decade it had risen to more than 16 per cent. In the rest of this section we discuss possible explanations for this. Focus is placed on three factors: regulation, shifts in worker preferences and unemployment.[9]

### The role of regulation

Is there any reason to expect that the regulatory changes have had important effects on the increase of LDCs during the 1990s? Legislation could have the effect of increasing the use of LDCs if either the regulation of the open-ended contract was tightened or the regulation of LDCs was liberalized. There have been no significant changes in the statutory regulation of the open-ended contract during the period under study. Focus should thus be placed exclusively on the regulation of LDCs.

The reforms in 1994 had at most a marginal effect on the regulation facing the firm; as is shown in Storrie (1995), the law did not affect the content of the existing collective agreements. Moreover, the law was repealed the following year. The law of 1997 was *potentially* a more significant piece of legislation. However, even if the removal of the requirement to motivate an LDC was of some importance, the use of the new contract was limited to five employees per establishment. There are no statistics on the incidence of this form of LDC. However, a governmental inquiry, directed to the social partners, reported that there are very few of this type of contract. The public employer associations stated that this was due to the typically large size of places of work in the public sector. The private employer association stated that many collective agreements prohibited their use; see SKr (1999/2000).

Moreover, when one considers that the 1997 law also restricted the use of leave replacements, there are grounds to argue that the restrictive element in the legislation may even have dominated the liberalizing element, particularly when one recognizes that leave replacements are by far the most common form of LDC in Sweden. Furthermore, during the decade, temporary work agencies went from (in practice) total prohibition to almost total deregulation. Evidence in Storrie (2002) shows that the replacement of absent employees is among the most important of reasons for employers to use agency workers. Thus both the restriction of leave replacements and the liberalization of temporary work agencies have reduced the opportunity to meet absenteeism with a limited duration contract relative to using agency workers and may have resulted in a shift from limited duration to open-ended contracts. Also, as was documented in the introduction to this chapter, the major increase in LDCs occurred prior to the reform of 1997.

What role then remains for regulation in explaining the evolution of LDCs in the 1990s? A distinct feature of employment protection in Sweden is the importance of the collective agreement for the formation of the rules at the workplace, in terms both of the range of permitted bargaining outcomes and of the almost universal coverage of collective agreements in the labour market. This gives rise to considerable leeway for 'negotiated flexibility' at the local level. There is at least some scattered evidence suggesting that the regulation of LDCs in collective agreements has become more lax (SOU, 1997). As the outcome of both collective bargaining and the subsequent agreement's day-to-day implementation at the local level is largely a result of relative bargaining power, one could expect the mass unemployment of the 1990s to have led to a more liberal regulation than previously was the case. The possibility for the employer to press successfully for greater flexibility was probably further enhanced by the 1997 law that permitted the agreement to be struck at the local level. Thus, if legislation played any significant role, I would argue that the shift to the local level of bargaining is the most likely candidate.[10]

Under the Swedish system of regulation which allows derogation from the law that can not only increase but also decrease worker protection, the actual content of regulation applied at the workplace may be very sensitive to changes in the environment that influence the relative bargaining power of the parties. The level of unemployment is a critical issue in this context and may have an impact on most regulatory regimes. However, the impact may be expected to be greater, or at least more rapid, in the Swedish regime compared to countries where statutory law is of more importance. This should be kept in mind when we return to the issue of unemployment below.

**Worker preferences**

In popular debate one hears of new preferences for LDCs. Often these are described in terms of a shift in preferences of the younger generation and loosely related to a new organization of work and family life. However, at least in the Swedish context, this hypothesis is one that research emphatically rejects. Apart from the fact that such a hypothesis is hardly rational, all empirical investigations of this show very strikingly that it is not the case.

The available evidence suggests that there is a very strong preference for job security in Sweden. For example, responses from a representative sample of Swedish employees in the International Social Survey Programme ranked job security as the most important of the factors listed (Edlund and Svallfors, 1997). Other evidence, in Furåker and Berglund (2001), suggest that having a limited duration contract has a highly significant negative effect on the perception that 'My job is secure'. This perceived relationship between contractual form and job security and the aversion to LDCs is obviously behind the very strong preference for open-ended contracts expressed in a number of Swedish surveys. Berlin (1995, 1997) reports on investigations asking representative samples of the labour force about the preferred contractual form. Over 95 per cent of the respondents expressed preference for open-ended contracts. Aronsson and Göransson (1999) present even more striking results from another questionnaire. They find that, of workers on open-ended contracts who were not working in their preferred occupation, only 25 per cent would prefer a limited duration contract in their desired occupation. Of those who had a limited duration contract in their desired occupation, 58 per cent would be willing to abandon their preferred occupation if they could obtain another job with an open-ended contract.

**Unemployment**

The most obvious empirical indication that unemployment lies behind the growth of LDCs is that both increased rapidly in the early-to-mid-1990s. Moreover, the broad evidence from other Nordic countries is also in line with this explanation (see Holmlund and Storrie, 2002). Among the other Nordic countries, only Finland has exhibited a similar growth in LDCs. Indeed, the Finnish experience during the 1990s has been even more dramatic than the Swedish one, with greater increases both in unemployment and in LDCs. The macroeconomic conditions in Denmark and Norway were much less volatile, with only modest increases in unemployment. It is striking that neither of those two countries experienced any significant rise in LDCs.[11]

In terms of flow accounting, the impact of unemployment on the increase in LDCs is simply due to the increase in the number of people in the major source states of flows into LDCs (non-participation and unemployment) with transition rates remaining more or less constant (see Holmlund and Storrie, 2002). They find that the increase in LDCs can in part be interpreted as purely a business cycle phenomenon; indeed Figure 4.2 illustrates such a cyclical pattern for probationary contracts.

There are a number of possible ways in which unemployment can affect the proportion of LDCs in the labour market. In periods of high unemployment, with many job seekers, high screening costs may provide a greater incentive for firms to screen through LDCs; Holmlund and Storrie (2002) provide some empirical support for this matching hypothesis. On the supply side there may be an increased willingness on the part of workers to accept LDCs when job offers are in short supply. Holmlund and Storrie also find tentative evidence of a trend increase in LDCs in the 1990s irrespective of business cycle conditions, amounting to two percentage points.

They argue that this may be due to increased product market volatility, but can provide no hard evidence for this.

Summing up this section, the increase in limited duration contracts in Sweden during the 1990s is not due to changes in statutory legislation or changes in individual preferences. Moreover, Holmlund and Storrie (2002) show that the increase cannot be due to shifts in the demographic composition of the labour force or sector shifts from low to high LDC-intensive groups or sectors. A significant part of the increase is related to the increase in unemployment. While there is no shortage of reasons why such a relationship may exist, there is no hard empirical evidence that can distinguish between the various hypotheses.

## SOME CONCLUDING REMARKS

The standard open-ended contract is still the typical employment relationship in Sweden. Among those defined as employed in the labour force survey, more than 75 per cent have an open-ended contract. Moreover, there has been no significant change in the regulation of open-ended contracts and an employment contract is presumed to be open-ended unless the employer explicitly states otherwise. However, it could be argued that the pace of deregulation of non-standard employment relationships (limited duration contracts and temporary agency work) in the 1990s has been greater in Sweden than in any other OECD country. The regulation of agency work, which before the 1990s could best be described as illegal, has now been almost totally deregulated. Moreover, since 1997, the employer is no longer required to provide a reason to employ for a limited duration.

There were two features of contingent labour that stood out in Sweden in the 1990s: the very rapid increase in the number of LDCs and the rapid and extensive growth of collective agreements for temporary agency work.

Temporary agency was made legal in the early 1990s and, by the end of the decade practically all agency workers were covered by collective agreements that awarded employees with a guaranteed monthly wage, regardless of the demand for assignments. This remarkable development can be attributed to the well-documented proactive stance of Swedish unionism to new forms of work organization and their general overall strength in the labour market. However, it is important not to underestimate the role of the employers in this context. The Swedish temporary work agency sector is the most concentrated in the European Union and these centralized employers have used the collective agreement, together with ethical codes and advertising campaigns, to improve radically the image of a sector that previously was viewed with some suspicion. In addition, rulings in the insurance courts have meant that employers have not been able to pass on the cost of flexibility to the social security system.

During the 1990s, LDCs increased from 10 to 16 per cent of all employment contracts. This increase occurred in all sectors and for all demographic groups. The increase was, however, accompanied by a change in the character of the contracts. There was a relative decline in the use of leave replacement contracts and a major increase in on-call contracts, which were shown to be the type of LDCs associated with the poorest of working conditions. In explaining the growth of LDCs we could quite clearly reject the hypotheses of shifts in demographic and industrial structure, increased preferences for LDCs and the role of statutory legislation. The increase in the use of these contracts is statistically strongly associated with the increase in unemployment. Exactly what this in turn is due to could not be firmly established.

It must be underlined that we have observed the growth of contingent employment at a time of very severe crisis in the labour market, with unemployment rates not seen since the Great Depression. If the labour market continues to improve it may be the case that both the weakened bargaining power of employers and the need to compete for scarce labour may see a greater propensity for the employer to offer open-ended contracts and the employee to reject limited duration contracts. Thus the current level of LDCs in Sweden may not be a long-term trend. The growth of temporary work agencies in the 1990s is potentially a more permanent phenomenon. Following deregulation, the sector has grown very rapidly, although it is still at a low level. Moreover, after the signing of collective agreements covering practically the entire sector, it is now firmly embedded in the institutions and culture of Swedish industrial relations. While the sector is unlikely to continue to grow at the rate of the late 1990s, neither will it fall back to the virtual non-existence of the early 1990s unless there is a repeal of the law. There is no indication that significant changes to the law will occur in the near future.

## NOTES

1. I would like to thank Ola Bergström for several useful comments.
2. See Storrie (2001) for a detailed account of the shifts in employment structure in OECD labour markets.
3. Indeed OECD (1999) quantitative measures of deregulation of temporary work indicate that the changes in Sweden have been greater than in any OECD country.
4. Earlier agreements in this sector gave lower guaranteed wages. The first collective agreement gave 50 per cent and one concluded in 1998 gave 75 per cent.

5. Intensity is defined as the number of limited duration contracts as a percentage of all contracts.
6. The diminished importance of leave replacements can be seen identified in Table 4.4 from the large decline in the share of LDCs in the Health and Care sector.
7. A detailed breakdown of LDCs by sector and type of LDC between 1987 and 1996 can be found in Storrie (1998).
8. In this context one should not underestimate the fact that the worker *may* opt to join an unemployment insurance scheme which is partly administered by the trade union. In this case the worker must join the union.
9. Before examining some of the candidates for explanation, it should be noted that shifts in industrial structure, away from low LDC intensity to high LDC intensity, do not explain the growth. This is indicated in Table 4.5. Moreover, Holmlund and Storrie (2002) report that neither is it due to demographic shifts in the labour force.
10. On the other hand, the liberalization of the statutory regulation of the temporary work agency sector has been a necessary condition for its rapid increase and, as these activities were previously more or less illegal and then were almost totally deregulated, the role of legislation has been vital. Moreover, the statutory tightening of the regulation of leave replacements may have opened up more opportunities for agency work.
11. Sweden, Norway and Finland have similar regulation of employment contracts. Denmark is closer to the more liberal regimes as in, for example, the UK.

# REFERENCES

Aronsson, G. (1999) 'Contingent workers and health and safety at work', *Work, Employment and Society*, 13(3), 439–59.

Aronsson, G. and S. Göransson (1999) 'Tillfälligt anställda och arbetsmiljödialogen', *Arbete och hälsa*, 3, Arbetslivsinstitutet, Solna.

Aronsson, G. and K. Gustafsson (1999) 'Kritik eller tystnad – en studie av arbetsmarknads- och anställningsförhandens betydelse för arbetsmiljökritik', *Arbetsmarknad & arbetsliv*, 5(3), hösten.

Aronsson, G., K. Gustafsson and M. Dallner (2000) 'Anställningsformer, arbetsmiljö och hälsa i ett centrum-periferiperspektiv', *Arbete och hälsa*, 9, Arbetslivsinstitutet, Solna.

Benavides, F. and J. Benach (1999) *Precarious Employment and Health-related Outcomes in the European Union*, European Foundation for the Improvement of Living and Working Conditions, Luxemburg: Office for Official Publications of the European Commission.

Bergmark, K. (1999) 'Privatanställda sjuksköterskor med bakgrund i offentlig sektor', Investigation commissioned by SAF and carried out by Demoscope AB, 17 December.

Berlin, E. (1995) 'Massiv majoritet för fast jobb', *Arbetsmiljö*, 4(7–8).

Berlin, E. (1997) 'Stor majoritet för fast jobb', *Arbetsmiljö*, 5(3–5).

Bertola, G., T. Boeri and S. Cazes (2000) 'Employment Protection in Industrialized Countries. The Case for New Indicators', *International Labour Review*, 139, 57–72.

CIETT (2000) *Orchestrating the Evolution of Private Employment Agencies Towards a Stronger Society*, Paris: International Confederation of Private Employment Agencies.

Edlund, J. and S. Svallfors (1997) 'Raw data from Work Orientation II', International Social Survey Programme, Umeo University.

Fahlbeck, R. (1984) 'Employment Protection Legislation and Labour Unions Interests: A Union Battle for Survival?', *Stanford Journal of International Law*, 20, 295–327.

Fahlbeck, R. (1999) 'Trade Unionism in Sweden', Labour and Society Programme, Discussion Paper, DP/109/1999, International Labour Organization.

Fridén, L., Y. Hedén and E. Wadensjö (2000), 'Personaluthyrningsföretag – en bro till arbetsmarknaden?', Bilaga 2 till Mångfaldsprojektet, Näringsdepartementet, Stockholm.

Furåker, B. and T. Berglund (2001) 'Employment in Relation to Work and Organizational Commitment', in B. Furåker (ed.), *Employment, Unemployment, and Marginalization. Studies on Contemporary Labour Markets*, Department of Sociology, Göteborg University, Stockholm: Almqvist och Wiksell International.

Holmlund, B. and D. Storrie (2002) 'Temporary Jobs in Turbulent Times: The Swedish Experience', *Economic Journal*, 112, 245–69.

Isaksson, K. and Bellaagh, K. (1999) 'Vem stöttar Nisse? Socialt stöd bland uthyrd personal', *Arbetsmarknad & arbetsliv*, 5(4).

OECD (1999) *Employment Outlook*, Paris: OECD.

SKr (1999/2000) 'Regeringens skrivelse 1999/2000', Skr. Anställningsformen Överenskommen visstidsanställning, 146.

SOU (1997) 'DELTA – Utredningen om deltidsarbete, tillfälliga jobb och arbetslöshets-ersättningen', 27.

Storrie, D. (1993) 'The Anatomy of Large Swedish Plant Closure', PhD thesis, Department of Economics, Gothenburg University.

Storrie, D. (1995) 'Reglering av visstidsanställningar i kollektivavtal: Konsekvenser av 1994 års lagstiftning' (The Regulation of Limited Duration Contracts in Collective Agreements: The Consequences of the Reforms in 1994), EFA, Arbetsmarknadsdepartementet, Stockholm.

Storrie, D. (1998) 'Flexible Employment Contracts in Sweden', *Flexibility in the Nordic Labour Markets*, Copenhagen: Nordic Council of Ministers.

Storrie, D. (2001) 'Service Employment, Productivity and Growth', in D. Anxo and D. Storrie (eds), *The Job Creation Potential of the Service Sector in Europe*, Employment Observatory Research Network, Luxemburg: European Commission.

Storrie, D. (2002) 'Temporary Agency Work in the European Union', Consolidated Report, European Foundation for the Improvement of Working Life and Living Conditions, March.

Stråth, B. (1986) 'Redundancy and Solidarity: Tripartite Politics and the Contraction of West European Shipbuilding Industry', *Cambridge Journal of Economics*, 10(2).

# 5. Contingent employment in Spain

**Manuel Pérez Pérez**

## INTRODUCTION

Like most developed countries, Spain suffered a major unemployment crisis between 1981 and 1993. However, since 1992, the Spanish market appears to be recovering even if unemployment is still high and the Spanish labour market is unusually flexible. The Spanish case, when compared to other OECD countries, is a representative case of a contradictory situation detected by the labour market analysts. Despite a highly dynamic economy, a flexible labour market and a high rate of job creation, unemployment has remained high. This situation may be explained by a number of very different factors. The first factor is the return of a great number of Spanish migrant workers from other European countries; the second, the strong increase in the entry of women to the labour market since the middle of the 1980s; the third, perhaps, the very protectionist and interventionist labour legislation of the past. This chapter analyses the development of the Spanish labour market and in particular the use of contingent employment. Contingent employment is defined in terms of limited duration contracts and temporary agency work. However, in Spain, there are no differences between the limited duration contracts and the contracts that can be used by an agency.

Several sources have been used in the writing of this chapter. Firstly, we have analysed the statistical data published by the Spanish Department for Labour and Social Affairs. These data come in turn from two main sources. On the one hand, there are the labour force sample surveys from the Spanish National Statistics Institute, which are the most complete statistical source in Spain. These surveys have been carried out quarterly from 1988 onwards. There is an abundance of data on temporary work agencies owing to the fact that Spanish law compels agencies to provide the employment authorities with data on every aspect of their activities on a monthly basis.

Secondly, we have used the specialized literature in the field, which is written mainly in Spanish but not solely by Spanish analysts (see Alcaide Castro and Quiros Tomas, 1998; Navarro, 1998; Viñals and Jimeno, 1997;

Martín, 1997). These works have focused on the interpretation of the Spanish situation in recent years, compared to other European Union and also North American countries from both international and private data sources.

## GENERAL TRENDS IN THE LABOUR MARKET

In the last 25 years Spain has seen several stages of economic expansion and stagnation as reflected in the main employment indicators, making it possible to identify the following stages in the economic cycle:

1. a long stage of stagnation from 1976 to 1984, with an average yearly growth which in real terms was less than 1.4 per cent;
2. a stage of strong expansion between 1984 and 1990, in which the Spanish economy reached an average yearly growth in real terms of above 4.5 per cent;
3. a stage of major economic decline from 1990 to 1993. Over this period all the sectors except the service industries experienced negative growth, while the Spanish economy as a whole performed poorly with average annual growth of 0.5 per cent in real terms;
4. from 1994 onwards the Spanish economy has seen a period of moderate growth, which is having a very positive effect on employment and has attained average yearly growth of almost 3.5 per cent (Alcaide Castro and Quiros Tomas, 1998).

In the mid-1970s, the Spanish unemployment rate was 3.5 per cent, which was in line with that experienced by other European Union member states. By 1985, unemployment had increased to 22 per cent in Spain and to 10 per cent in the rest of the EU countries. The Spanish and EU unemployment rates have since then behaved in a similar way, in spite of the gap between them.

The unemployment rate was first accompanied by a strong increase in the inflation rate in the first half of the 1970s, peaking around 26 per cent in 1977, compared to 14 per cent in the rest of the EU countries. Lately we have seen a stage of steady decrease in inflation, which has allowed for a high degree of nominal convergence with most of the EU countries (Viñals and Jimeno, 1997).

### Activity Rates and Trends in Labour Supply

The increase in the participation of people aged between 16 and 64 years has been relatively greater than in the rest of the EU. The Spanish participation rate (labour force as percentage of the population between 16 and 64), which in the mid-1980s was considerably lower than that of the rest of the EU, has increased towards, but still has not reached, the EU average. The growth of the labour force has put pressure on the labour market in recent years, and in particular during the stages of economic expansion, as a result of both the natural increase in the working age population and women's entry into the labour market (see Martín, 1997).[1]

However, the Spanish activity rate is still amongst the lowest in the EU. In 1992, the rate was 48.9 per cent and by the first quarter of 2000 had risen to 51 per cent. Another notable feature, which will be dealt with in the remaining analysis, is the large gap in the activity rate between men and women. In 1992, the activity rate amongst men was almost double that of women. Although there is a trend towards the narrowing of the gap, it is still considerable (see Figure 5.1).

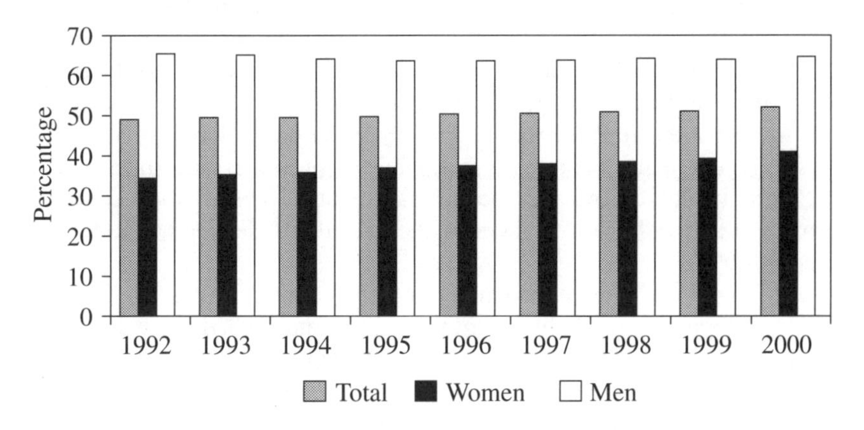


*Figure 5.1 Activity rate, by gender*

**Changes in the Employment Rate**

The number of employed in the last quarter of 1996 was almost the same as 20 years before, despite a significant increase in labour supply. However, profound changes have taken place in the productivity and employment structure.

First, between 1992 and 2000, the apparent productivity of work increased considerably. Taking GDP (gross domestic product) and employment figures for 1976 as 100, we observe that, once the effects of inflation have been eliminated, Spanish GDP has increased by 60 per cent, with the same number of employed people as in 1976. Second, despite the fact that the number of employed people in the year 2000 is slightly higher than in

1992, the Spanish economy has seen stages of both outstanding job creation and losses in accordance with the swings in the economic cycle. Third, Spain has a substantial hidden labour supply, which emerges in the expansion stages owing to the fact that the activity rate is relatively low. Between 1996 and 2000, the hidden economy increased its percentage of GDP from 15 to 21.2 per cent (*El Pais*, 2001).

If we compare job creation with unemployment reduction, we find that during the period of economic expansion, 1995–6, the strong job creation had almost no impact on unemployment. The 800000 new jobs created resulted in a reduction in unemployment of barely 200000. This seemingly contradictory situation originates from the fact that Spain has a substantial hidden labour supply which, in the economic expansion stages, passes from inactivity to activity in statistical terms, but without being unemployed: most of the job creation involves people who appeared in the statistics as inactive rather than as unemployed. In addition, the sector structure of employment has changed greatly, with an outstanding increase in the importance of the service sector, to the detriment of the industry sector and especially the primary sector (agriculture, fishing and mining). Whereas the primary sector has suffered constant job loss in recent years, the service sector has enjoyed a strong stage of job creation, while the industry sector has created jobs in the economic growth stages only to lose them in the periods of decline (Alcaide and Quiros, 1998).

Looking at the relative tendencies and percentages, we can say that the total employment rates between the years 1992 and 2000, despite the three-point increase from 48 per cent to 51 per cent, have merely gone back to the relative employment figures of the period prior to 1992. This is clearly reflected in the increase in the employment rate of females, which rose from 25.5 per cent in 1992 to 31.0 per cent in 2000 (see Table 5.1). Amongst men, this tendency is less apparent as the employment rate has gone from 55.4 per cent in 1992 to 57.6 per cent in the year 2000.

In the 1986–96 period, Spain had the lowest employment rate within the EU. Unlike the previous years, however, we must highlight that the Spanish economy saw an outstanding period of job creation, growing by 12 per cent over that decade.

Another peculiar feature of the Spanish labour market is the importance of limited duration contracts (LDCs) in relation to open-ended contracts. Starting from the fact that in 1985 the LDCs amounted to 8 per cent of the total, it is hard to understand how this figure has quadrupled in 10 years, reaching 37.3 per cent in 1998. This percentage has since tended to decrease at a low yearly rate of around 0.5 per cent (see Table 5.2).

Labour insecurity has not affected all sectors equally. Some sectors have

*Table 5.1* *Employment rate, by gender and age (%)*

| | 1992 | | 1993 | | 1994 | | 1995 | | 1996 | | 1997 | | 1998 | | 1999 | | 2000 | |
|---|---|---|---|---|---|---|---|---|---|---|---|---|---|---|---|---|---|---|
| | M | W | M | W | M | W | M | W | M | W | M | W | M | W | M | W | M | W |
| 16–19 | 21.5 | 14.7 | 16.3 | 11.8 | 15.0 | 10.2 | 14.6 | 10.1 | 14.9 | 8.9 | 14.8 | 8.7 | 17.4 | 9.4 | 19.2 | 11.7 | 21.6 | 12.2 |
| 20–24 | 49.5 | 36.0 | 42.8 | 31.8 | 41.2 | 30.9 | 42.5 | 31.0 | 41.9 | 30.7 | 43.6 | 32.3 | 64.1 | 33.2 | 50.5 | 36.4 | 52.9 | 39.5 |
| 25–54 | 81.9 | 38.8 | 78.5 | 38.5 | 77.5 | 38.8 | 78.3 | 40.2 | 78.8 | 41.8 | 79.9 | 43.4 | 81.8 | 44.8 | 84.0 | 47.6 | 85.2 | 50.8 |
| 55+ | 27.3 | 8.6 | 25.3 | 8.3 | 23.0 | 7.6 | 22.4 | 7.6 | 22.8 | 7.4 | 22.6 | 7.3 | 23.0 | 7.3 | 22.3 | 7.3 | 23.4 | 7.6 |
| Total | 55.4 | 25.5 | 52.1 | 24.6 | 50.8 | 24.5 | 51.3 | 25.1 | 52.0 | 26.0 | 52.9 | 26.9 | 54.5 | 27.7 | 56.1 | 29.5 | 57.6 | 31.0 |

*Source:* Active population survey, Spanish Labour and Social Affairs Department; Estadísticas/BEL/EPA.

*Table 5.2 Limited duration contracts and open-ended contracts (thousands)*

| | 1992 | 1993 | 1994 | 1995 | 1996 | 1997 | 1998 | 1999 | 2000 |
|---|---|---|---|---|---|---|---|---|---|
| Total | 6465 | 5987 | 5872 | 6024 | 7901 | 8301 | 8891 | 9487 | 9881 |
| OEC | 4333 | 4161 | 4030 | 4127 | 5048 | 5210 | 5571 | 5997 | 6250 |
| LDC | 2081 | 1827 | 1841 | 1897 | 2853 | 3091 | 3320 | 3499 | 3631 |
| LDC (%) | 32.2 | 30.5 | 31.4 | 31.5 | 36.1 | 37.2 | 37.3 | 36.9 | 36.7 |

*Source:* Ministry of Labour and Social Affairs; Estadísticas, BEL.

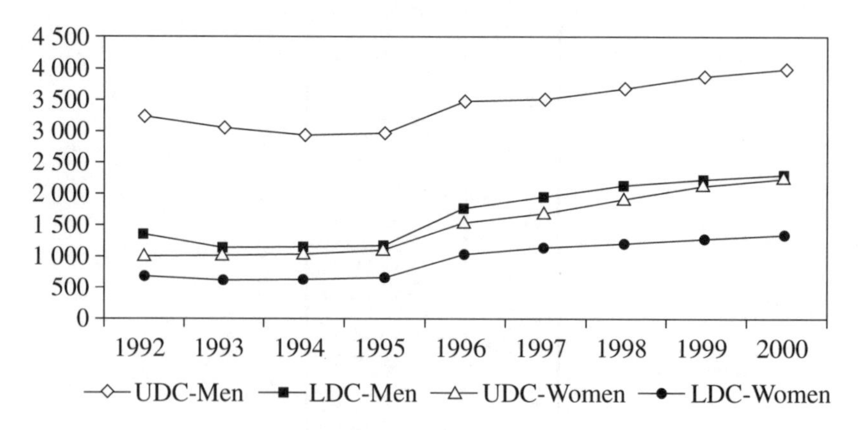


*Figure 5.2 Workers according to contract types, by gender*

had a rate that has not exceeded 19 per cent (mining, motors, energy, iron and steel, shipbuilding and chemical industries, among others). The sectors where rates of temporary contracts have not exceeded 29 per cent include electric material, paper, machinery and hardware and petrochemical industries, among others. The industries with the highest rates of job insecurity are those where LDCs have reached a rate of 37 per cent (fashion, footwear, food and furniture industries, among others). The building industry must be accounted for separately because of its unusually high rate of LDCs – 65.7 per cent in 1995 (Álvares Aledo, 1997).

According to analysts, this growing trend of LDCs has been slowed lately by a disproportionate use of part-time contracts. The part-time open-ended contracts have thus multiplied by five, growing from 102900 in 1992 to 528300, whereas the part-time LDCs have grown from 173000 in 1992 to 683300, in the year 2000. We observe that men account for most LDCs. On the other hand, the relative proportions favour women, as the ratio between LDCs and open-ended contracts amongst men is 3 to 1, whereas amongst females this ratio is 2 to 1 (see Figure 5.2).

### Unemployment

The most problematic feature of the Spanish labour market is the still unusually high unemployment rate, which has negative effects on both the economy and society. We must remember that this trend has by no means been steady: between 1976 and 1985, unemployment figures increased fivefold; from 1994 onwards the economic expansion has allowed for a constant decrease in unemployment.

Unemployment rates vary between the sexes. Unemployment occurs more amongst women. Unemployment rates were well above 20 per cent during the 1990s and peaking (at 31.4 per cent) in the year 1994. Over the same period, the unemployment rate amongst men swung between 12 per cent in 1990 and 10.5 per cent in the first quarter of the year 2000, reaching its peak (at 19.8 per cent) in 1995. Unemployment declines with age.

When analysing the unemployment rate by sector we see that it has only increased in the agriculture sector, which grew from 13.4 per cent in 1992 to 17 per cent in the year 2000. The overall unemployment rate in the remaining sectors decreased from 12.4 per cent in 1992 to 9 per cent in the year 2000. In the industry sector this rate went down from 11.7 per cent to 7 per cent in 2000, while in the construction sector it saw a sharp decrease, going from 22.2 per cent to 10.8 per cent over the same period. However, the unemployment rate in the services sector has remained almost the same as in 1992, although it has undergone ups and downs.

Finally, analysing the unemployment data by Autonomous Communities we note that the highest unemployment rates are shared by Andalusia (24.5 per cent) and Extremadura (23.7 per cent), while Navarra (5.9 per cent) and the Balearic Islands (7.2 per cent) are the lowest.

## INSTITUTIONAL FRAMEWORK AND EMPLOYMENT REGULATION

The current situation of employment in Spain is in all probability the consequence of a number of factors which could provoke individually a sequence of negative effects on the economy, but whose actual relevance remains unknown when studied as a whole. For this reason a mere account of isolated factors cannot give a proper view on this issue, although this is all we can do for now, as there is still no way to measure scientifically the effects of these interrelated factors. From this limited starting point, we will proceed now to study the context of contingent employment in Spain, dealing in the first place with the institutional background, later with the legal regulation of contracts and finally with the social security system.

## The Institutional Framework

The current institutional framework regulating industrial relations in Spain is just 20 years old. In an effort to safeguard the dictatorship, the effects of the 1973 oil shock in Spain were not made apparent until Franco's death in 1975, causing them to coincide with the dismantling of the previous repressive regime's political, economic and industrial structures, and the passing of a new Constitution in 1978.

All these changes vary in importance. For instance, the granting of fundamental civil rights, such as the right of assembly, the freedom to join a union or the right to strike, made possible the establishment of a labour movement assembly and the creation of a number of workers' and employers' associations. Parliament drafted the Union Law (passed in 1985), which granted the largest unions a number of powers – the 'more representative' concept[2] – which went beyond strict worker representation, in order to ensure their silence while the bill on the duration of contracts was being discussed. The reform consolidated the two main unions in Spain, namely the Comisiones Obreras (CCOO), formerly Communist-led, and the Union General de Trabajadores (UGT), formerly influenced by the Socialist party, the PSOE. Over the last decade, these unions have preferred close mutual cooperation rather than a collaboration with their political counterparts. As for the main employers' federations, the CEOE (*Confederación Española de Organizaciones Empresariales*) represents the most influential banking and industry companies nationwide, whereas the small and medium-sized undertakings are represented by nationwide federations (CEPYME) or sector associations (ASAJA, UAGA, COAG).

### Collective bargaining

Collective industrial agreements in Spain generally affect all those theoretically involved in an agreement. According to Spanish labour legislation, trade unions (who represent 10 per cent of a sector's workforce) have the right to take part in negotiations. This situation has caused hostility on the part of the minor unions that fail to reach this threshold. This may be regarded as an effort to have themselves recognized as valid negotiation partners by means of provoking conflicts to be resolved later.

The workers' rights in Spain are governed by either the collective labour agreements of the sector or a company's own agreement, with the exception of drop-out groups (that is, sub-Saharan and North African immigrants) who work mainly in the construction sector and on greenhouse crops on the Mediterranean coast, and self-employed workers. Consequently, the last two groups experience high job insecurity. Several agreements have been reached by the main trade unions and the employers' association since 1996. First, there were the agreements on the solution of labour conflicts (ASEC, 1996) and work stability (AIEE, 1997). These agreements aimed at reducing the high rate of temporary contracts and encouraging permanent contracts. Secondly, there was the general agreement on collective bargaining (AINC, 1997) and the agreement on the coverage of legal vacuums, (AIVC, 1997). Finally, there were the Madrid and Toledo agreements, aiming at streamlining social security pensions.

### The legal system

The Constitutional Court is the driving force of the modern, progressive interpretation of the rights granted by the Constitution, both collective (freedom to join a union, right to strike) and individual (legal protection against discrimination, judicial protection). The Constitutional Court has established a number of principles that make up the major part of the Trade Union Law of 1985, and constitute the core of the draft bill on strikes in essential national services discussed between 1992 and 1994.

The new decentralized 'State of Autonomies' implies that the industrial relations system is plural and on different levels, and even has shared powers. This situation makes the Spanish system of industrial relations extremely complicated, and also contributes to altering the market laws through protectionist employment policies in each region. The regional governments introduced a new administrative level between the central and local governments, which greatly increased the demand for workers in the public service. However, instead of objectively assessing merits and abilities, the regional administrations apply discriminatory rules against candidates from other parts of Spain (promotion of regional languages, Catalan, Basque, Galician and of their own regional administration employees). This situation has provoked a number of labour market distortions in certain Autonomous Communities, which in turn involve a labour rigidity that affects both the public and the private sectors: there is considerable reluctance towards mobility within Spain.

### The public service reforms

We need to highlight the public service reforms carried out in the 1980s and 1990s, which in an effort to render the management of public administration more efficient have 'labourized' the Spanish public service when the concept of a Labour Law was in crisis in the private sector. Thus, apart from the rules on public servants' union collective rights such as representation and the settling of working conditions, we stress that the relations between the administration and its employees are similar to those envisaged by the Labour Law, especially concerning the civil servants' rights and duties and the disciplinary system. This might convey an idea of the scope of the Spanish Labour Law; and also, it is a great achievement in light of the extremely stable posts of the civil service in the early 1980s.

This review of the institutional framework of the Spanish labour market would be incomplete without mention of two traditional agencies in the industrial relations system: the Spanish Office of Employment (INEM), and the Advisory, Conciliation and Arbitration Service (IMAC). Both agencies were intended to speed up the two most critical stages of industrial relations and make them more flexible: these were the job search by INEM and the cancellation of contracts through IMAC. These two agencies are being strongly challenged as they have been supplanted by private institutions, namely temporary work agencies, private recruitment agencies and, to a lesser extent, private non-profit employment agencies. The public employment agencies now confine themselves to updating the employment statistics or making the official announcements of public posts, rather than dedicating most of their efforts to matching labour supply and demand, which was their role until 1994, when the employment agencies' monopoly ended. The power of IMAC is limited to the management of the incorrectly termed 'trade union' polls, where the posts for the unitary representation of each company are elected every four years, and this only in the regions where this area has not been handed over to the Community government. Their regional counterparts, the Mediation, Arbitration and Conciliation Centres, supervise the conciliation processes regarding individual redundancies, although this supervision is not compulsory. The mediation, arbitration and conciliation functions are, however, carried out by the General Mediation and Arbitration Service (SIMA), which was created in 1996 through a collective agreement between the most relevant social partners nationwide. This service deals with the collective industrial conflicts between social and economic organizations or the unions.

The Labour Inspectorate carries out the supervision of industrial relations during the period of validity of contracts. The Labour Inspectorate has been criticized because of its laxity, especially since the Popular Party took over office; for example, the administration's *laissez-passer* policy has caused a sharp increase in labour accident rates since 1996.

### The Legal Framework

The legal framework of Spanish industrial public and private relations originated as the development of the Constitution's provisions in the last

20 years, and to a lesser extent as a consequence of Spain's entry into the EEC in 1986. Moreover, a considerable number of rules have resulted from the government's aim to reduce unemployment as well as from monetary and inflation-tackling policies.

The Workers' Act of 1980 (law 8/1980) includes the regulations on individual industrial relations, participation and representation of workers in companies, collective bargaining and labour offences. This legislation originates directly from article 35.1 of the 1978 Constitution, so the Workers' Act was passed according to the political situation prior to the economic crisis, when stability was the priority. This Act was preceded by an extensive agreement amongst the major unions' and employers' associations, and has been subsequently modified in 1984, 1994, 1997 and 2001.

As far as collective rights are concerned, apart from the Trade Union Law of 1985, we must mention Royal Decree 17/1977 on industrial relations which governs lock-outs, collective industrial conflicts and the right to strike as ratified by the Constitutional Court in 1981.

In addition to the above, the Constitution also envisaged a Public Service Act. However, the recruitment of the Public Service has been determined by a number of minor reforms intended to make it more efficient and, more importantly, by the constant transfer of civil servants from the central to the regional administrations as a consequence of the more favourable working conditions in the latter.

**The regulation of open-ended contracts**

The open-ended contract is considered as a relic of the Second Republic's legal system, which established two types of contracts: open-ended and limited duration.

The open-ended contract has been the standard model of contract in Spain. However, since 1994 there has no longer been any open-ended contract presumption. The practice of considering that the contract had an undetermined duration has turned into an option between the parties who enter into a contract of employment as the two types (open-ended and temporary) are not regarded as equally favourable for both parties.

Law 8/1980 of the Workers' Act establishes three types of considerations which can be put forward in the cancellation of a contract. First, there are the *economic, technical and organizational or production reasons* (large-scale redundancy). This measure must contribute to overcoming a difficult economic situation in the company. Second, there are the *objective considerations* which affect employees individually and are divided into four types:

- incompetence after a trial period;
- lack of adaptation to the technical changes in a post, provided that

the said changes are justifiable and at least two months have passed since the modifications;
- necessary and justified cutback on staff for economic, technical, organizational or production reasons; and
- absenteeism from work, even when justified, whenever it is intermittent and amounts to 20 per cent of working days in two months, or 25 per cent of working days in any four months in a period of 12 months, and provided that the overall absenteeism rate is higher than 5 per cent over the same period.

These first two types are similar to the third case of objective redundancy if 10 per cent of the staff are affected. In addition, the redundancy payment is similar in both cases: 20 days' salary for each year of service with a maximum of 12 monthly payments, provided that the reasons for dismissal were valid. For the dismissals under objective considerations, the employer must give notice 30 days in advance.

The third type of dismissal is due to *disciplinary considerations*. Disciplinary considerations are defined as grave breaches of contract on the part of the employee: absenteeism or lack of punctuality; disobedience or lack of discipline in work; verbal and physical offences against the employer, other employees or their relatives; breach of trust in contract or work; continuous and voluntary decrease in output in work; continuous drunkenness and drug abuse which has a negative effect on work.

If the court deems disciplinary dismissal appropriate, the dismissed employee is not entitled to a redundancy indemnity. However, if it is inappropriate, the indemnity can amount to 45 days' salary for each year of service with a maximum of 42 monthly payments. The same indemnity is due if the judge considers that an objective dismissal is inappropriate. Despite the employers' criticism of the high costs of dismissals, they actually prefer to seek individual court judgments, knowing full well that they stand no chance of success, for fear of the loss of prestige that a large-scale dismissal judgment might provoke.

The Spanish government endorsed the general agreement on work stability with two Royal Decree, 8/1997 and 9/1997.[3] These measures resulted in the creation of a new type of contract denominated *contract for the promotion of open-ended contracts*, also called 'stable' contracts. These are open-ended contracts which can be cancelled for objective considerations. If the court declares the dismissal inappropriate, instead of receiving the indemnity for inappropriate disciplinary dismissal, the employee is only entitled to receive 33 days' salary for each year worked, with a maximum of 24 monthly payments. These reforms are considered positive by the major Spanish unions.

**The regulation of contingent employment**

In Spain there is no homogeneous set of rules governing contingent employment. The most cohesive regulation is that of temporary contracts, both agreed directly by the employer or through an agency. The rest of contingent employment situations follow sociological or economic considerations rather than strictly legal ones and are governed by a different regulation. For instance, the situation of freelance workers is not governed by the regulations of employees.

In addition, some insecure employment situations known as 'black' or illicit work affect not only social dropout groups such as North African and sub-Saharan immigrants, but also people who, because of an urgent need for a wage, agree not to register in the social security registry (especially in domestic service). These situations are considered an infringement of labour law, which may give rise to a civil penalty (that is, a fine) or even be considered a crime under Spanish Penal Law.[4] However, they are not the subject of further discussion here, and we will focus now on limited duration contracts and those agreed through temporary work agencies.

*Regulation of limited duration contracts* Limited duration contracts (LDCs) needed to be based on legal grounds following the industrial and legal tradition of the Spanish Second Republic (1931–6) and, above all, the dictatorship's protectionist industrial relations system which was established to make up for the lack of free trade unions and a democratic system.

The law originally envisaged five cases of temporary contracts: (a) for a particular service or work; (b) for production reasons or excess of demand with a maximum duration of six months within a period of 12 months; (c) as an interim substitute for a worker who will later resume work; (d) exceptionally, as part of employment promotion policies; and (e) to carry out open-ended work, but on a discontinuous basis; a sixth case (f) Royal Decree 5/2001 was introduced as the so-called *insertion contract* for an unemployed person to collaborate in social or general interest work (a) for a particular service or work.[5]

All these LDCs are fully envisaged by specific royal decrees, which originate as the development of the regulation contained in the Workers' Act. However, these regulation developments cannot establish rules without a previous law, but specify the existing law. A well-known case of excess of this power was the Government taking advantage of this faculty by developing the legal regulation of the *launch new activity* contract. This has now been discontinued. This was done in 1984 by means of introducing an extremely important change: the approval of LDCs *in order to launch a new activity*. Many major banks and commercial and services companies have extensively used this form of LDC for up to three years, rather than open-ended contracts. In 1997, this type of contract disappeared from the Workers' Act.

Recently, we have also seen new modalities such as takeover contracts and the return of part-time jobs. Along with the above, there were other existing types of LDCs like the training or apprenticeship contracts (commonly referred to as 'rubbish contracts'[6] by young people) or work experience contracts.

**Changes in the legislation**

The government's rather flippant attitude regarding this issue is that a temporary contract is better than no contract at all. More importantly, between 1984 and 1993, the employer could choose, at his or her discretion, to recruit people as temporary workers rather than entering into an open-ended contract. When the Spanish legislature changed the law and introduced the economic promotion of some open-ended contracts, as a measure to improve the labour market, the trend changed and the employers' preference was no longer only for temporary contracts. However, before this change took place there was a significant decline in the number of open-ended contracts relative to limited duration ones. Furthermore, the widespread use of temporary contracts rather than trial periods became a major abuse of the law as this helped employers avoid the strict duration terms established by the Workers' Act for trial periods of two weeks, three months or six months, depending on the worker's technical skill. In practice, the legal proof period has disappeared.

**Interpretation of the law**

Despite the strong criticism by Spanish experts of LDCs (Moradillo Larios, 1998; Sempere Navarro and Cardenal Carro, 1996; Vicente Palacio, 1996), the Supreme Court's case law has been significantly flexible in interpreting the law and rules. In particular, regarding the cancellation of LDCs, it has established doctrines that clearly favour employers. For instance, in the case of contracts for a particular service or work, which are mainly used in the construction and shipbuilding industries, the termination of the contract depends on the completion of the actual work. The Supreme Court has made a distinction between the end of the whole job and the end of its stages. As the employer is usually the person who knows when each stage and the whole job are finished, the termination of contracts is at his or her discretion. The same can be said of the law's provisions for the cases when a replaced permanent employee fails to resume work after the period established by law; usually, the interim worker would take the vacant post, but the Supreme Court's interpretation in this field clearly favours the companies.

However, the Supreme Court's interpretation regarding the eventual LDCs is stricter to avoid the excesses of so-called market reasons, that is, more demand or supply. These contracts have a maximum duration of six months during a period of up to 12 months in order to prevent abuse in terms of repeatedly entering into contingent contracts to avoid entering into an open-ended one. The rigidity of these contracts was determined by three law reforms in 1994, 1997 and 2001, which allowed for changes in the maximum duration and the maximum period within which these contracts could take place by virtue of an agreement signed by the employers' associations and the main unions (no limits, 13.5 months and, finally, 12 months).

The use of LDCs to replace employees who are temporarily absent has also undergone some changes that make it possible to recruit an interim worker to occupy a vacant post while the selection of the permanent substitute is in process. This last modality of contract has been widely used by the local and regional administrations, as the selection of the most suitable candidate must meet some publicity requirements; this could take a long time, during which the post cannot remain vacant. Regarding this issue, most field experts consider that, according to the strict interpretation of the Workers' Act, should the administration commit an irregularity (such as exceeding the maximum period) it would be compelled to enter into an open-ended contract. In spite of the above, the Supreme Court's law reports show us that it has tended to favour the public administration and not to order an open-ended contract. It is also interesting to highlight that the LDCs agreed for a period shorter than the maximum one established by law are considered to be extended up to the legal maximum if the employer fails expressly to give notice of its cancellation in due time. For LDCs, notice of the cancellation must be given at least 15 days in advance and, if the employer fails to give notice, the salary corresponding to this period is considered as a small redundancy indemnity.

Law 11/1994 amended article 15 of the Workers' Act and abrogated the traditional presumption of law that open-ended contracts were the rule and accepted for the first time both modalities of contracts as options. Nonetheless, this does not imply that the two types of contracts are considered to be equal, as LDCs need to prove the existence of a just cause to be legitimate.

In 1997, a number of important legal reforms were made in order to improve temporary contracts. This was achieved through laws 63/1997, *on urgent measures to improve the labour market and encourage open-ended contracts* and 64/1997, *on social security and fiscal incentives to promote open-ended contracts*. These abrogated the controversial '*in order to launch a new activity*' modality contracts, leaving just three types of LDCs (for a particular service or work, temporary because of an excess of demand, and interim as a substitute), plus the two training contracts (apprenticeship and work experience).

One year later, article 12 of the Workers' Act was amended through Royal Decree 15/1998, which had a direct impact on part-time contracts and discontinuous open-ended contracts.

*Regulation of temporary work agencies* Temporary work agencies (TWAs) were introduced in Spain in 1994. However, the short lapse of time since then has been enough to attract the analysts' attention owing to the huge number of jobs they have created in the Spanish labour market. These agencies used to be governed by law 14/1994, which has been amended almost every year since the Popular Party took over the government in 1996. Finally, this law was totally restructured in 1999 by virtue of two laws: first, law 29/1999, which amended 11 out of the 21 articles of the former legislation; second, law 45/1999, which introduced for the first time in Spain the regulation on cross-border activity of European TWAs. In addition, Royal Decree 4/1995 established the guidelines on the relations between the TWA and the labour authorities.

The Spanish legislation on this issue has been greatly influenced by the Germanic model, though there are requirements copied from all three existing models in an effort to comply with European legislation (Del Rey Rodriguez, 2000; Escudero Rodriguez and Mercader Uguina, 2000; Molero Marañon, 2000; Pérez Pérez, 2001). Spanish legislation on TWA establishes only the minimum requirements to enter into a limited duration contract and can be later improved through a collective agreement.

The Spanish law is extremely interventionist. The government tries to control every aspect of TWAs. As soon as a TWA is set up, the labour authorities must issue an ad hoc permit prior to the beginning of business. Furthermore, a security deposit must be placed with a public body, a private organization or a public registry (central or regional) which then carries out an almost daily review of the TWA activities. Once the TWA is operating, it is compelled by law to present reports on the number of jobs created or any relevant fact in the agency itself (change in partners, increase in the corporate capital and so on) to the labour authorities on a monthly basis. The authorities' control ends only when the agency no longer exists, as even the termination of a TWA involves a complex registration process for the refunding of the aforementioned security deposit.

The Spanish TWA can recruit both permanent and temporary workers, but they can only enter into the types of LDCs envisaged by article 15 of the Workers' Act and not all those available to employers who recruit their workers directly (namely, contracts for a particular service or work, those due to an excess of demand and interim workers). In recent years the TWAs have tried to combine all the advantages granted by the different types of LDC (for example deciding when a service or work is finished) applying them to the termination of the temporary contracts with a maximum duration of six months. Furthermore, these agencies have claimed that the termination date is the employer's responsibility on the grounds that the contract between the TWA and its client is different from the contract of employment and no such date was stipulated in the direct recruitment. In order to tackle these schemes, both the Supreme Court (decision taken 4 February 1999) and the legal reforms carried out in the summer of 1999 by virtue of law 29/1999 have settled the controversy in a decisive manner. The TWA can only enter into the same kinds of temporary contracts and under the same conditions and requirements as established for other employers by article 15 of the Workers' Act and Royal Decree 2720/1998. In addition, a number of prohibitions were added. The four prohibitions on hiring agency workers are (i) to replace strikers; (ii) to perform dangerous tasks as laid down by Royal Decree according to several European directives; (iii) to fill a position that had been abolished in the previous year, according to the law; and (iv) to transfer the worker to another TWA. In the case of contracts that infringe these requirements and prohibitions, the TWA will be authorized to accept the original temporary contract, converted into an open-ended one. This is the typical penalty used by the Spanish law against fraudulent temporary contracts.

**TWAs and collective agreements in Spain**

Currently there are two collective agreements operating: first, a nationwide agreement which came into force in January 2000 and will be valid until December 2002 in which minimum requirements are set; second, an agreement in Catalonia that is valid between December 2000 and December 2001.

The role of collective bargaining has been crucial not only for the institutionalization of industrial relations in the TWA sector but also for these agencies to become creators of stable jobs. According to the nationwide collective agreement, the Spanish TWAs undertake that 50 per cent of their staff (according to the number of employees by 31 December of the previous year) will be employed under open-ended contracts, leaving out of the calculation those part-time contracts in which the working hours amount to less than 50 per cent of a full-time one. The TWAs that fail to meet this requirement will not be granted the power to extend temporary contracts to the maximum duration of 12 months. The new Catalan collective agreement regulates, in article 14(A) for the agency staff (personnel who permanently, or temporarily, work within the agency and are not transferred to any other user), two criteria to measure the obligation of stable employment. The first criterion relates to the number of workers in the agency; the second to the number of workplaces in the work centre of the agency (see Peréz Peréz, 2001).

**Enforcement of the regulation of TWAs**

Given that Spanish legislation of TWAs is so rigid, it is not difficult to infringe the rules contained in law 14/1994, which have recently been added to Royal Decree 5/2000. This law envisages three types of offence: those related to bureaucracy are considered as petty/minor offences; those related to employment contracts and information are deemed serious breaches of the regulations; finally, the violation of explicit prohibitions of the law is a very serious offence. However, it is extremely easy to deny all liability on the grounds that the user might be responsible for the 'errors' committed by the TWA. Furthermore, the Labour Inspectorate's laxity in recent years has contributed to the fact that these offences are rarely punished. This is the conclusion that we can draw from the small number of cases taken to the courts (six in the last eight years). It is common knowledge that all cases on labour offences are appealed systematically. The appeals are generally upheld on the ground that the offence was trivial. The legal penalties increase gradually according to the importance of the offence. However, the administration punishes these infringements of the law by the more subtle means of not extending the necessary permission for the second or third year of activity or even the suspension of the agency when the infringement is repeated.

## Social Security

The Spanish social security system does not differentiate between permanent and temporary workers, at least with respect to the nature and importance of the benefits granted by the system. Thus both the social security system and its governing law protect all employees who render their services in compliance with the conditions established by the Workers' Act, whether temporary or permanent, even on a discontinuous basis, regardless of the professional category, the size of the salary or the specific governing legislation of the activity.

In a social security system strongly based on contributions, like the Spanish one, with the exception of almost universal medical care, the degree of protection is a function of the contribution period. This could be extremely important in some circumstances (for example, disability, old age, inability to work, unemployment and so on).

Furthermore, although social security contributions vary among workers there are both advantages and disadvantages. The advantage for temporary contracts is that the regulation of part-time contracts stipulates a minimum contribution of €3.62 per hour for engineers and university graduates and of €2.42 per hour for the eight lower qualification categories out of a total of 11. Contribution rates are also established for the training contracts (for university graduates) and work experience contracts (non-graduates) which are respectively €35 per month (€4.80 paid by the worker) and €32 per month (€3.94 paid by the worker). The disadvantages with temporary contracts are: (i) the contribution for unemployment benefit increases both for the employer and for the temporary worker;[7] (ii) when the contract has a limited duration, and is endorsed by a TWA to transfer the employee to the client firm, the contribution amounts to 9.3 per cent (7.7 + 1.6) or 7.55 per cent of real salary when the employee has a degree of disability over 33 per cent.

## CONTINGENT EMPLOYMENT IN SPAIN

### Limited Duration Contracts

We begin this section by mentioning three ideas introduced earlier (p. 111). First, LDCs are extremely important in Spain compared to other countries. Second, the relative importance of LDCs tends to decrease in comparison to open-ended contracts. Third, temporary employment has not affected all sectors equally. The fashion, non-metallic minerals, food, furniture, shoe and leatherwear industries account for most of the LDCs, to say nothing of the building industry, whose environment is the natural and logical home of LDCs for a particular piece of work.

In addition to the above, we stress the fact that, although slowly decreasing in relative importance, this type of contract has grown in absolute terms in the largest sectors (namely industry, construction and service). However, LDCs have not grown equally in the different subsectors. According to the Interim Labour Survey, whereas the open-ended contracts have increased by 44 per cent between 1992 and 2000, the LDCs grew by 74 per cent over the same period. Part-time and full-time contracts have not grown at the same rate. As far as unlimited duration contracts are concerned, full-time contracts have increased by 34 per cent whereas part-time contracts have risen by 465 per cent; within LDCs full-time contracts have grown by 54 per cent and part-time contracts have increased by 294.7 per cent.

**LDCs and the economic sector**

When analysing limited duration contracts by sector of activity we note that the service sector has seen the greatest relative and absolute increase, which indicates that the service sector is the most important in the Spanish economy. The building sector is second in LDC creation, followed by the industry sector (see Figure 5.3). When we observe the trends of LDCs, we see that temporary contracts achieved an overall increase of 20 per cent from 1992 to 2000 in the industry sector, while they increased by 86.7 per cent in the service sector and by an outstanding 110.51 per cent in the building sector. If we focus on sub-sectors of activity we see the features indicated in Table 5.3 regarding limited duration contracts in the year 2000.

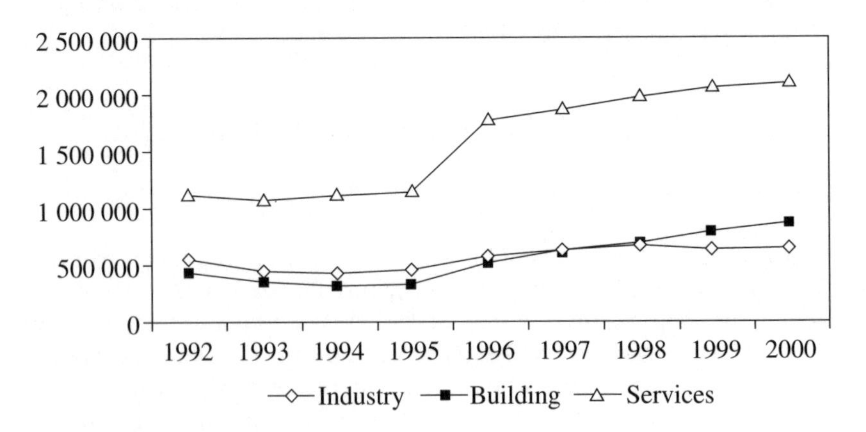


*Figure 5.3 LDCs, by economic sector*

*Table 5.3 LDCs, by sub-sectors (year 2000)*

| Sub-sectors | LDC (year 2000) | Change (1992/2000, %) |
|---|---|---|
| Manufacturing | 622700 | 20.88 |
| Mining and extraction | 12800 | −2 |
| Electric water & gas power prod. | 9300 | 52 |
| Commerce and repair | 598000 | 57 |
| Real est., leas. & comp. services | 526500 | 198.1 |
| Hotel & catering trade | 244900 | 103 |
| Health, vet. & social services | 224500 | 87.86 |
| Education | 190000 | 102 |
| Transport, storage & communic. | 165800 | 105.7 |
| Personal services & household | 159500 | 91.4 |

If we now analyse the Registered Labour Movement data on the type of LDCs, we see that, in the year 2000, those due to an excess of demands and contracts for particular work or a particular service represented over three-quarters of the total. These are followed, far behind, by provisional contracts to substitute workers who will later resume work and the remainder are divided between the other types of LDCs (see Table 5.4).

*Table 5.4 Type of limited duration contracts (year 2000)*

| Types of LDC | % of LDC (2000) |
|---|---|
| Excess of demands & circumstances of market | 46.0 |
| Particular work or service | 39.5 |
| Replacement of workers/selection process | 7.2 |
| Reminiscences of former legislation | 4.0 |
| Training temporary contracts | 1.57 |
| Work experience contracts | 0.9 |
| Contract for disabled workers | 0.2 |
| Replacement of retired workers | 0.029 |

*Source:* Ministry of Labour and Social Affairs; Estadísticas, BEL, MLR 37a.

However, there have been different trends in the 1992–2000 period: whereas LDCs have quadrupled, the contracts for a specific service or piece of work have only increased by 2.5 per cent, replacement contracts have doubled and the remainder have decreased by 300 per cent. In turn, training contracts have undergone both ups and downs: for instance, apprenticeship contracts have increased by 11 per cent, whereas work experience contracts have decreased by 13.5 per cent over the same period.

## Agency Workers

In Spain the number of TWAs boomed from 1995 to 1998. In 1998, there were 435 TWAs. Following a modification of the law, the number of TWAs decreased to 411 towards the end of 1999 and fell further, to 364, in December 2000, when the law underwent a major amendment.

During the 1994–2000 period, the number of transferred workers increased from 301 344 in 1995 to 1 362 208 in 2000, which means that the current figure is 4.5 times higher than at the beginning of the period. The data registered by the Spanish National Employment Office show that, in 1997, the figure increased by 68.3 per cent over the 1996 data and in 1998 the increase amounted to 35 per cent compared to the year 1997.

However, we know that not all contracts of availability between the TWAs and their clients imply that a worker is transferred to the client, as these data deal with contracts between the two employers and not with the actual worker. This is why we do not know whether the workers stay within the TWA or are not recruited at all (see Figure 5.4).

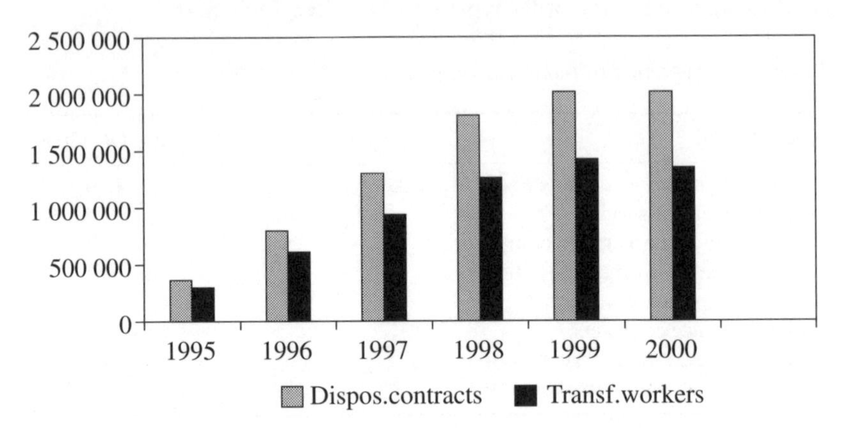


*Source:* Ministry of Labour and Social Affairs. Estadísticas. BEL/ETT/ett1.

*Figure 5.4 Disposal contracts and workers transferred by TWAs*

If we now focus on the kind of contract, we find that, out of 2005132 contracts of availability in 2000, 1027873 contracts were temporary through excess of demand and market circumstances, which is 51 per cent of the total. These were followed by contracts for a particular service or work, with 874906 contracts (43 per cent); next came the contracts to replace a worker, which amounted to 131909 (5 per cent of the total) (see Figure 5.5).

When analysing data by sector of activity, we find that 55 per cent of agency workers were in the service sector in 1999 and 35 per cent in the industry sector. In spite of the fact that it is strictly forbidden in the building industry, the sector had 4.6 per cent of agency workers. Finally, the agricultural sector took 4.7 per cent of agency workers.

If we now analyse the data by the sub-sector of the user company, the hotel and catering sector has 346240 contracts (17 per cent of all the contracts managed by TWA). This sector is difficult to study, not only because it includes restaurants, bars and cafés but also because of the seasonal behaviour of many hotels and restaurants which open either during the high season or only at week-ends. In 2000, the food, beverage and tobacco industries employed 170401 agency workers (8 per cent) and retailing and domestic

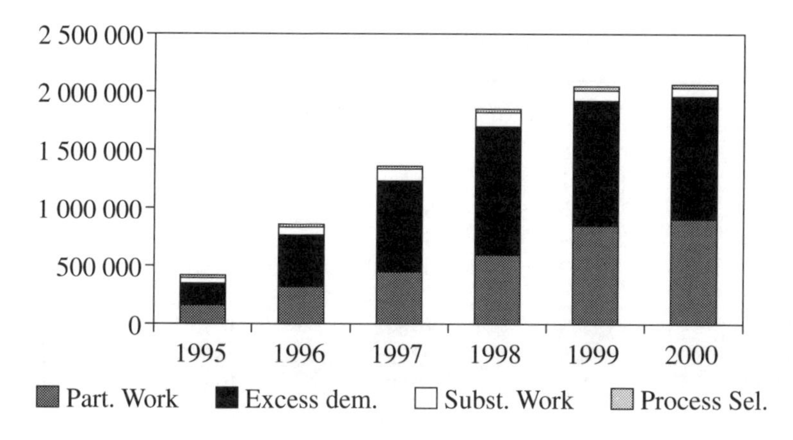


*Source:* Ministry of Labour and Social Affairs. Estadísticas. BEL/ETT/ett1.

*Figure 5.5 Type of temporary contracts*

repairs 119570 contracts (6 per cent). All sectors have a percentage of contracts managed by TWAs. The financial and insurance companies recruited 71659 agency workers, and the health and veterinary services plus the social services accounted for 10058 contracts; finally, amongst computing activities and research and development, the number of contracts was also low, at 13813.

Of the total agency contracts in 1997 and 1998, 37.9 per cent and 37.6 respectively were for those between 20 and 24 years of age. If we take into consideration the fact that this age group is followed by those aged between 25 and 29 and between 16 and 19, we arrive at the conclusion that three out of four agency workers in Spain are young people (see Table 5.5).

If we analyse the data by level of qualification, we find that most agency workers have an intermediate level of education. The graphic representation of this trend adopts the shape of a diamond. The groups with higher and lower levels of education are placed at the ends of the graph and have low relative percentages of recruitment. This may give us an idea of the kind of people sought by TWAs in Spain. The group with the highest number of agency contracts is that of people who have completed primary education (41.5 per cent in 1998, 42.5 per cent in 1999), followed by those who have a school-leaving certificate (22.7 per cent in 1998, 22.5 per cent in 1999). This group is followed by those who have completed secondary education or the equivalent. Next comes the group of people who have completed professional training at a technical college and this group is followed, far behind, by that of higher education (see Table 5.6).

*Table 5.5 TWA contracts, by age*

| Age | 1997 | 1998 | 1999 | 2000 |
|---|---|---|---|---|
| 16–19 | 149456 | 222525 | 264192 | 249859 |
| 20–24 | 485991 | 648669 | 710655 | 658321 |
| 25–29 | 299955 | 389691 | 420514 | 390650 |
| 30–34 | 137959 | 185566 | 202674 | 186885 |
| 35–39 | 79792 | 108766 | 122546 | 116676 |
| 40–44 | 50612 | 72069 | 83389 | 77811 |
| 45–49 | 32243 | 44843 | 48808 | 45370 |
| 50–54 | 16749 | 23755 | 26571 | 24216 |
| 55–59 | 6232 | 9696 | 10555 | 10333 |
| 60+ | 1635 | 2262 | 2380 | 2659 |
| Total | 1260524 | 1707842 | 1892284 | 1762780 |

*Source:* Ministry of Labour and Social Affairs; Estadísticas, 1996, 1998 and 2000.

*Table 5.6 TWA contracts according to qualification*

| | 1997 | 1998 | 1999 | 2000 |
|---|---|---|---|---|
| No education | 1186 | 3199 | 5535 | 5793 |
| Primary education | 9472 | 18759 | 21585 | 21480 |
| School certificate | 264639 | 388239 | 427047 | 388284 |
| General education | 514038 | 708896 | 807109 | 754852 |
| Secondary education | 213341 | 276765 | 310174 | 299092 |
| Professional train. | 177521 | 218819 | 215276 | 186529 |
| Middle univ.stud. | 40141 | 47505 | 52059 | 50113 |
| High univ.stud. | 40186 | 45660 | 53499 | 56637 |
| Total | 1260524 | 1707842 | 1892284 | 1762780 |

*Source:* Spanish Office of Employment (INEM).

The male percentages for each group are closer to the overall average than those of females, which, having achieved 38.3 and 39.5 per cent during this period, are well below those of males (43.67 and 44.8 per cent). It is also striking that amongst males the group with upper secondary education has exceeded that of lower secondary education, which is a feature which does not appear either in the overall or in the females percentages. Finally, the agency contracts amongst females with intermediate and higher qualifications are double those amongst males with the same qualification. According to contracts by *sex*, the same groups repeat the order of importance, with the sole exception in 1999 that contracts for a specific piece of work or service amongst males exceeded temporary agency contracts, owing to a major increase in 1999 (47 per cent higher than in 1998).

As regards average duration of contracts, the largest group is that of 'one month or less' duration, followed by indefinite duration contracts. Next are those of one to three months' duration (see Table 5.7). If we examine these data by gender, we see that the same percentages are repeated, except for two features. First, one month or less duration, which is the most common agency contract amongst women, amounting to 60.1 per cent in 1998, decreased to 47.4 per cent in 1999. The same applies for men, with a decrease from 53 per cent in 1998 to 40.9 per cent in 1999. This relative loss has been made up mainly by open-ended contracts.

*Table 5.7 TWA contracts, by contract duration*

| | 1999 | 2000 |
|---|---|---|
| 1 month or less | 825277 | 719507 |
| 1/5 days | 524326 | 468554 |
| 6/10 days | 97252 | 77519 |
| 11/15 days | 65269 | 55930 |
| 16 days/1 month | 138430 | 117504 |
| 1/3 months | 107893 | 98603 |
| 3/6 months | 25978 | 19418 |
| 6 months/1 year | 1260 | 1057 |
| More than 1 year | 192 | 118 |
| Indeterminate (particular work or service) | 928372 | 921818 |
| Open-ended | 3312 | 2259 |
| Total | 1892284 | 1762780 |

*Source:* Spanish Office of Employment (INEM).

Finally, when we analyse by *the type of work or assignment carried out* in the user company, the posts for workers with no qualifications stand out, taking 59 per cent of the total in 1998 and 61.1 per cent in 1999. It is especially striking that management posts, either for companies or in public administration only take 0.03 per cent in both years and that only 0.7 per cent in 1998 and 0.6 in 1999 of agency workers were used for technical, scientific and intellectual tasks. With all this evidence it seems quite clear that the TWAs manage almost exclusively the lower-quality jobs in Spain (see Table 5.8).

*Table 5.8 TWA contracts, by type of work*

| | 1997 | 1998 | 1999 | 2000 |
|---|---|---|---|---|
| Managers | 572 | 646 | 625 | 540 |
| Sci. technicians | 12059 | 12429 | 11752 | 10340 |
| Prof. technicians | 24947 | 32534 | 34156 | 33595 |
| Clerks | 181002 | 229274 | 236024 | 211780 |
| Qualified workers | 5548 | 6637 | 7599 | 7845 |
| Handicrafts | 70813 | 87558 | 81252 | 60265 |
| Operators | 39861 | 82646 | 90837 | 78713 |
| Restaurant serv. | 182281 | 248789 | 274214 | 259416 |
| Unqualified | 743441 | 1007329 | 1155825 | 1100286 |
| Total | 1260524 | 1707842 | 1892284 | 1762780 |

*Source:* Ministry of Labour and Social Affairs Yearbooks, 1996, 1998 and 2000.

## Casual/Seasonal Workers

Whereas there are no specific data on casual workers, except that related to agency workers with contracts with less than six days' duration, casual workers are legally considered as permanent workers on a discontinuous basis. This means that this group of workers appear in statistics under the category of open-ended contracts, because of the duration of their contracts, and also under the category of part-time workers, because of the duration of their working day. Thus there are no specific data on this type of worker. Despite this, we can shed some light on the distribution and working conditions. For instance, in Spain a quite large proportion of this group of workers are employed in hotels on the coast. These hotels may be open all year or just during the high season. In the first case the hotel management employs a resident/core staff plus a number of workers who start working in April and finish in October. In the second case, the hotel staff is made up of permanent workers on a discontinuous basis who are entitled to be called upon, in order of years in service, at the beginning of the high season. The hotel business, which is permanent and discontinuous by nature, recruits the largest part of this category of workers.

This type of contract is also frequently used by businesses related to the food and beverage industries. In the small family-run olive oil mills along the Guadalquivir valley, this is the usual modality of contract. Also the processing and packing of fruit during the summer months and, to the south, in the province of Cádiz, the processing and packing of tuna and the bottling of soft drinks during spring and summer, rely on a major use of seasonal workers.

However, the Spanish jurisprudence has made quite clear that jobs related to sales, which employ a great deal of contingent labour in department stores, are not a genuine permanent and discontinuous activity but rather an excess of demand or orders. This is the reason why article 12, section 3(b) of the Workers' Act, by incorporating court rulings, has established that it is the task to be accomplished, and not the contract, that needs to be permanent and discontinuous.

## CONCLUDING REMARKS

It is not easy to give an explanation for the features of the Spanish labour market outlined above. If the field experts have problems in explaining these phenomena, we may have even more difficulty as we have included some ideological elements, which are very hard to assess. What is the importance of legal changes when in some cases they help to create only 1800 new contracts each year (as is the case of takeover contracts) and in others (contracts to launch a new activity) cause the temporary employment rates to soar, growing from a yearly 8 per cent to 35 per cent when the temporary work agencies were given the green light? It seems crystal clear that the legal changes in Spain are relatively important for the market trends and changes; but so also is the will of the authorities to cope with the real problems of the market without yielding to the permanent and unquenchable demands of employers.

## NOTES

1. This study gives an activity rate of 60.1 per cent for the year 1996, based on data obtained from OECD (Labour Force Statistics and Quarterly Labour Force Statistics) and the European Studies Department of the Fundación de Cajas de Ahorro (savings banks' foundation). Unlike the Spanish National Statistics Institute (INE), these take into account the population aged between 15 and 64, not from the age of 16. Nonetheless, the forecasts made by Martín in 1997 for the forthcoming years can be assumed to be accurate as they have been confirmed by subsequent statistics.
2. The 'more representative trade union' is a legal term in Spain and is a fundamental element of the political system designed by the Spanish Constitution. It describes the process of selecting between several trade unions those who best represent the workers and who are then chosen to represent the public interest (that is, to negotiate with public bodies, to participate in the organization of institutions and protection of public buildings, to organize elections to ensure trade union representation in the company, to settle collective disputes, and so on). Every four years there are polls in every Spanish company (of six workers or more) to elect the shop steward(s) or company committee members. According to the final election results only those trade unions gaining more than 10 per cent of the votes at the national level can be regarded as representative. At the regional level, 15 per cent of the votes are required and at the branch level, 10 per cent.
3. Later these Royal Decree became laws 63/1997, on urgent measures to improve the labour

market and promote open-ended contracts, and 64/1997, on social security and fiscal incentives to promote open-ended contracts.

4. The Spanish Penal Code punishes employers who, by means of deceit or abuse, oblige workers to accept labour conditions which damage or suppress the rights granted by law, the collective or individual agreement and the people who deal illegally with workers, recruit employees offering deceptive working conditions or encourage and favour the illegal immigration of foreign workers. The cases above are punished by law with the same prison term of between six months and three years and a penalty of between six and 12 months in prison.
5. Introduced as a new type of temporary contract by Royal Decree 5/2001, 2 March, and converted into law by law 12/2001, 9 July, as new art. 15.1(d) of the Workers' Act. This type of insertion contract is exclusive to the Public Administration and non-profit organizations and cannot be used by private employers.
6. The name 'rubbish contract' comes from the adverse legal working conditions of the original apprenticeship contract in a law, introduced in 1993, which allowed this contract for young people between 16 and 25 years old, lasting from six months to three years and with salary reductions of 30 per cent, 20 per cent and 10 per cent below the minimum and no social security for each year of the contract. The three levels of reduction are determined according to the different situations of unemployment that diverse groups (the elderly, woman and young people) can fall into. The Spanish Constitution and the Workers' Act authorize the government to improve the labour conditions of 'dropped-out' groups. This form of contract disappeared in 1997.
7. From 7.55 per cent (6 per cent paid by the employer and 1.55 by the employee), which is the percentage established for open-ended contracts, to 8.3 per cent (6.7 + 1.6) or even 9.3 per cent (7.7 + 1.6) when the contract is temporary and part-time.

# REFERENCES


Alcaide Castro, M. and J. Quiros Tomas (1998) 'La evolución del mercado de trabajo español durante los últimos veinte años', Temas Laborales no. 46, 3.

Álvarez Aledo, C. (1997) 'Nuevas dualidades del mercado laboral', *Sistema*, no. 140–41, 199.

Del Rey Rodriguez, I. (2000) 'La contratación a través de empresas de trabajo temporal: tendencias normativas y jurisprudenciales', *Tribuna Social.*

*El Pais* (2001) Supplement Negocios, 5 August.

Escudero Rodriguez, R. and J.R. Mercader Uguina (2000) 'La Ley 29/1999, de reforma de la Ley 14/1994, sobre empresas de trabajo temporal: un empeño a medio camino', *Relaciones Laborales* (2000-I).

Martín, C. (1997), 'El mercado de trabajo español en perspectiva europea: un panorama', *Papeles de Economía española*, no. 72, 2.

Molero Marañon, M.L. (2000), 'La reforma del contrato de puesta a disposición', *Relaciones Laborales* (2000-I).

Moradillo Larios, C. (1998) *Los contratos de trabajo temporales e indefinidos*, 2nd edn, Madrid: Editorial CISS.

Navarro, V. (1998) 'Los mercados laborales y la cuestión social en la Unión Europea', *Sistema*, no. 143, 5.

Pérez Pérez, M. (2000) *El artículo 45 del Convenio Colectivo Estatal de Empresas de Trabajo Temporal, Comentarios al convenio colectivo estatal de empresas de trabajo temporal*, Mercia: Editorial Laborum.

Pérez Pérez, M. (2001) 'Empresas de Trabajo Temporal y Relaciones Laborales', Mercia: Editorial Laborum.

Sempere Navarro, A.V. and M. Cardenal Carro (1996) *Los contratos temporales ordinarios en el ordenamiento laboral*, Madrid: Editorial La Ley-Actualidad.
Spanish Labour and Social Affairs Department (Ministerio de Trabajo y Asuntos Sociales) (2000) 'Estadísticas/BEL', Encuesta de Población Activa (EPA), active population survey.
Vicente Palacio, A. (1996), *El contrato de trabajo temporal para obra o servicio determinado*, Valencia: Tirant lo blanc.
Viñals, J. and J.F. Jimeno (1997), 'El mercado de trabajo español y la unión económica y monetaria europea', *Papeles de Economía española*, no. 72, 21.

# 6. Contingent employment in Germany

**Thomas Peuntner**

## INTRODUCTION

In Germany, as with several other countries in Europe, most of the 1990s were a period of low economic growth, increasing unemployment and a perception of crisis. The growing international interdependence of capital, the breaking down of national borders, the rapid speed of technical progress and the resulting increase in national and international competitive pressure have posed major new challenges to the German economy (Eichenberg and Wiskemann, 1997, p. 142).

This crisis is often described as being manifested by the transition from a stable industrial society to a constantly changing information society, characterized by the increasing use and importance of information and communication technology (see, for example, Oechsler, 2000b, pp. 28f). These structural changes are accompanied by discontinuity and uncertainty.

In the wake of the growing international competition, the discontinuity and the ensuing uncertainty, companies initially responded by reducing their workforce. This downsizing, together with both a concentration process within the German economy and an increase in the number of insolvencies, led to an appreciable increase in unemployment.

A further response to the new circumstances facing companies was the flexibilization of the workforce. Companies need to adjust to the ever more rapid changes in their environment by developing a more flexible work organization (ibid., pp. 29f). This need for flexibility affects all activities in the company, such as production, the supply chain and human resources. As growth was no longer certain, companies gave up the practice of usually recruiting employees on open-ended contracts, but started to increase the use of limited duration contracts, temporary work agencies and subcontracting.

## ECONOMIC AND LABOUR MARKET TRENDS

The German economic context during the 1990s was mainly influenced by increasing global competition, the unification of Eastern and Western Germany and a weak economic development in Europe compared to a long period of dynamic growth in the United States. Currently a re-creation of the economic development in Germany can be observed. Economic growth in 2000 reached a level of 3 per cent and the unemployment rate is going down. Beyond that a tax reform has just been introduced (1999) that aims to create a better climate for employers and to increase their readiness to employ more people.

Labour costs in Germany are not only high in terms of pure wages but also in terms of payroll fringe costs. These payroll fringe costs represent a share of about 80 per cent of the wages that are only paid for real working time (excluding paid leave, sick pay, holiday pay and so on). This high share is a result of legal regulations, collective agreements and company agreements that contain, for example, the social insurance, paid leave or employee pension schemes. But high labour costs are not a problem if the productivity of the workers can compensate for it so that unit labour costs can be kept at an adequate and competitive level. Productivity in Germany is at a high level, but it is not able to compensate the high labour costs completely. Even with regard to the unit labour costs, Germany has one of the highest levels compared to other industrialized countries (o.V. 2000a, pp. 4–5). In 1997 and 1998, there was a slight decrease in unit labour costs in Germany, but this trend changed in 1999 (OECD, 1999; German Council of Economic Experts, 1999).

The German labour market cannot be analysed as a single labour market owing to the problems of the transformation of Eastern Germany from a planned to a market economy. This process has led to an appreciably higher unemployment rate in the eastern part of Germany. This problem – after 10 years of a unified Germany – still exists and will probably continue to exist for some time in the future. This is mainly because labour productivity in the eastern *länder* of Germany is rising more slowly than income that, mostly for political reasons, converges on the income level in the western German *länder*. Moreover, unification did not only affect the eastern part of Germany. During the first years of unification (from 1990 to 1992/3) West Germany experienced a so-called 'unification boom'. This led to operating at full national production capacity and a remarkable rise in employment. However, these positive employment effects of unification concealed structural problems in the German economy and its institutional setting. These problems appeared after the end of the unification boom and still remain. Economic policy, in particular, has failed to introduce the reforms necessary to promote economic growth and create employment (German Council of Economic Experts, 1997, p. 151).

Table 6.1 shows the development of employment in Germany from 1990 to 1999. It can be seen that unemployment rates went up during the 1990s, from 7.2 per cent in 1990 to 11.7 per cent in 1999. The number of employed also decreased during this period, except for the major increase in 1991 that was due to the unification. The labour force was almost constant. The employment rate of men in the relevant age group went down during the 1990s from 82.7 to 80.3 per cent, while female participation rose from 58.5 to 63.8 per cent. The main part of the increase in the female employment rate can be explained by the high employment rate of women in East Germany.

An analysis of the structure of the labour force by gender and age in 1998 (see Table 6.2) indicates that, up to the age of 55 years, 55 per cent of each age group is male and 45 per cent female. Beginning with the age group from 55–60 years, the share of men goes up to 60 or even 70 per cent of the labour force. This structure has not really changed compared to the year 1991. In 1998, 8.7 per cent of the labour force were foreign (1991, 7.3 per cent).

The German economy is moving steadily towards service industry. The share of the service industry increased from 55.8 per cent in 1990 to 63.3 per cent in 1998 (Figure 6.1). The share of the manufacturing industry went down from 40.5 per cent in 1990 to 33.8 per cent in 1998. Agriculture and fishing play a minor role in the German economy and are decreasing slightly from a low level of about 3 per cent.

In 1999 and the first half of 2000, the economic situation and the situation on the labour market improved. These positive developments were mainly a result of an economic recovery based on rising domestic demand, rising investments and a recovery of the export situation after the end of the international financial crisis. Regardless of these successes, it has to be stated that researchers, as well as political parties, unions and companies, still see a need for structural reforms in the labour market, the tax system and the social security system (German Council of Economic Experts, 1999, pp. 1–3). A reform of the tax system was decided in July 2000. This reform is designed to relieve both private households and companies in order to create employment from the demand side and the supply side. The overall opinion of the tax reform – from managers as well as economic scientists – with regard to its expected effects on the labour market is generally positive. A reform of the social security system, especially the state pension insurance system, is at this time the next important topic of political discussion. Reforms of the labour market system cannot be expected at the moment, because the government is focusing on other problems, such as the reform of the state pension insurance system. Beyond, that a positive development in unemployment rates can be observed that reduces the

*Table 6.1* *Development of employment in Germany, 1990–99 (thousands)*

| | 1990 | 1991 | 1992 | 1993 | 1994 | 1995 | 1996 | 1997 | 1998 | 1999 |
|---|---|---|---|---|---|---|---|---|---|---|
| Employed | 29334 | 37445 | 36940 | 36380 | 36076 | 36048 | 35982 | 35805 | 35860 | 36402 |
| Unemployed | 1971 | 2642 | 3186 | 3799 | 4160 | 4035 | 4003 | 4475 | 4402 | 4106 |
| Labour force | 31305 | 40087 | 40126 | 40179 | 40236 | 40083 | 39985 | 40280 | 40262 | 40508 |
| Unemployment rate | 7.2 | 7.3 | 8.5 | 9.8 | 10.6 | 10.4 | 11.5 | 12.7 | 12.3 | 11.7 |
| Men (15–65 years) | 82.7 | 82.9 | 82.0 | 81.3 | 81.3 | 81.0 | 80.3 | 80.0 | 80.2 | 80.3 |
| Women (15–65 years) | 58.5 | 62.1 | 62.5 | 62.3 | 62.7 | 62.6 | 62.3 | 63.0 | 63.0 | 63.8 |

*Source:* Federal Statistical Office (1992–9), data from Microcensus and Federal Office for Labour.

*Table 6.2 Labour force in Germany (thousands)*

| Age | 1991 | | | | | 1998 | | | | |
|---|---|---|---|---|---|---|---|---|---|---|
| | Men & women | Men | % | Women | % | Men & women | Men | % | Women | % |
| 15–20 | 1768 | 987 | 55.8 | 780 | 44.1 | 1464 | 838 | 57.2 | 626 | 42.8 |
| 20–25 | 4645 | 2466 | 53.1 | 2179 | 46.9 | 3191 | 1768 | 55.4 | 1423 | 44.6 |
| 25–30 | 5475 | 3031 | 55.4 | 2444 | 44.6 | 4501 | 2483 | 55.2 | 2019 | 44.9 |
| 30–35 | 5166 | 2975 | 57.6 | 2191 | 42.4 | 5847 | 3334 | 57.0 | 2513 | 43.0 |
| 35–40 | 4834 | 2735 | 56.6 | 2100 | 43.4 | 5678 | 3210 | 56.5 | 2468 | 43.5 |
| 40–45 | 4568 | 2600 | 56.9 | 1969 | 43.1 | 5181 | 2860 | 55.2 | 2322 | 44.8 |
| 45–50 | 4298 | 2483 | 57.8 | 1815 | 42.2 | 4900 | 2699 | 55.1 | 2201 | 44.9 |
| 50–55 | 5020 | 2984 | 59.4 | 2036 | 40.6 | 3837 | 2178 | 56.8 | 1659 | 43.2 |
| 55–60 | 3007 | 1950 | 64.8 | 1057 | 35.2 | 4180 | 2472 | 59.1 | 1707 | 40.8 |
| 60–65 | 980 | 724 | 73.9 | 256 | 26.1 | 1114 | 787 | 70.6 | 327 | 29.4 |
| 65+ | 326 | 189 | 58.0 | 137 | 42.0 | 368 | 234 | 63.6 | 134 | 36.4 |
| Labour Force | 40087 | 23125 | | 16962 | | 40262* | 22864 | | 17399 | |

*Note:* * Differences may be due to the method of the Microcensus, where 1 per cent of the whole population takes part in the inquiry and the figures are then projected to the whole population.

*Source:* Federal Statistical Office (1999, p.101), Federal Statistical Office (1993, p.110); data from the Microcensus.

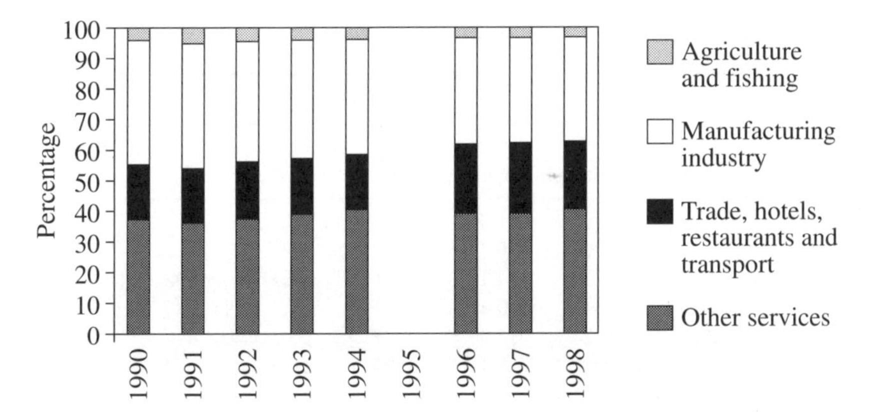


*Note:* There are no data in published statistics available for 1995.

*Source:* Federal Statistical Office (1992–9); data from Microcensus.

*Figure 6.1 Employment structure, by industry, in Germany, 1990–98*

pressure to introduce labour market reforms. One attempt to achieve progress in the labour market is the initiative called the 'alliance for employment, education and competitiveness' (Bündnis für Arbeit, Ausbildung und Wettbewerbsfähigkeit).[1] This alliance was initiated by Chancellor Gerhard Schröder in December 1998 and is based on the cooperation of the main labour market actors, unions, employers' associations and representatives of industry and the state.

Table 6.3 indicates that the number and share of limited duration contracts has increased slightly from 1991 to 1999, as did the number of apprentices from 1991 to 1998. The share of temporary work agency employees has doubled from 0.4 per cent to 0.8 per cent of total employment, but is still at a comparatively low level. There are still more family workers than TWA employees, but numbers of family workers have decreased steadily from 522000 in 1991 to 311000 in 1999. Part-time workers increased from 5.8 million in 1991 to 9.0 million in 1998 and now represent 25.2 per cent of total employment. It has to be pointed out that the definition of part-time work used here is due to statistical availability as far as these categories are stable over the years. The definition of part-time work used in the official statistics in Germany changed from jobs with a regular working time of less than 36 hours in 1991 to less than 32 hours in 1998. Using this definition, there were only 5.2 million part-time workers in 1991 and 7.7 million in 1998, representing a share of total employment of 14.0 per cent and 21.4 per cent.

*Table 6.3 Contingent employment in Germany*

| | 1991 | | 1998 | | 1999* | |
|---|---|---|---|---|---|---|
| | 1000s | % of total employment | 1000s | % of total employment | 1000s | % of total employment |
| Limited duration contracts[a] | 2500 | 6.7 | 2500 | 7.0 | 2800 | 7.7 |
| Apprentices | 1523 | 4.1 | 1601 | 4.5 | n.a. | |
| TWA employees[b] | 134 | 0.4 | 253 | 0.7 | 286 | 0.8 |
| Part-time workers[c] | 5822 | 15.5 | 9031 | 25.2 | n.a. | |
| Self-employed | 3037 | 8.1 | 3594 | 10.0 | 3594 | 9.9 |
| Family workers | 522 | 1.4 | 388 | 1.1 | 311 | 0.9 |
| Employees | 33887 | 90.5 | 31878 | 88.9 | 32497 | 89.3 |
| Total employment[d] (employees, self-employed, family workers) | 37445 | 100.0 | 35860 | 100.0 | 36402 | 100.0 |

*Notes:*

* The Statistical Yearbook 2000 was not available at the time this table was produced. Data are taken from the official homepage of the Federal Statistical Office (*www.statistik-bund.de*), especially the sites containing data from Microcensus, 1999.

[a] Data from Microcensus, 1998, 1999.

[b] Social Consult (1998, p. 22); data from the Federal Office of Labour (Bundesanstalt für Arbeit).

[c] Employees, self-employed and family workers, working from less than 15 to 35 hours. See Federal Statistical Office (1993, p. 116), Federal Statistical Office (1999, p. 106). The range from fewer than 15 hours of weekly working time to 35 hours has been taken because it can be found regularly in the national statistics and a breakdown on gender and economic sector is available. The definition of part-time work in the national statistics has changed. In 1990, all employees working fewer than 36 hours were classified as part-time workers, whereas in 1998 workers working less than 32 hours were put in this category.

[d] Totals may not sum due to rounding differences.

## INSTITUTIONAL FRAMEWORK AND EMPLOYMENT REGULATION

### The Legal Framework

#### The regulation of open-ended contracts

Before describing the regulation of contingent employment, the standard working contract has to be explained in order to see the relation and differences between them. The standard working contract in Germany is still an open-ended contract on a full-time basis. The most distinctive feature of the standard working contract in relation to contingent employment is dismissal protection which, together with some social security matters, is the major focus of this section.

The termination of an employment contract requires advance notice. The notice period, according to the German Civil Code, has to be at least four weeks and increases with seniority, up to seven months' notice when the contract continued for 20 years. However, the Dismissal Protection Act, which applies to all companies with more than five employees and for employment contracts lasting more than six months, requires the employers to specify socially justified reasons for the dismissal. There are three kinds of acceptable reasons for a dismissal: first, reasons relating to the individual employee, for example the employee is no longer able to carry out the job; second, reasons relating to the behaviour of the employee, such as breaches of the employment contract, but not sufficient for a dismissal without notice;[2] and third, reasons relating to the company, such as adjusting the size of the workforce to the level required, if it is economically necessary. It is important to mention that, owing to the so-called '*ultima ratio* principle', the interests of employer and employee have to be balanced. Dismissal is regarded as the last possible step on a list of alternatives, such as reasonable training or continued employment at a different workplace with changed (normally less favourable) working conditions.

If the employee is of the opinion that the reasons are not valid or not sufficient for a dismissal, he/she may go to court in order to start an action against unlawful dismissal. If the court shares the opinion of the employee, the employer can be required to pay severance pay of up to 12 months' salary. The severance pay may even be higher for older employees that have been employed in the company for more than 15 years.

A topic strongly related to dismissal issues is the duration of a probationary period, because during this period the working contract can be terminated by both parties without any reason and with a notice period of two weeks. Some employers may want to avoid dismissal protection through a longer probationary period, but this is not possible, as the maximum duration of probationary periods in Germany is six months and after being employed for six months the dismissal protection law is applicable.

It should also be mentioned that there are special dismissal protection laws for specific types of employees, such as pregnant women, parents on child-rearing leave, the severely handicapped, apprentices and those who are on military or civilian service. Furthermore, members of the works council are particularly protected against dismissal during and after their term of office.

Finally, with regard to dismissals, the works council has specific rights to participate in the process. According to the Works Constitution Act, in companies with regularly more than 20 employees, the works council has to be involved in the decision-making process on redundancies, when there is a considerable reduction in the workforce. They are entitled to negotiate in order to accommodate conflicting interests and draw up a social plan. This social plan normally contains redundancy payments for the dismissed workers.

**The regulation of limited duration contracts**

Limited duration contracts (LDCs) in Germany can be based on two different laws. According to the German Civil Code the employer must name an objective reason (for example, for a specific project, seasonal work or leave replacement) why the contract is made only for a limited duration (Oechsler, 2000a, p. 272). This jurisdiction implies that a court could convert an LDC into an open-ended contract if the reason is not accepted. As many employers do not want to take this risk, jurisdiction prevented this kind of LDC from being an instrument for employers to increase numerical flexibility.[3]

The Employment Promotion Act of 1985 made it possible for employers to hire on an LDC without an objective reason and was explicitly designed to create more employment (Deutscher Bundestag: BT-Drucksache 10/2102, pp. 1, 14–22). However, the rules of the German Civil Code were not repealed. Thus, if the employer wants to make use of the German Civil Code or the Employment Promotion Act, that is, to hire on an LDC without giving a reason, the legal basis of each LDC has to be declared explicitly in the (written) contract. This Act has gone through modifications in 1990, 1994 and 1996. Since the last modification in 1996 it is possible to make LDCs up to a maximum duration of 24 months. In cases of an objective reason there is generally no legal limit for the duration of LDCs (OECD, 1999, pp. 104–6).

The Employment Promotion Act was only valid until 31 December 2000.[4] The unions would like to cancel the Employment Promotion Act completely as they are of the opinion that it has not achieved its aims, especially in creating new employment. They claim that employers just recruit on a limited duration basis in order to avoid the dismissal protection laws through revolving working contracts on an LDC basis.

**Regulation of temporary agency work**

Job leasing in Germany is legally based on the Personnel Leasing Act (Arbeitnehmerüberlassungsgesetz) as amended in 1997. Job leasing is a three-party arrangement between the temporary work agency, the temporary work agency employee and the user company. The basis of the relationship between the TWA employee and the temporary work agency is a regular employment contract. This contract can be open-ended or of limited duration. The user company and the temporary work agency make a personnel-leasing contract that obliges the client to pay the personnel-leasing fee and gives him/her the right to instruct the TWA employee. During the leasing period the TWA employee is an employee of and is paid by the temporary work agency. The maximum duration of hiring TWA employees is, since January 1997, 12 months (OECD, 1999, pp. 107–8).

Legal permission is required to establish a temporary work agency and is not permitted in the construction industry.[5] Moreover, the state has the right to withdraw permission, if a temporary work agency repeatedly employs TWA employees on a limited duration basis that is as long as the first leasing period.

Most TWA employees are not covered by collective agreements. The agreements that exist are usually to be found at some of the larger temporary work agencies. New approaches for a further liberalization of the regulation of temporary work are being discussed that aim to combine a further liberalization with collective agreements: only temporary work agencies that are amenable to a collective agreement would be able to make use of this new rule.

The legal framework of temporary work agencies has been the subject of deregulation. This can be seen especially in the historic development of the maximum duration of personnel leasing from three months in 1972, to six months in 1985, nine months in 1993, up to the current maximum duration of 12 months in 1997 (Rudolph and Schröder, 1997, p. 103). A further reform, which aims to deregulate the existing law, is currently being discussed in parliament. It should lift the ban on temporary work in construction and should present proposals to link the reform with regulations by collective agreement (Klös, 2000, p. 21).

## Social Security

Social security is regulated at the national level. All employees earning more than €320 per month are obliged to pay contributions to the social security system. The maximum contribution is reached at a wage of €4400 (East Germany €3630). Beyond this earnings ceiling the contribution is based on €4400. This earnings ceiling is higher for employees in the mining industry; civil servants do not have to pay contributions to the social security system. Employees earning less than €320 can pay contributions on a voluntary basis in order to get full social protection.

Contributions that have to be paid are for health insurance, pension insurance, unemployment insurance, nursing care insurance and accident insurance. Contributions for the accident insurance are fully paid by the employer; the other contributions are paid half by the employer and half by the employee. The compulsory contributions total about 20 per cent of the gross wage of an employee and have to be paid for contingent workers as well. Thus they get basically the same social protection with regard to social security as non-contingent workers.

## The Institutional Framework

The institutional framework may have important implications for the use of contingent employment. It can influence employment strategies of companies as well as being able to create new forms of employment. Before describing the legal framework of contingent work, first the general system of employment relations in Germany will be briefly explained in order to get an overview of the labour law context.

The German system of employment relations can be divided into three parts: first, the legal determinants of the employment relations, that is, the national regulations; second, the regulations in collective agreements and worker participation at the company level in the supervisory board. This second level of regulation will be called the strategic level because, at this level, strategic decisions are taken; third, worker participation at a plant level, which is mainly concerned with the introduction and implementation of human resource instruments. The national regulations set minimum or maximum standards that have to be met by companies, such as maximum working hours or minimum annual leave, and collective agreements can only improve worker protection.

The whole set of national regulations, and especially dismissal protection in Germany, is relatively restrictive and a source of complaint for employers.[6] Restrictive firing rules are one of the reasons for the increased demand for changes in the labour law to provide more flexibility (Emerson, 1988, pp. 775f). One important example of a change in the labour law is the new regulation for LDCs through the introduction of the Employment Promotion Act in 1985 and its reforms in 1990, 1994 and 1996. This law permitted longer maximum duration of LDCs without the employer being required to provide an objective reason. Another example is the change of the Personnel Leasing Act in 1997, raising the maximum cumulative duration of hiring TWA employees to 12 months and introducing further minor deregulations. These changes in the labour law aim to create a less restrictive context that gives more flexibility to the companies in order to create new employment.

### Strategic level

Collective bargaining is especially important at the strategic level. Most wages are negotiated at this level; only the unions, together with the employers' associations, or sometimes single employers, are responsible for wage determination in a sector or a company. Working conditions in collective agreements have to meet at least the minimum standards of the national laws, but they may, and often do, exceed the national regulations. Collective agreements have the status of a law; that is, they are legally binding for the signatory parties and their members. Collective agreements may have so-called 'opening clauses' in order to make company-specific agreements possible, otherwise, company-specific agreements on matters that are already regulated in a collective agreement are legally forbidden.

The state generally has no right to take part in the collective bargaining process. This is an important principle that is guaranteed by the German Constitution. The government is only able to appeal to the collective bargaining partners as it has done for example in the alliance for employment, education and competitiveness described above, or in exceptional cases to set collective agreements for entire industries. Consequently, changes in the collective agreements are a matter for the unions and the employers or their associations. There is currently a trend towards company agreements, that is, collective agreements between a union and a single employer, instead of industry-wide collective agreements. Moreover, a number of companies have resigned from the employers' associations in order to avoid being bound by a collective agreement. However, a survey by the Institute for Labour Market Research in 1998 shows that there is still a high proportion of employees covered by collective agreements (Kohaut and Schnabel, 1999, pp. 63ff). In the western part of Germany, 75.8 per cent of all employees work under the conditions of collective agreements[7] and in the eastern part of Germany this share is 63.2 per cent. An examination of the companies' collective bargaining coverage shows that only 52.5 per cent of the companies in the western part of Germany and 33.4 per cent of the companies in the eastern part are bound by a collective agreement (Kohaut and Schnabel, 1999). This reflects the fact that smaller companies are less often covered by collective agreements.

High social standards, for example in paid leave and working hours, and wages set by collective agreements may be a reason for companies to make use of different forms of contingent workers. Collective agreements that are valid for the employees of a company do not apply to TWA employees and this means, for example, that they regularly earn less.[8] Thus temporary work agencies allow the employer to employ workers at below the wage level of the collective agreement, which would be impossible with their own employees. This is also true for the dependent self-employed: as long as they are legally classified as self-employed, collective agreements are not valid for them, whereas employees with LDCs and part-time workers are included in collective agreements.

Codetermination procedures give employees the right to participate in the supervisory board, which is responsible for the appointment and dismissal, as well as the permanent supervision, of the board of directors.[9]

**Plant level**

In companies with five or more employees, the employees have the right to elect a works council. Works councils have the right to information on personnel planning and work organization, the right of participation in personnel matters and the right of codetermination in social matters, such as temporary reduction or prolongation of working hours or health and safety issues (Schreyögg *et al.*, 1995, p. 333). This means that especially human resource management has to pay attention to these rights when, for example, implementing new compensation systems, introducing flexible work time or dismissing employees. If an employer has decided to make use of contingent employment, the codetermination rights of the works council have to be respected. But these rights differ sometimes from those of non-contingent workers. TWA employees, for example, are not represented in the works council of the client company but may elect a works council in the temporary work agency.[10] If an employer replaces non-contingent workers with TWA employees, it weakens the basis of the works councils in the client company, and the works council may not be in favour of TWA employees. The works council represents employees with LDCs. They are allowed to take part in the election of the works council in the same way as employees with open-ended contracts or part-time workers.

## CONTINGENT EMPLOYMENT IN GERMANY

### Limited Duration Contracts

The most recent micro census in Germany[11] shows that, in 1999, 2.8 million people (excluding apprentices) worked on limited duration contracts. This is 9 per cent of employees and 7.7 per cent of total employment (employees, self-employed and family workers). In 1991, this share was 7.5 per cent in relation to all employees and 6.7 per cent in relation to total employment.[12]

The previously mentioned east–west divide in the German labour market is also reflected in the distribution of LDCs. In the eastern *länder*, in 1999, 14 per cent of employees had an LDC, while in the west the corresponding figure was only 8 per cent (see Table 6.4).

The micro census also shows that young employees, up to 30 years of age, more often have LDCs, as in 1999 nearly 20 per cent of this group worked

*Table 6.4 Development of limited duration contracts in Germany, 1990–99*

| | 1990 | 1991 | 1992 | 1993 | 1994 | 1995 | 1996 | 1997 | 1998 | 1999 |
|---|---|---|---|---|---|---|---|---|---|---|
| Number of LDCs (×1000) (without apprentices) | 1839 | 2431 | 2495 | 2221 | 2322 | 2388 | 2356 | 2453 | 2500 | 2842 |
| LDC intensity* | 7.0 | 7.2 | 7.5 | 6.8 | 7.2 | 7.4 | 7.3 | 7.7 | 8.5 | 9.0 |
| West Germany | 7.0 | 6.1 | 6.3 | 5.7 | 6.1 | 6.2 | 6.2 | 6.7 | 7.0 | 8.0 |
| East Germany | n.a. | 10.9 | 12.6 | 11.4 | 11.6 | 12.5 | 11.9 | 11.8 | 12.0 | 14.0 |
| Men (% of all male employees) | 7.3 | 7.4 | 7.6 | 7.0 | 7.3 | 7.6 | 7.8 | 8.1 | 9.0 | 10.0 |
| Women (% of all female employees) | 6.7 | 6.9 | 7.3 | 6.4 | 7.1 | 7.2 | 6.7 | 7.2 | 7.0 | 9.0 |

*Note:* *Per cent of all employees.

*Source:* Data from Microcensus, 1990–99.

on a limited contract, and that men are slightly more often confronted by LDCs (1999: men 10 per cent, women 9 per cent).

The educational level of employees working on LDCs is only slightly different from the educational level of all employees. A significant difference can only be seen in the share of university degree holders: 18.9 per cent of the employees working on an LDC basis hold a university degree. This is a very high proportion compared to 10.5 per cent of all employees holding a university degree (see Figure 6.2). This difference can be explained by the high use of LDCs for scientific assistants employed in universities and the increasing use of them for job beginners. This affects university graduates in the same way.

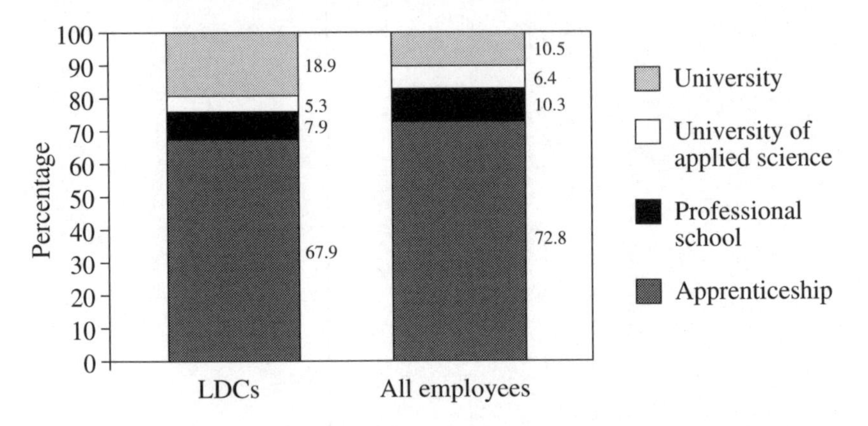


*Source:* Federal Statistical Office (1999b, pp. 92–9); Böhlich (1999, p. 26), data from Microcensus.

*Figure 6.2 Education of employees with LDCs, compared to all employees*

Data about the distribution of LDCs in the different economic sectors show that there is a high proportion of LDCs in agriculture, in extraterritorial organizations and bodies, in hotels and in education, among others. There has been a high proportion of such contracts in these industries, with little deviation, since 1995 (see Table 6.5). A low proportion of LDCs can be observed in the financial intermediation industry, in households and in the mining and quarrying industry. This low level has also been almost constant over the last five years.

It is of interest to know whether employees are voluntarily or involuntarily on a limited duration contract. This question is closely related to the reasons for working on an LDC. Along with the employees' reasons, it is of interest to know the reasons for the employers using limited contracts. The

*Table 6.5 Limited duration contracts, by industry*

| | Share of LDCs (%) | | | | |
|---|---|---|---|---|---|
| | 1995 | 1996 | 1997 | 1998 | 1999 |
| Agriculture, hunting and forestry | 27.5 | 31.5 | 30.9 | 29.4 | 33.9 |
| Fishing | 19.3 | 26.7 | 7.5 | 9.1 | 0.0 |
| Mining and quarrying | 10.0 | 8.7 | 6.6 | 7.9 | 8.7 |
| Manufacturing | 8.1 | 8.3 | 9.1 | 10.5 | 10.8 |
| Electricity, gas and water supply | 7.5 | 6.1 | 9.4 | 9.2 | 11.9 |
| Construction | 12.4 | 15.0 | 16.3 | 16.5 | 17.8 |
| Wholesale and retail trade | 9.6 | 10.4 | 11.6 | 12.0 | 14.0 |
| Hotels and restaurants | 16.9 | 17.2 | 19.4 | 21.1 | 21.2 |
| Transport, storage and communication | 6.9 | 8.0 | 7.4 | 7.9 | 8.4 |
| Financial intermediation | 8.2 | 8.2 | 8.7 | 9.5 | 9.3 |
| Real estate, renting and business activities | 11.4 | 12.0 | 12.7 | 13.5 | 13.7 |
| Public administration and defence | 15.7 | 16.7 | 16.4 | 15.8 | 17.0 |
| Education | 16.7 | 17.6 | 19.8 | 21.0 | 23.2 |
| Health and social work | 16.8 | 18.0 | 18.2 | 19.3 | 20.9 |
| Other community, social and personal service activities | 16.9 | 17.0 | 18.3 | 18.6 | 20.4 |
| Private households with employed persons | 11.8 | 5.5 | 12.2 | 9.1 | 8.1 |
| Extraterritorial organizations and bodies | 22.0 | 15.1 | 26.1 | 26.7 | 36.3 |

proportion of employees working voluntarily on an LDC basis in Germany is 1.7 per cent. This is a very small rate compared to that of other European countries, where the average rate is 7.6 per cent (Eurostat, 1997, pp. 148f). But it has to be added that in Germany nearly half of the employees with a limited contract work as apprentices and all apprenticeship contracts are hired on a limited duration basis. Thus it has to be stated that these contracts cannot be declared as involuntary LDCs as it is normal and widely accepted that apprenticeship contracts in the German system of vocational education are made for the duration of the apprenticeship. Consequently, apprenticeship contracts should not be seen as contingent labour. This is even more the case because of special dismissal protection of apprentices.

Other reasons that appeared in empirical studies included family considerations. Middle-aged women especially often start working after a 'family period' on an LDC. But they more often start on a part-time job with an open-ended contract. Other groups often working on LDCs are pupils and students.

In a research project that was financed by the Federal Ministry of Labour, employers that make use of LDCs were asked (in an adequate sample) for the reasons to use LDCs. More than one answer was possible;

the figures indicate the frequency of the reasons named by the employers (as a percentage of the answering employers). The main reasons for employers to recruit on an LDC basis resulting from this research project are shown in Figure 6.3.

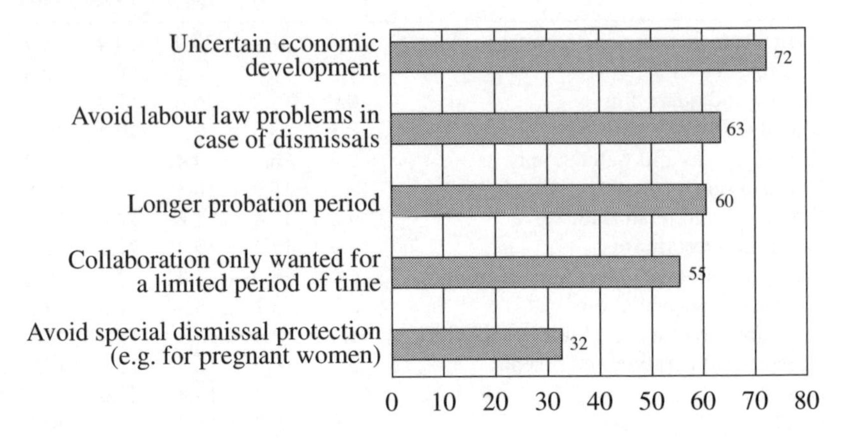


*Source:* Bielenski *et al.* (1994, p. 31).

*Figure 6.3 Reasons for employers to hire on LDCs*

The figure shows that the uncertain economic development is regarded as the most important reason for employers to use LDCs. Beyond that it can be seen that employers try to avoid labour law problems in the case of necessary dismissals. These reasons may be explained by the labour law in Germany, especially the law connected with dismissals, which is often seen as restrictive by employers, although an international comparison by Emerson shows that it is just the average in Europe (Emerson, 1988, p. 783). The third reason, getting a longer probationary period, must also be regarded in the labour law context. The maximum legal probationary period is six months. If it happens that there is an unsatisfactory performance after this period, it is not easy to end the contract. Thus a longer legal probationary period (together with an open-ended contract) may be an alternative instrument to limited duration contracts.[13]

Some companies may more easily and, at an earlier stage, more willingly make contracts on a limited duration basis instead of an open-ended contract in order to reduce their risk. However, they often become interested in open-ended contracts after getting to know the employee better and being surer about the permanent manpower requirements. One empirical study has shown that about 30 per cent of the employees working on an LDC basis are transferred to an open-ended contract (Büchtemann and Höland, 1989, pp. 331ff). An empirical analysis of the effects of the Employment Promotion Act of 1994 even showed that every second employee with an LDC based on the Employment Promotion Act is transferred to an open-ended contract (Bielenski, 1997, pp. 535–6). The results of these studies may lead to the assumption that LDCs are often the door to open-ended contracts and thus may have positive effects on the labour market.[14]

**Temporary Work Agency Employment**

Agency work in Germany has become the most rapidly growing form of employment over the last few years. The growth rate in the number of TWA employees was 72 per cent from June 1990 to June 1997 (Social Consult, 1998, p. 6), but in relation to the workforce (which is obliged to pay social insurance, that is, mainly employees) it is still a minor form of employment with a share of 0.9 per cent in 1997. This share increased to a level of 1.1 per cent in 1999, with 285000 TWA employees (Klös, 2000, p. 6). In relation to total employment (employees, self-employed and family workers) in 1999, this is a share of about 0.9 per cent. (See Table 6.6.)

The growth of temporary work in Germany can be seen not only from the number of TWA employees but also from the development of the number of temporary work agencies. Figure 6.4 shows the development of the temporary work agencies in Germany. It is obvious that, parallel to the increase of TWA employees, an increase in the number of temporary work agencies took place. An analysis of the structure of temporary work agencies in 1999 shows that the major part of these are small and medium-sized firms. Of the temporary work agencies, 57.4 per cent have fewer than 10 TWA employees and more than 50 TWA employees can only be found in about 15.8 per cent of the temporary work agencies (Deutscher Bundestag: Bundestags-Drucksache 14/4220, p. 8).

Temporary agency work is a male-dominated form of employment with a share of about 80 per cent of all TWA employees. This reflects the main areas of use of temporary work, which are production industries, where the share of female employees is traditionally small. Table 6.7 shows that women are employed primarily as administrative and office workers (1990: 63.1 per cent; 1997: 54.8 per cent). Beyond that there is a high proportion employed as unskilled workers (8.2 per cent; 16.0 per cent, respectively) and in the transport industry (8.5 per cent; 10.0 per cent). The proportion of female TWA employees working in these industries is clearly above the proportion of women with these professions over all industries.

Male TWA employees are mainly employed as mechanics (1990: 34.3 per cent; 1997: 27.8 per cent), electricians (13.0 per cent; 12.8 per cent), unskilled workers (11.6 per cent; 19.6 per cent) or workers in the transport industry

*Table 6.6 TWA employees in Germany, 1990–99*

| | 1990 | 1991 | 1992 | 1993 | 1994 | 1995 | 1996 | 1997 | 1998 | 1999 |
|---|---|---|---|---|---|---|---|---|---|---|
| TWA employees | 123378 | 133734 | 135827 | 115058 | 128577 | 161995 | 159889 | 190868 | 232242 | 285362 |
| Male | 99755 | 107698 | 108830 | 91983 | 104351 | 130845 | 128509 | 151949 | 184174 | 222760 |
| Female | 23623 | 26036 | 26997 | 23075 | 24226 | 31150 | 31380 | 38919 | 48068 | 63602 |
| TWA employee intensity | 0.5 | 0.4 | 0.4 | 0.4 | 0.4 | 0.5 | 0.5 | 0.6 | 0.8 | 0.9 |

*Source:* Social Consult (1998, p.22); data from Federal Office for Labour.

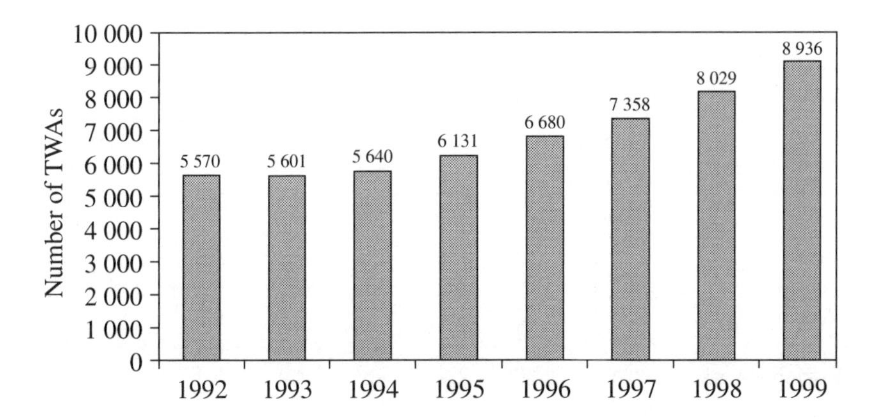


*Source:* Deutscher Bundestag: Bundestagsdrucksachen 13/5498, 14/4220, data from Federal Office for Labour.

*Figure 6.4 Development of TWAs in Germany, 1992–9*

(7.9 per cent; 9.0 per cent). The proportion of male TWA employees working in these industries is generally higher than the proportion of men with these professions over all industries, except the transport industry.

It is noteworthy that TWA employees are mainly full-time employees. Only 0.7 per cent of the male and 6.9 per cent of the female TWA employees worked part-time in 1997. This is a very small share compared to the general share of part-time working employees in relation to all employees (men: 6.5 per cent; women: 18.4 per cent) in 1997 (Social Consult, 1998, p. 27; Federal Statistical Office, 1998, p. 109). The idea of an open-ended contract in a temporary work agency as an alternative to an open-ended contract in a 'normal' company or revolving LDCs has obviously not become reality: 12.3 per cent of the TWA contracts are terminated after less than one week, 52.4 per cent after one week to three months and 35.3 per cent after more than three months (Klös, 2000, p. 13).

Regarding the wages of TWA employees, a study showed that, in 1995, these were on average 63.4 per cent of the overall wage level (Rudolph and Schröder, 1997, p. 117). These data are based on a comparison of men in the age group from 25 to 35 years, working full-time. A comparison of wages in different kinds of jobs shows that the low-qualified jobs have an average wage level of only 60 per cent, and even office workers, who have the best wage relation of the TWA employees, lose 21.8 per cent compared to the wages of comparable jobs in Germany (Table 6.8). The development of the wage relationship from 1980 to 1995 indicates that the wage differences have grown. The wage relation went down from 77.4 per cent in

*Table 6.7 Professions of TWA employees, by gender (%)*

| Profession | Men | | | | Women | | | |
|---|---|---|---|---|---|---|---|---|
| | Temporary work | | All industries | | Temporary work | | All industries | |
| | 1990 | 1997 | 1990 | 1997 | 1990 | 1997 | 1990 | 1997 |
| Chemicals worker | 0.4 | 0.3 | 2.7 | 2.1 | 0.8 | 0.5 | 1.5 | 0.9 |
| Metal-worker | 6.4 | 4.7 | 4.9 | 3.4 | 0.3 | 0.1 | 0.9 | 0.4 |
| Mechanic | 34.3 | 27.8 | 13.4 | 12.4 | 0.4 | 0.5 | 0.8 | 0.8 |
| Electrician | 13.0 | 12.8 | 4.8 | 4.6 | 0.3 | 0.6 | 0.5 | 0.4 |
| Assembly worker | 4.1 | 3.8 | 2.3 | 1.9 | 4.0 | 3.3 | 3.0 | 1.6 |
| Construction jobs | 0.7 | 1.5 | 6.0 | 7.2 | 0.1 | 0.1 | 0.1 | 0.2 |
| Joiner | 2.0 | 1.2 | 1.9 | 1.9 | 0.0 | 0.0 | 0.1 | 0.1 |
| Painter | 4.2 | 4.4 | 1.7 | 1.8 | 0.1 | 0.4 | 0.2 | 0.2 |
| Trade controller | 1.7 | 1.5 | 1.7 | 1.4 | 3.6 | 2.1 | 2.0 | 1.4 |
| Unskilled worker | 11.6 | 19.6 | 1.1 | 1.4 | 8.2 | 16.0 | 0.5 | 0.7 |
| Machinist | 0.7 | 0.7 | 1.5 | 1.4 | 0.5 | 0.1 | 0.0 | 0.1 |
| Engineers, chemists, physicists, mathematicians | 1.6 | 1.5 | 3.6 | 4.1 | 0.2 | 0.4 | 0.3 | 0.6 |
| Technician | 3.7 | 2.1 | 6.6 | 6.2 | 3.2 | 1.8 | 2.1 | 2.3 |
| Jobs in transport | 7.9 | 9.0 | 10.4 | 10.6 | 8.5 | 10.0 | 2.8 | 2.5 |
| Administrative and office worker | 4.8 | 5.4 | 11.0 | 12.0 | 63.1 | 54.8 | 30.7 | 31.3 |
| Service jobs in general | 1.1 | 1.8 | 1.9 | 12.7 | 2.3 | 6.0 | 11.4 | 37.7 |
| Further professions | 1.8 | 1.9 | 24.5 | 14.8 | 4.4 | 3.3 | 43.1 | 18.9 |

*Source:* Social Consult (1998, pp.25–6); data from the Federal Office for Labour.

1980 to 63.4 per cent in 1995, showing that there is no convergence of the overall wage level and the wages of TWA employees.

The qualifications of TWA employees fit into the picture of the typical professions of TWA employees. As the typical jobs require a professional qualification, a large proportion of TWA employees (60.9 per cent) hold a secondary school qualification and have completed vocational training successfully (Table 6.9). But there is also a sizeable proportion of TWA employees that has just a secondary school qualification (27.2 per cent). It may be supposed that these TWA employees are mainly employed as unskilled workers. The differences in the qualification levels of men and women are small. It may be concluded that the qualification levels of the female TWA employees are slightly higher than those of their male

*Table 6.8 Average monthly income of TWA employees in relation to all employees (%)**

| Type of job | 1980 | 1990 | 1995 |
|---|---|---|---|
| Low qualified worker | 74.3 | 67.6 | 59.7 |
| Qualified worker | 82.8 | 77.5 | 71.4 |
| Workers (altogether) | 79.3 | 73.2 | 65.4 |
| Office workers (altogether) | 89.2 | 85.8 | 78.2 |
| Low qualified | 73.4 | 67.7 | 59.4 |
| Qualified | 82.3 | 76.5 | 70.0 |
| Employees (altogether) | 77.4 | 71.7 | 63.4 |

*Note:* Full-time, men, 25–35 years old.

*Source:* Rudolph and Schröder (1997, p.117); data from Federal Office for Labour.

*Table 6.9 Qualifications of TWA employees in 1997*

| | Men (frequency, %) | Women (frequency, %) |
|---|---|---|
| Secondary school qualification only | 27.2 | 27.3 |
| Secondary school qualification and professional education | 60.9 | 52.0 |
| A levels only | 0.9 | 2.2 |
| A levels and professional education | 1.6 | 6.0 |
| University of applied sciences degree | 1.5 | 1.6 |
| University degree | 1.1 | 3.1 |
| Qualification unknown | 6.9 | 7.8 |

*Source:* Social Consult (1998, p.28); data from Federal Office for Labour.

colleagues. The structure of the qualifications of TWA employees has been quite stable over recent years and so it will be sufficient to restrict the analysis to the data from 1997.

The role of temporary work agencies in the labour market has been widely discussed (see, for example, Keller and Seifert, 1995; Deutscher Bundestag: Bundestags-Drucksache 14/4220, pp.25–7). TWAs may be regarded as a way for employees to enter the labour market. Several studies support this claim (for example, Rudolph and Schröder, 1997). Research shows that, before being employed by the temporary work agency, about 60 per cent of the TWA employees were unemployed (Deutscher Bundestag: Bundestags-Drucksache 14/4220, p.94; Klös, 2000, p.11). About a fifth of these unemployed were unemployed for more than a year or had never been employed before (Deutscher Bundestag: Bundestags-Drucksache 14/4220, p. 94; Klös, 2000, p. 11).

A second support for the argument is provided by the transfer rates from TWA employment into non-contingent work. There are no official statistics referring to this issue, but non-official estimations from the Institute for Labour Market and Profession Research (research department of the Federal Institute for Labour) cite transfer rates from 18.5 per cent to 30 per cent (Klös, 2000, p. 12). Thus it can be said that in Germany temporary work agencies serve as a bridge into the labour market.

## CONCLUDING REMARKS

During the 1990s, contingent employment in Germany increased, but it is still at a comparatively low level as its share of total employment was 7.1 per cent of total employment in 1991 and 7.7 per cent in 1998, if we add together LDCs and agency workers. The share of LDCs only grew from 6.7 per cent in 1991 to 7 per cent in 1998, whereas the share of temporary work agency employees almost doubled in the same period, going from 0.4 per cent to 0.7 per cent of the total employment, although remaining at a low level.

The analysis of LDCs in Germany showed that there are differences between the eastern part of Germany, where in 1999 14.5 per cent of all employees worked on an LDC basis, whereas the figure in the western part of Germany was 8 per cent. Young employees up to 30 years of age are more often confronted by LDCs, with almost 20 per cent of this group having an LDC. Men are only slightly more often confronted by LDCs than women are.

Agency work has become the most dynamic form of employment in Germany but is still a minor form of employment, with an increase from 0.4 per cent in 1991 to 0.8 per cent of total employment in 1999. In 1999, 285 000 employees were working for a temporary work agency. Temporary work is male-dominated, with a share of 80 per cent of all TWA employees. This is a consequence of the main areas of use of agency workers in the typical production industries, where the proportion of female employees is traditionally small. It is surprising that agency work offers full-time jobs in the first place. Only 0.7 per cent of the male and 6.9 per cent of the female TWA employees worked part-time in 1997. The average wage of TWA employees in 1995 was 63.4 per cent of the overall wage level. Agency work often serves as a bridge into the labour market. About 60 per cent of the TWA employees have been unemployed and seeking a job before being employed in a temporary work agency. Official transfer rates from TWA employees into non-contingent work do not exist. Estimations cite transfer rates from 18.5 to 30 per cent.

At first sight, these developments can be put down to the changes in the legal, economic and social context, as described above. And there are certainly strong links between these external developments and the use of contingent employment in Germany. The greater proportion of working women, the changing individual needs of workers and changes in environment (such as the globalization of markets, with consequent greater flexibility needs for the companies or the deregulation of the labour market) characterize the use of contingent employment in Germany. Another important factor may be the crisis that many companies experienced, especially during the 1980s. The crisis changed the attitude of many firms that used to be very successful in the past. They, employers *and* employees, had grown used to success and were shocked by the speed and the profound influence of the evolving problems. Since then, they seem to be more careful when employing people on an open-ended contract and have tried to build up a flexible workforce (as part of the whole workforce in a company) that can be reduced more easily than a workforce with open-ended contracts.

Companies in Germany often complain about the restrictive labour law context and the lack of missing flexibility, especially in terms of wages and dismissals. But contingent employment does not seem to be the solution, or is not accepted as a solution to these problems, because the use of contingent work is certainly increasing, although still relatively small. This could be due to several reasons, such as company values, resistance to changes in employment policies or simply economic reasons, making the use of TWA employees uneconomical. Thus there is still a need for further research to discover the explanations for the use as well as for the resistance to the use, of contingent work in Germany.

## NOTES

1. See *http://www.buendnis.de*.
2. A dismissal without notice is possible if an employee causes a serious breach of his/her obligations and duties that makes the continuation of employment, in particular for the period of notice, impossible. In this case the employee has to be told of the problem and warned of the legal consequences of not amending his/her behaviour before he/she is dismissed.
3. Empirical studies on the impact of the new rules of the Employment Promotion Act 1985 and 1990 regarding LDCs showed that many employers made use of the new rules because these rules are easier. In many of the cases the LDCs would have been possible under the former rules as well. The studies came to the conclusion that the employment effects of the simplification of the law were greater than the direct effects of the additional possibilities of making LDCs (Büchtemann and Höland, 1989, pp. 281–4; Bielenski *et al.*, 1994, p. 47).

4. Since 1 January 2001, there has been a new law called the Part-time and Limited Duration Contract Law (Teilzeit- und Befristungsgesetz) containing rules that were formerly part of the Employment Promotion Act. The possibility of entering into LDCs without giving a reason is still valid.
5. But building companies have been allowed to rent out workers to each other since 1994.
6. This type of collective agreement ('Tarifvorrang') is currently under discussion, because it often restricts flexibility for companies, as the collective agreements in Germany most often are valid for a whole economic sector. Thus they often cannot respond to company-specific flexibility needs.
7. The major part of these collective agreements (67.8 per cent) is industry-wide. Usually, unions and employers' associations are the partners of these agreements, of which 8 per cent are firm-wide; that is, with a single employer and a union making an agreement.
8. The average wage of TWA employees is 63.4 per cent of the overall wage level (see Rudolph and Schröder, 1997, p. 117).
9. There are three different laws regulating codetermination in Germany (the Company Constitution Act 1952, the Montan Constitution Act 1951 and the Constitution Act 1976). See Schreyögg *et al.* (1995, p. 333).
10. The new Works Constitution Act (2001) gives TWA employees (under certain conditions) the right to take part in the election of works councils (elections are held every four years).
11. In Germany each year the Federal Statistical Office carries out a micro census. One per cent of all households take part in this statistical inquiry, whose purpose is to get a database for political and economic decisions at a micro level (Federal Statistical Office, 2000).
12. In the following the figures are related to all employees and not to total employment as the original data are related to employees and a transfer is not always possible.
13. Probationary periods cannot be seen as an LDC. Open-ended contracts regularly start with a probationary period.
14. The studies of Büchtemann and Höland (1989) and Bielenski *et al.* (1994) showed that a proportion of the LDCs would have been open-ended contracts if the Employment Promotion Act did not exist. But *beyond* this effect, they both found positive employment effects of this law.

# BIBLIOGRAPHY

Bielenski, H. (1997) 'Deregulierung des Rechts befristeter Arbeitsverträge', Enttäuschte Hoffnungen, unbegründete Befürchtungen, in *WSI-Mitteilungen*, bk 8, pp. 532–7.

Bielenski, H., B. Köhler and M. Schreiber-Kittl (1994) 'Befristete Beschäftigung und Arbeitsmarkt. Empirische Untersuchung über befristete Arbeitsverträge nach dem Beschäftigungsförderungsgesetz', Eine Untersuchung der Infratest Sozialforschung GmbH im Auftrag des Bundesministeriums für Arbeit und Sozialordnung, Munich.

Böhlich, S. (1999) *Neue Formen der Beschäftigung*, Wiesbaden: Gabler.

Büchtemann, C.F. and A. Höland (1989) *Befristete Arbeitsverträge nach dem Beschäftigungsförderungsgesetz 1985* (BeschFG 1985), vol. 183 of the series 'Forschungsberichte', edited by Bundesminister für Arbeits- und Sozialordnung, Bonn.

Bundesanstalt für Arbeit (ed.) *Presse Information der Bundesanstalt für Arbeit*, No. 38/2000.

Deutscher Bundestag: Bundestags-Drucksache 10/2102.

Deutscher Bundestag: Bundestags-Drucksache 14/4220.
Eichenberg, S. and G. Wiskemann (1997) 'Personnel Management', in N. Reeves and H. Kelly-Holmes (eds), *The European Business Environment: Germany*, London: International Thomson Business Press, pp. 124–51.
Emerson, M. (1988) 'Regulation or Deregulation of the Labour Market. Policy Regimes for the Recruitment and Dismissal of Employees in the Industrialised Countries', *European Economic Review*, 32, 775–817.
Eurostat (1997), *Erhebung über Arbeitskräfte, Ergebnisse 1996*, Luxemburg.
Federal Statistical Office (ed.) (1992) *Statistical Yearbook 1992 for the Federal Republic of Germany*, Stuttgart.
Federal Statistical Office (ed.) (1993) *Statistical Yearbook 1993 for the Federal Republic of Germany*, Stuttgart.
Federal Statistical Office (ed.) (1994) *Statistical Yearbook 1994 for the Federal Republic of Germany*, Stuttgart.
Federal Statistical Office (ed.) (1995) *Statistical Yearbook 1995 for the Federal Republic of Germany*, Stuttgart.
Federal Statistical Office (ed.) (1996a) *Bevölkerung und Erwerbstätigkeit*, Fachserie 1 Reihe 4.1.1, Stand und Entwicklung der Erwerbstätigkeit.
Federal Statistical Office (ed.) (1996b) *Statistical Yearbook 1996 for the Federal Republic of Germany*, Stuttgart.
Federal Statistical Office (ed.) (1997) *Statistical Yearbook 1997 for the Federal Republic of Germany*, Stuttgart.
Federal Statistical Office (ed.) (1998) *Statistical Yearbook 1998 for the Federal Republic of Germany*, Stuttgart.
Federal Statistical Office (ed.) (1999a) *Statistical Yearbook 1999 for the Federal Republic of Germany*, Stuttgart.
Federal Statistical Office (ed.) (1999b) *Bevölkerung und Erwerbstätigkeit*, Fachserie 1, Reihe 4.1.1, Stand und Entwicklung der Erwerbstätigkeit, Stuttgart (and volumes from 1990–97).
Federal Statistical Office (ed.) (2000) *Leben und Arbeiten in Deutschland, Ergebnisse des Mikrozenszus 1999*, Wiesbaden.
German Council of Economic Experts (ed.) (1997) *Wachstum, Beschäftigung, Währungsunion – Orientierungen für die Zukunft*, Jahresgutachten, 1997/98, Stuttgart.
German Council of Economic Experts (ed.) (1999) *Wirtschaftspolitik unter Reformdruck*, Jahresgutachten 1999/2000, Stuttgart.
Institut der deutschen Wirtschaft (ed.) (1999) *Industrielle Arbeitskosten im internationalen Vergleich 1980/98*, Cologne.
Institut der deutschen Wirtschaft (ed.) (2000) *Zahlen zur wirtschaftlichen Entwicklung der Bundesrepublik Deutschland*, Cologne.
Keller, B. and H. Seifert (1995) *Atypische Beschäftigung. Verbieten oder gestalten*, Cologne: Bund-Verlag.
Klös, H.P. (2000) 'Zeitarbeit – Entwicklungstrends und arbeitsmarktpolitische Bedeutung', *iw-trends*, 1/2000, 5–22.
Kohaut, S. and C. Schnabel (1999) 'Tarifbindung im Wandel', *iw-trends*, 2/1999, 63ff.
OECD (1999) *Employment Outlook*, June, Paris.
Oechsler, W.A. (2000a) *Personal und Arbeit. Grundlagen des Human Resource Management und der Arbeitgeber-Arbeitnehmer-Beziehungen*, 7th edn, Munich and Vienna: Oldenbourg.

Oechsler, W.A. (2000b) 'Workplace and workforce 2000+ – the future of our work environment', *International Archives of Occupational and Environmental Health*, supplement to vol. 73, June, 28–32.
o.V. (2000a) 'Lohnstückkosten. Noch nicht am Ziel', *iwd*, 26. Jg., 4–5.
o.V. (2000b) 'Trend zur Selbständigkeit', *Sozialpolitische Umschau*, 10, July, 32.
Rudolph, H. and E. Schröder (1997) 'Arbeitnehmerüberlassung: Trends und Einsatzlogik', *Mitteilungen aus der Arbeitsmarkt- und Berufsforschung*, 1, 102–26.
Schreyögg, G., W.A. Oechsler and H. Wächter (1995) *Managing in a European Context*, Wiesbaden: Gabler.
Social Consult (1998) 'Wirtschaftliche Bedeutung und arbeitsmarktlicher Beitrag der Zeitarbeit in Deutschland 1990 bis 1997', Studie im Auftrag des Bundesverbandes Zeitarbeit Personal-Dienstleistungen e.V., Bonn.

# 7. Flexible employment in the USA

**Kay McGlashan, Rebecca Ellis and Doug Glasgow**

## INTRODUCTION

In this chapter, we examine the state of contingent and alternative work in the United States. The situation in the USA is not necessarily an increase in flexible work, but a significant change in the way that work is being arranged (Micco, 1999). Employee–employer contracts are more varied in design than the typical permanent work contract. The USA has also seen a tremendous growth in staffing services and alternative work agencies (that is, temporary help agencies, independent contracting firms, outsourcing), as a result of a changed 'mindset' about employment in the USA. According to the US Bureau of Labor Statistics, in February 2001 approximately 4 per cent of workers considered themselves to be contingent workers, and 9.4 per cent considered themselves to be in alternative employment arrangements.

We first examine the larger labour market context in the USA, including a discussion of the general economic and employment trends during the 1990s. We then describe the institutional framework, including industrial relations and the legal framework and regulations surrounding employment. Next we turn to an in-depth examination of the existing data on the demand for alternative employment (that is, the distribution of these arrangements across general industry and occupational categories), as well as the supply of alternative employment (that is, demographic characteristics of gender, race, age, education, full-time versus part-time status, wages and benefits, and worker preferences regarding employment arrangements). These data are taken from the special supplements to the Current Population Survey conducted by the Bureau of Labor Statistics during February of 1995, 1997, 1999 and 2001. We conclude with a general discussion and future research opportunities.

## GENERAL TRENDS IN THE US LABOUR MARKET

After a period of recession in the early 1990s, the United States has enjoyed an unprecedented period of expansion and good economic conditions (Hatch and Clinton, 2000; *Report on the American Workforce*, 1999). Over the past decade, the US labour force grew at a steady pace. From 1990 to 2000, total non-farm employment grew by 20.4 per cent, to 131.8 million workers. In recent years, unemployment rates have been at three-decade lows. Unemployment in 1990 was 5.6 per cent, in 1992 peaked at 7.5 per cent, and by 2000 decreased to 4.0 per cent.[1]

In 2000, the US labour supply was 51.6 per cent male and 48.4 per cent female, contrasted with 1990, when the labour force was 47.4 per cent female. The employment population ratio for females in 1990 was 54.3 per cent, increasing to 57.7 per cent in 2000. The male employment population ratio decreased slightly from 72.0 per cent in 1990 to 71.8 per cent in 2000.[2] The growth in female participation rates in the US labour market reflects a general increase in dual wage-earner couples and single-parent families. However, females still lag behind males considerably in overall labour force participation.

The workforce is ageing, owing to the influence of the baby-boom generation (persons born between 1946 and 1964). At the same time, the youth labour force (age 16 to 24) is expected to grow at a faster pace than the overall workforce for the first time in a quarter-century (Fullerton, 1999). The 25 to 24 and 35 to 44 age categories are expected to have decreasing shares of the labour force over the next 10 years.

As of 2000, the employment population ratio for whites was 65.1 per cent, up from 63.7 per cent in 1990. Blacks and Hispanics also reflected increases, with blacks' ratio moving up from 56.7 per cent in 1990 to 60.8 per cent in 2000, and Hispanics increasing from 61.9 per cent to 64.7 per cent during the same time period. Overall, the ethnic make-up of the employed civilian labour force for 2000 was 83.9 per cent white, 11.3 per cent black and 10.7 per cent Hispanic.[3] Contrasted with 1990 percentages of 86.1 per cent white, 10.2 per cent black, and 8.3 per cent Hispanic, we note that minorities constitute a greater proportion of the workforce than they did 10 years ago.

The USA continues its shift to a service economy, with the services industry in 1990 having 25.5 per cent of total non-farm employment, increasing to 30.7 per cent by 2000. Manufacturing lost 3.4 per cent of employment during the time period, with 14 per cent in 2000. Retail trade stayed relatively steady, with 17.7 per cent of employment in 2000, while government employment declined by 1 per cent to 15.7 per cent in 2000.

Along occupational lines, the dominant occupational groups in terms of percentage of civilian employment in 2000 were managerial and professional specialty at 30.2 per cent (up 4.6 per cent from 1990) and technical/sales/administrative support at 29.2 per cent (down 1.9 per cent from 1990). Service occupations comprised 13.5 per cent of 2000 employment (unchanged), operator/fabricator/labourer held 13.5 per cent (down 1.7 per cent from 1990), precision production/craft/repair had 11 per cent (down 0.6 per cent), and farming/forestry/fishing held the remaining 2.5 per cent in 2000 (down 0.4 per cent from 1990).

## INSTITUTIONAL FRAMEWORK AND EMPLOYMENT REGULATION

In the following sections, we present a discussion of the US institutional and legal frameworks within which contingent or flexible employment exists. The institutional framework includes a description of the historical context of employment in the USA, as well as discussion of the industrial relations context (unionization and labour movements) in the 20th century. Then we present a discussion of the legal framework pertaining to the employment relationship, including employment laws and case law pertaining to the issue of flexible employment.

### The Institutional Framework

This section will review the broader sociopolitical context within which contingent employment has developed, with emphasis on the historical interplay of business, government and labour unions. Following this, we will discuss the posture towards contingent work that has been adopted historically by the labour movement, and identify some novel approaches that have recently emerged. Finally, we will take a closer look at legal developments, particularly with respect to case law on job security that may have implications for the use of contingent workers.

#### The historical context

The USA has had a 'secondary' or peripheral workforce since at least the mid-1800s. What has changed (more than its size) is its occupational/demographic composition, with 1980s 'downsizing' bringing more professional/managerial/white males in, so that the 'social status' of peripheral work has gone up. Barker and Christensen (1998) say the status change was symbolized by the change in terminology from 'peripheral' to 'contingent' worker. It still contains disproportionate numbers of people from several traditionally marginalized groups, but the stereotyping and stigmatization have lessened.

Historically, however, non-standard employment (for example, part-time and temporary work, lack of a guaranteed income and benefits, and a loose or triangulated relationship between employer and employee) was as much the norm as the exception in the USA before the New Deal (Cobble and Vosko, 2000). For instance, 19th-century manufacturing was largely dependent on a loosely coupled system of production that used skilled craft workers and their helpers to contract for the production of a specific product rather than sell their labour by the hour. The 19th-century craft-based models of employment centred on marketable skills possessed by the worker, who gained considerable economic independence as a result. However, following early 20th-century applications of Taylorism and the principles of Scientific Management to manufacturing, the modern factory was born and the craft system of production declined. Thus this early independent contracting system was ultimately replaced by bureaucratic mass production, just as craft unionism, organized on an occupational basis, gradually gave way to industrial unionism. The industrial unionism model organized all workers regardless of occupation at a plant- or industry-wide level, a model that better suited large bureaucratic organizations and mass production.

As the methods of production were changing, so too were social attitudes. The 'Social Darwinism' of the late 1800s made for a laissez-faire economy, where individual entrepreneurs were admired and government saw little social role for itself in regulating the economy. The Progressive political movement for reform, roughly continuing from 1900 to 1920, held that irresponsible actions by the rich were corrupting both public and private life. This was the beginning of the view that there was an appropriate regulatory role for government in the economy, and in labour market conditions. The sea change in public opinion, though, and a new activist view of the social role of government was to come with President Franklin D. Roosevelt's New Deal, an extended effort to deal with the crushing economic effects of the Great Depression of the 1930s. During the next 20 years, the bulk of US labour law was written, the Social Security system was begun, and 'Social Darwinism' was largely discredited. It seemed self-evident that the plight of working men and women during the Depression was not solely their own fault, or even primarily due to lack of individual enterprise.

The New Deal initiated legislation that would shape the US labour relations system for the next 65 years. Beginning with the National Labor Relations (Wagner) Act of 1935, Roosevelt's policies expressed open encouragement of labour unions. Before this time, employer rights went essentially unchecked by federal legislation. With profound implications for the marginalization of contingent workers, the New Deal industrial relations model was built upon the assumed predominance of large, bureaucratic organizations as the major employers of labour, with a basic building block of the permanent job (Kunda *et al.*, 1999). Other New Deal statutes with impacts for contingent labour included the Federal Insurance Contribution Act, better known as the Social Security Act (1935), and the Fair Labor Standards Act of 1938 which mandated minimum wages and restrictions on maximum hours of work. Ultimately, access to health insurance, pensions and unemployment insurance all became tied to the legal framework that held employers responsible for fulfilling legally prescribed obligations to a permanent workforce (Kunda *et al.*, 1999). The use of independent contractors became one way businesses could reduce labour costs, since firms that employed them were not responsible for payroll taxes or benefits.

Although basic labour law remains unchanged since the 1930s, the public policy posture towards unionism was to take another turn in the early 1980s when then President Ronald Reagan fired striking air traffic controllers. The legislation of the New Deal had sought to equalize the power of employers and employees by institutionalizing unionism, but to many, unions ultimately became viewed as too powerful. Reagan's action reflected this shift of public opinion, and ushered in an era of increased employer resistance to unions. Indeed, some present-day observers believe the use of contingent workers is a deliberate employer tactic to avoid unionization.

As the example of craft-based independent contracting cited above indicates, the social history of each form of flexible employment (such as temps, independent contractors or part-timers) is as distinct as their social/employment relationships and organizational functions. Thus each form of contingent employment is likely to have its own unique social history, reflecting a complex interplay of governmental, industry and labour market forces. A second historically interesting development regarding contingent employment, from a sociopolitical perspective, is the emergence and rapid growth of the modern temporary help industry in the years shortly after the Second World War.

Industry actors fought a protracted battle in the courts and in state legislatures for recognition as the legally constituted employer of the workers sent on to client industries. According to sociologist George Gonos (1998), the fledgling industry began as an offshoot of employment agencies and job placement firms, which were being heavily regulated in the post-war era. To distinguish themselves from placement firms was seen as advantageous in two respects: it might relieve them of increasing regulation, and at the same time allow them to continue to make money as long as the workers they placed continued working. The key marketing appeal for employers was the change in the nature of the employment relationship. If temps were legally the employees of temp agencies, then the user (that is, the client firm) could escape increasingly burdensome legal and social obligations to workers that also began to appear in the post-war period.

The first industry association to be mobilized on a national level was the Institute for Temporary Services, in 1966, later renamed the National Association of Temporary Services, then the National Association of Temporary and Staffing Services, and most recently (1999) renamed the American Staffing Association. This group became a very effective lobby at a state level, ultimately successfully distinguishing itself from placement services one state at a time. The protracted battle was necessary because most early court decisions were not in favour of the industry's preferred designation of itself as employer of record. The major industry wedge in this fight was contradictory and/or conflicting de facto regulations promulgated by government agencies. Most notable was the Internal Revenue Service (IRS), which found tax collection from temp agencies far easier than tax collection from myriad independent contractors. State Unemployment Insurance tax collectors were similarly eager to accept monies sent from temp agencies claiming themselves to be 'employers'. Recent court cases (for example, Microsoft) suggest that the fights over who should be designated employer of record and who is a 'common law' employee are far from over. However, the temporary help industry is here to stay, and is far less regulated than in any other industrialized country.

**The industrial relations context**

As a people, Americans are well known as the standard-bearer for the cultural trait of individualism (as opposed to collectivism) as articulated by Geert Hofstede in the 1980s (Hofstede, 1980). This cultural glorification of individual achievement may be one reason for union activity in the USA having always been viewed with some suspicion, if not outright hostility. As alluded to in the previous section, unionism did not gain legal status in the USA until President F.D. Roosevelt insisted on it as a matter of public policy, with passage of the 1935 Wagner Act establishing the right of employees to form unions, to bargain collectively and to strike. Prior to the New Deal, unions were treated in common law, first, as criminal conspiracies, and later as illegal conspiracies in restraint of trade. Nor did it take long for public opinion to weigh in on the Wagner Act. In 1947, the Taft–Hartley Act introduced six unfair union labour practices to counterbalance the five unfair employer practices specified in the Wagner Act, and, in 1959, the Landrum–Griffin Act sought to check perceived union leadership power abuses. It is instructive to note that, even at the absolute zenith of union power and influence in American society, only 33 per cent of the workforce was organized in the mid-1950s. In short, the American labour movement has never been particularly strong. Another relatively distinctive feature of the American labour scene is the 'business unionism' perspective on collective bargaining, whereby unions focus narrowly on bread-and-butter issues of specific, pragmatic interest to union members, rather than broader social–political issues.

The US labour movement has suffered years of membership decline since its heyday in the 1950s, with membership in 2000 at approximately 14 per cent of the labour force. Progressive leaders of the labour movement have called for several changes in the labour agenda, chief among them reaching out for membership gains among the least protected, most needy segments of the workforce, which would necessarily include many contingent workers. These workers have proved to be very difficult to organize under existing labour laws such as the Wagner Act. Such laws were written with the New Deal Industrial Relations model at their core; that is, the expectation of a long-term relationship between a single-site employer and a largely immobile workforce.

As noted above, the Wagner Act was designed to protect employee rights to form and join unions, and to engage in activities such as strikes, picketing and collective bargaining. Among other things, the Wagner Act created the National Labor Relations Board (NLRB), a five-person independent federal agency appointed by the president (with the advice and consent of the Senate) that is charged with administering US private sector labour law. The NLRB's primary functions are (1) to administer certification elections, that is, secret ballot elections that determine whether employees want to be represented by a union, and (2) to prevent and remedy unlawful acts called 'unfair labour practices'. It is with respect to the first of these functions that the NLRB has played a role in the contingent employment landscape. For, in order to conduct an election, the Board must first determine which workers have a sufficient 'community of interest' to justify placing them in a single 'appropriate bargaining unit'. Only members of this NLRB-determined unit are allowed to vote for union representation. Historically, the NLRB has held temporary employee interests to be generally different enough from those of permanent workers. They argue that they should automatically be excluded from the unit, unless both employers (the temporary help agency that referred them and the client to whom they were temporarily assigned) agree that they should be included. This ruling was reversed on 25 August 2000. Henceforth, temporary employees need not get the permission of their joint-employers to be eligible to vote, although they must still satisfy the Board's criterion of a sufficient 'community of interest' in order to join a bargaining unit with permanent workers performing similar tasks or functions.

At the same time, this change in regulatory agency guidelines does nothing to change the underlying statutory framework of regulations, which were passed at a time when there was little contingent employment as we know it today. While many interested and informed observers continue to advocate major revisions of existing labour law (for example, Kochan, 1999), the two dominant political parties tend not to agree on the tack that reform should take. As neither party has been able to amass a clear and consistent majority in either house of Congress, the chances of new legislation in the short term are slim. Therefore, if the labour movement is to survive and thrive, it will have to do so without a major overhaul of US labour laws. It will need to find ways to work around the existing labour legislation.

The historical union approach to contingent work, in line with special-interest business unionism, has been to preclude or at least limit management's ability to use such workers, under the reasoning that they will take work away from bargaining unit members. A recent (1997) strike against United Parcel Service (UPS) illustrates this approach, with strikers pressing the company to convert more part-time workers into full-time employees.

While suppression of contingent work is undoubtedly still the norm among union activists, there are nonetheless several interesting alternatives that have surfaced recently. The new directions involve efforts at organizing outside the federal legal framework of the NLRB and changing the traditional sorts of things unions seek to negotiate under collective bargaining. Among the new initiatives are attempts to include contingent workers in bargaining units (with separate status), bargaining for parity in wages and benefits for part-time and contingent workers who are members of the unit, and bargaining for schedule flexibility for *all* bargaining unit members – both in and out of the contingent workforce, as life events make alternative work arrangements more or less desirable from the individual worker's perspective.

In terms of organizing, there have also been some notable successes in organizing on a local, geographically limited basis, bringing potential union members in a general occupational group together to face multiple, distributed employers in a geographically proximate area (for example, a metropolitan area). Examples include the successful SEIU (Service Employees International Union) campaign regarding 'Justice for Janitors' in Las Vegas, and the organization of over 70000 home health care workers in Los Angeles in 1999. In line with exhortations by current AFL–CIO (American Federation of Labor and Congress of Industrial Organizations) president Sweeney, it would seem that labour organizers have taken to heart the new economy dictum: organize people before jobs. The successful geographically local organization of erstwhile difficult-to-organize contingent workers calls for a new social activism on the part of labour unions. Instead of concentrating on a particular worksite or a single employer, these new initiatives have sought to bring together a coalition of interests, both public and private. It is a community-based effort that has worked in the few local areas where it has been tried.

## The Legal Framework

Traditionally, workers in the USA have been divided into two broad categories: employees[4] and independent contractors. How workers are categorized has important legal ramifications for the employer. The legal distinction between these two categories has blurred over the past decade because of the increasing use of alternative work arrangements such as leased workers who often have characteristics of both employees and independent contractors. This section will discuss the legal distinction between employees and independent contractors. We then move on to discuss the law with respect to the use of employees and after that the law regarding the use of independent contractors. Finally, we will discuss how the law has been applied to alternative work arrangements.

Theoretically, it is employers who categorize workers as either employees or independent contractors, but, in practice, the law determines how the workers are categorized. Because of the legal advantages of using independent contractors, employers would categorize most of their workers as independent contractors if they were free to do so. For instance, in the USA, employers must withhold federal taxes, provide workers' compensation insurance for injuries, pay for unemployment insurance and pay social security and medicare taxes for employees. They are not required to do so for independent contractors. Attempts by employers to classify numerous categories of their workers as independent contractors have met stiff resistance from the IRS. The IRS lists 20 factors used to determine whether a worker is categorized as an independent contractor or as an employee. These factors focus on the right of the employer to control the actions of the worker. The greater is the control, the more likely the worker will be deemed an employee. A few of these factors are listed here, in no particular order of importance.

- The extent of the employer's control over the hours and times worked.
- The ability of the worker to work concurrently for other employers: for instance, performing courier services for several employers would indicate that a worker is an independent contractor.
- The way in which the pay of the worker is calculated, such as by the hour or by the job.

- The risk of gain or loss to the worker based upon the worker's performance. For instance, normally an independent contractor would receive less compensation for work that was poorly performed.

The IRS determination of employment status is often used to determine the application of other federal employment law.

**Employees and open-ended contracts**

Workers that are in employee relationships with their employers receive the greatest level of regulatory protection. However, the level of protection against being wrongfully dismissed by an employer is different depending upon whether the employee is replaced in a job that is continuing or whether the employee's job is eliminated. Jobs may be eliminated by employers for a variety of reasons. Demand for products may change, changes in technology may alter the capital–labour ratio in production, and, often, reorganization and downsizing may lead to the elimination of jobs. Also firms may shift production to other countries to take advantage of their comparative advantage in labour-intensive production.

Congress has been reluctant to create rights for employees with respect to job eliminations because of their potential effect on the economic efficiency and competitiveness of US firms in world markets. In 1988, Congress passed the Worker Adjustment and Retraining Notification Act (WARN) in order to provide advance notification of layoffs to employees. However, WARN only requires employers to give employees 60 days' advance notice of plant closings or layoffs and only applies to employers with 100 or more employees. Furthermore, employer exemptions are granted in emergency cases where there has been a major loss of orders or the firm is 'faltering'. It is unlikely that WARN has had any effect on the number of plant closings.

State legislatures have also been reluctant to pass laws preventing employers from adjusting their employee numbers. States compete with each other to attract employers into the state and would be less attractive if they had job elimination protections that could reduce the competitiveness and efficiency of employers located there.

In the USA, 'employees' are similar to workers with open-ended contracts in EU countries. Although the law varies from state to state, there are two basic types of employee relationships: employment-at-will and employment-by-contract. The difference between them is the amount of job security that each affords. Theoretically, the employment-at-will relationship continues as long as it is at the will of both the employer and the employee. Either the employer or the employee can terminate the employment relationship for any non-discriminatory reason or no reason at all.

While this may seem to offer little in the way of job security, it has long been recognized that markets punish employers who gain a reputation for dismissing productive employees. These employeres experience increased costs of hiring, training and retaining employees who want job security. At least in competitive industries, it is the employer's expertise and market survival that are brought to bear in making employment decisions.

Inefficient or unfair dismissals of employees can occur because of a lack of competition in an industry, asymmetry of information or mistakes by employers. Since most of the law concerning employment-at-will is common law, most state courts have been active in extending job security to employees-at-will, causing a serious erosion in the freedom of employers to dismiss employees without liability. Between 1973 and 1995, 46 state courts decided cases that restricted employers' discretion to dismiss at-will employees, often finding an implied understanding of continued employment or an implied contract of employment (Autor, 2000). These judicially created contracts can arise from the circumstances surrounding the employment environment such as longevity of service, a history of promotion or salary increases, general employee policies, or even typical industry practices.[5] The uncertainty of the obligations owed to employees has led to numerous successful lawsuits against employers. In California, for example, employees have prevailed in 52 per cent of implied employment contract actions against their employers (Dertouzos and Karoly, 2000; Jung, 1997).

Employees who are not at-will are employees-by-contract, either expressed or implied. Employees who work under collective bargaining agreements between a union and an employer are employees-by-(expressed) contract. Employees at-will who are deemed by courts to have implied understandings of continued employment would be considered employees-by-(implied) contract. Employees-by-contract have more job security than employees-at-will because they can be dismissed for one of only three reasons: (1) for breach of the expressed or implied employment contract, (2) for 'just cause' which is a good faith reason related to productivity, or (3) if the job itself is eliminated. The law does not regulate the terms of these contracts with respect to hours or duration but does require the employer, under most circumstances, to provide all employees with such benefits as minimum wages and overtime pay, family and medical leave, and some religious and disability accommodations.

Discharged employees may bring legal actions against their former employers for wrongful termination of employment and usually, particularly with regard to employees-by-contract, the burden of proof is upon the employer to prove the dismissal was for a legal reason. This often requires accurate record keeping, consistent disciplinary procedures and extensive litigation expenses. A win by the employer means only the loss of legal expenses. A loss by the employer adds compensatory and possibly punitive damages to the bottom line. In California, for example, the average and median compensatory damage awards to employees who won wrongful termination of employment lawsuits against employers were \$586000 and \$268000, respectively. In another study, legal fees averaged \$98000 in cases where the employer prevailed and \$220000 in cases where the former employee prevailed (Jung, 1997). Because of the cost of litigation and potential liability, the vast majority of these lawsuits are settled out of court. Today it is common to give a severance package to dismissed employees, which may include a bonus paid to the dismissed employee in exchange for a waiver of liability against the employer for wrongful termination of employment.

Federal law protects employees from discrimination by their employers on the basis of race, colour, gender, religion, national origin, pregnancy, age and disability. The law of some states further protects employees from discrimination on the basis of sexual preference, marital status and family status. Employees may file discrimination complaints against their employers through the Equal Employment Opportunity Commission, a federal agency, which represents them against their employer, free of charge.

Legally, employers can avoid much of the risk of litigation by using leased or agency workers whom they can return to the leasing agent or temporary help agency if they are dissatisfied. In most cases, there are no legal consequences to the employer because leased workers are the employees of the leasing company, not of the client employer. Autor (2000) found a causal link between increased job security for at-will employees and the increased use of temporary help agencies. This form of alternative work arrangement will be discussed below (see p. 175).

**Independent contractors**

Independent contractor relationships are created by implied or express contracts and are governed by the common law of contracts. Independent contractors are similar to limited duration contract workers in EU countries. There are some legal advantages to the use of independent contractors in addition to the reduced tax liability and the reduced risk of wrongful termination lawsuits that were discussed earlier.

The use of independent contractors reduces the employer's potential liability to third parties. Under the law of all states, employers, with few exceptions, are automatically liable to third parties for injuries caused by the negligent or intentional acts of their employees while acting within the scope of employment. Subject to some exceptions, employers are not liable for the acts of independent contractors unless the employer was negligent in hiring them or their actions were directed by the employer. State courts use a common law test focusing on the employer's control over the worker to determine whether the employer should be held liable.

Federal labour laws dealing with union–management relations do not apply to independent contractors. While there have been efforts by unions to organize other types of contingent workers, such as part-time workers, independent contractors are not covered by labour laws and are not permitted to unionize. A union of independent contractors could also be viewed as an illegal cartel under the antitrust laws because the union could provide a means by which prices for independent contractor services could be fixed. This restriction on independent contractors does not apply to other types of contingent workers such as part-time workers and leased or agency employees. Recent decisions have given these workers the right to unionize under certain conditions.

**Contingent workers and other alternative work arrangements**

As protections for employees have increased, employers who cannot use independent contractors because of control issues have turned to alternative work arrangements in an effort to reduce their legal liability exposure. State legislatures and Congress have been unable to keep up with the hybrid forms of work arrangements and have left it to the courts to attempt to extend conventional employment protections to unconventional employment relationships. Courts are hampered by the fact that state and federal statutes, which are often the basis of employee protections, are often vague in their definitions of 'employee' and 'employer'. Courts are left to use a blend of employment law, agency law and contract law to determine the liability of employers.[6]

Contingent workers whom employers have attempted to classify as independent contractors in order to reduce their potential liability have brought lawsuits against their employers seeking status as employees in order to obtain protection under state and federal employment law.[7] Cases that were decided in favour of contingent workers against employers have certain facts in common. The workers were hired under vague contract terms concerning the duration of their project. They were employed longer than expected, often for years longer. Their employer often trained them. When employers treat independent contractors and other contingent workers like employees, exert the same control over such workers as they do over employees, and hire contingent workers under vague contracts, they run the risk of having the workers deemed employees.

A relatively new legal concept is being applied to leased and agency workers. In some cases, the staffing company and the client company have been deemed joint employers for purposes of certain laws. Recent decisions under the Fair Labor Standards Act (which requires a minimum wage and overtime pay) and the Family and Medical Leave Act (which requires unpaid leave for worker emergencies) have made the staffing company and the client company jointly liable for worker benefits. The impact of these decisions on alternative work arrangements remains to be seen.

## CONTINGENT AND ALTERNATIVE EMPLOYMENT

### Flexible Staffing Arrangements

It is within the general labour context discussed in the previous section that contingent and alternative employment exist. Freedman (1985) first referred to 'contingent work' to describe conditional, transitory employment arrangements. Subsequently, others used the term in various ways and included or excluded certain types of employment arrangements such as temporary, contract or part-time work (Houseman, 1999). Houseman coined the term 'flexible staffing arrangements' to encompass these types of employment. Flexible, or contingent, labour implies an explicitly defined short-term relationship between employer and employee (Kunda *et al.*, 1999).

Prior to 1995, no time series data on US employment in contingent and alternative arrangements exist, with one exception. The Current Employment Survey (CES), also conducted by the Bureau of Labor Statistics (BLS), began keeping statistics on employment in the temporary help supply services industry segment (Standard Industry Classification code 7363) in 1982. According to the CES, the share of non-farm payroll employment in this sector grew from 0.5 per cent in 1982 to 2.3 per cent in 1998. Employment in the sector includes temporary workers placed through agencies, as well as the staff of the agencies themselves.[8] These data suggest growth in temporary work in the USA over the past two decades, but the data do not represent the numerous other types of contingent and alternative arrangements that workers might hold.[9]

With a lack of employment data on flexible employment arrangements in general, some researchers have examined employment in the industry category of business services, US standard industry classification code 736 (which encompasses SIC code 7363 from above) to find further evidence of growth in flexible staffing arrangements (Clinton, 1997; Houseman, 1999). A trend towards 'market-mediated work arrangements' such as 'outsourcing' of various functions and use of temporary workers or of leased workers may explain the tremendous growth (5.8 per cent annually from 1988 to 1997) in employment in business services in recent years (Clinton, 1997). Jobs that were once counted in an organization's industry employment are increasingly being counted as employment in the business services industry.

Other researchers have at times estimated that as much as 25 to 30 per cent of the US workforce was in a contingent employment arrangement (Belous, 1989). Polivka and Nardone, in 1989, criticized researchers' expansion of the concept of contingent work to include workers in all part-time and self-employed arrangements, when many of these workers enjoyed long-term and stable employment. They suggested two key criteria for classifying a worker as contingent: (1) a low degree of job security, and (2) variability in hours worked. Using these criteria, many workers who would otherwise be considered contingent would instead be classified as non-contingent workers.

Owing to the increased visibility and disagreement surrounding the concept of contingent work, the BLS, within the US Department of Labor, began collecting survey data on these workers in February 1995 as a supplement to the Current Population Survey (CPS). Subsequent surveys were conducted in February 1997, 1999 and 2001. The goal of these surveys was to measure such arrangements more accurately in response to the 'overly broad estimates' by some researchers in the 1980s and early 1990s (Houseman, 1999).

However, two caveats must be mentioned at this point. First, the nature of the BLS survey requires workers to classify themselves as contingent and/or alternative, based on their own perceptions of their current situations. The data do not reflect actual contracting arrangements between the employee and employer, as US companies are not required to report any information regarding their use of contingent or alternative workers. Second, the BLS incorporated the first of Polivka and Nardone's (1989) criteria for contingent employment, a low degree of job insecurity, while the second criterion, variability in hours worked, was not incorporated (Houseman, 1999). This may affect the accuracy of the data. As an example, only 57 per cent of agency temps classified themselves as contingent in the 1997 BLS survey, because hours variability was not used as a criterion. Therefore the BLS data should be interpreted with these points in mind. Nonetheless, according to the BLS, contingent workers are 'individuals who do not perceive themselves as having an implicit or explicit contract for ongoing employment'.[10]

The percentage of US workers who considered themselves contingent decreased from 4.9 per cent in 1995 to 4.0 per cent in 2001. This may be a reflection of the decreasing unemployment rate, which has caused employers to compete for scarce labour. Workers may be in a better position to negotiate permanent (that is, ongoing or open-ended) contracts in the current economy. It is also possible, as employees report their status themselves, that in better economic times individuals' responses reflect greater optimism about their continued employment.

Rather than contingent work, it may be more useful for us to focus our attention on the issue of alternative work arrangements in the USA. The BLS distinguishes these arrangements as separate from the contingent/non-contingent dichotomy. A worker may consider his or her employment arrangement to be alternative and, at the same time, either contingent or non-contingent. The four alternative classifications established by the BLS are the following:

1. *Independent contractors*: workers who were identified as independent contractors, independent consultants or freelance workers, whether they were self-employed or wage and salary workers.
2. *On-call workers*: workers who are called to work only as needed, although they can be scheduled to work for several days or weeks in a row.
3. *Temporary help agency workers*: workers who were paid by a temporary help agency, whether or not their job was temporary.
4. *Workers provided by contract firms*: workers who are employed by a company that provides them or their services to others under contract, and who are usually assigned to only one customer and usually work at the customer's worksite.

Table 7.1 summarizes the statistics from 1995 to 2001 for these alternative work arrangements in the USA. Independent contractors have the highest percentage of total employed of the four alternative arrangements. However, the proportion of employees classified as independent contractors fell slightly across the time period, while the other three categories remained relatively unchanged.[11]

Workers in alternative employment arrangements may or may not consider themselves contingent. Table 7.2 summarizes this relationship. Percentages vary across alternative arrangement categories. Table 7.2 shows that virtually all independent contractors consider their arrangements to be more permanent, similar to the proportions of traditional workers across the time period. Workers provided by contract firms only classified themselves as contingent approximately 17 per cent of the time in 2001. Temporary agency workers were twice as likely to have classified themselves as contingent in 1995, but in 2001 the percentage was closer to 50 per cent. The percentage of on-call workers and day labourers who considered themselves contingent decreased over the time period to one in four in 2001.

We now turn to a more in-depth examination of the demographics underlying alternative employment arrangements in the USA. We structure

*Table 7.1 Percentage of employed in alternative work arrangements in the USA*

| | 1995 | 1997 | 1999 | 2001 |
|---|---|---|---|---|
| Independent contractors | 6.7 | 6.7 | 6.3 | 6.4 |
| On-call workers and day labourers | 1.7 | 1.6 | 1.5 | 1.6 |
| Workers paid by temporary help agencies | 1.0 | 1.0 | 0.9 | 0.9 |
| Workers provided by contract firms | 0.5 | 0.6 | 0.6 | 0.5 |
| Total | 9.9 | 9.9 | 9.3 | 9.4 |

*Note:* While the CES (Current Employment Survey) probably overstates employment in the temporary help supply services sector (see note 9), the CPS (Current Population Survey) probably understates temporary agency employment (Houseman, 1999). The CPS counts workers whose main jobs are in the temporary help industry. Furthermore, some respondents to the CPS may have answered incorrectly that the client firm was their employer, rather than the temporary agency. The contingent and alternative survey is a supplement to the CPS.

*Table 7.2 Percentage of alternative/traditional workers classifying themselves as contingent*

| Arrangement | 1995 | 1997 | 1999 | 2001 |
|---|---|---|---|---|
| Independent contractors | 3.8 | 3.5 | 2.9 | 4.1 |
| On-call workers and day labourers | 38.1 | 26.7 | 28.0 | 24.6 |
| Temporary help agency workers | 66.5 | 56.8 | 55.9 | 55.4 |
| Workers provided by contract firms | 19.8 | 16.7 | 20.2 | 17.1 |
| Traditional workers | 3.6 | 3.4 | 3.2 | 2.9 |

the discussion by first discussing the demand for flexible workers in terms of occupation and industry categories in which the employment occurs. We then present a more detailed examination of the supply of alternative workers in terms of their underlying demographic characteristics. We also discuss particulars of the employment relationship itself in terms of status (full-time or part-time), wages and benefits, and workers' preferences regarding their employment arrangements.

## The Demand for Contingent and Alternative Labour

### Occupation

Table 7.3 summarizes employment in the various occupational categories for workers in alternative and traditional arrangements. The highest percentage of traditional workers in 2001 was in the occupational categories

*Table 7.3 Occupational categories for workers in alternative and traditional arrangements, 1995 and 2001 (%)*

| Occupation | Independent contractors | | On-call workers and day labourers | | Temporary help agency workers | | Workers provided by contract firms | | Workers with traditional arrangements | |
|---|---|---|---|---|---|---|---|---|---|---|
| | 1995 | 2001 | 1995 | 2001 | 1995 | 2001 | 1995 | 2001 | 1995 | 2001 |
| Executive, administrative & managerial | 18.6 | 19.4 | 2.9 | 5.5 | 6.5 | 6.7 | 5.7 | 13.1 | 13.6 | 15.1 |
| Professional speciality | 16.3 | 16.8 | 20.9 | 25.9 | 8.3 | 10.4 | 25.6 | 25.4 | 14.7 | 16.0 |
| Technicians & related support | 1.1 | 1.2 | 1.5 | 4.2 | 3.7 | 6.5 | 6.9 | 9.1 | 3.4 | 3.5 |
| Sales occupations | 18.8 | 15.6 | 6.0 | 6.6 | 2.6 | 7.7 | 3.2 | 3.1 | 11.7 | 12.0 |
| Administrative support, including clerical | 3.8 | 3.9 | 9.5 | 8.7 | 30.1 | 29.5 | 4.8 | 4.4 | 16.0 | 14.8 |
| Service occupations | 10.6 | 10.7 | 19.7 | 18.8 | 9.0 | 7.6 | 27.8 | 18.6 | 13.6 | 13.3 |
| Precision production, craft & repair | 19.2 | 19.5 | 14.3 | 13.0 | 5.6 | 7.5 | 14.6 | 19.3 | 10.1 | 10.3 |
| Operators, fabricators & labourers | 6.5 | 7.3 | 20.5 | 15.0 | 33.2 | 23.2 | 10.4 | 6.3 | 14.6 | 13.3 |
| Farmers, forestry & fishing | 5.1 | 5.6 | 4.7 | 2.2 | 1.0 | 0.9 | 0.9 | 0.7 | 2.4 | 1.8 |

of professional specialty, administrative support, and executive/administrative/managerial occupations. The distribution of employment for traditional workers across occupational categories remained relatively stable from 1995 to 2001.

The percentage distributions across occupational categories showed much more variability within each of the alternative arrangements. For independent contractors, the occupational category with the highest percentage in 1995 was precision production/craft/repair. By 2001, this category led by only 0.1 per cent over the second-ranked executive/administrative/managerial category which increased by 0.8 per cent to 19.4 per cent. One other category showing noticeable change from 1995 to 2001 was sales, down 3.2 per cent over the period.

In the on-call worker and day labourer category, professional specialty reflected the largest proportion over the time period. In 2001, the percentage was 25.9, up 5 per cent from 1995. Service occupations, with the second-highest percentage in 2001 at 18.8 per cent, was down 0.9 per cent from 1995. Other notable increases included a 2.6 per cent increase in the executive/administrative/managerial category and a 2.7 per cent increase in the technician/related support category. A significant decrease occurred in the operator/fabricator/labourer category, 5.5 per cent.

Temporary help agency workers reflected by far their largest percentages in the administrative support and operator/fabricator/labourer categories. The percentage of temporary agency workers classified in the administrative support category was 29.5 per cent in 2001, down 0.6 per cent from 1995. The operator/fabricator/labourer category percentage in 2001 was 23.2 per cent, down 10 per cent from 1995. Several categories showed relatively large proportional gains during the time period, including professional specialty, technicians, and sales occupations.

Finally, for the alternative arrangement of workers provided by contract firms, the occupation with the highest percentage in 2001 was professional specialty at 25.4 per cent, little changed from 1995. The previously top-ranked category of service occupations fell to second place with 18.6 per cent, down a significant 9.2 per cent. The executive/administrative/managerial category gained 7.4 per cent from 1995 to 2001, with 13.1 per cent of contract firm workers in 2001.

**Industry**

Referring to Table 7.4, by industry category the distribution of workers with traditional arrangements changed little between 1995 and 2001. The largest percentage of traditional workers was employed in the services industry, at 36.3 per cent in 2001 (up 1.9 per cent from 1995). Wholesale/retail trade had the second-highest proportion, 21.3 per cent in 2001,

*Table 7.4 Workers with alternative and traditional arrangements, by industry category, 1995 and 2001 (%)*

| Industry | Independent contractors | | On-call workers and day labourers | | Temporary help agency workers | | Workers provided by contract firms | | Workers with traditional arrangements | |
|---|---|---|---|---|---|---|---|---|---|---|
| | 1995 | 2001 | 1995 | 2001 | 1995 | 2001 | 1995 | 2001 | 1995 | 2001 |
| Agriculture | 5.0 | 5.7 | 4.4 | 2.1 | 0.4 | 0.5 | 0.3 | 0.5 | 2.4 | 1.8 |
| Mining | 0.2 | 0.3 | 0.5 | 0.4 | 0.2 | 0.9 | 2.4 | 1.1 | 0.6 | 0.4 |
| Construction | 21.2 | 19.6 | 15.2 | 10.1 | 2.8 | 2.9 | 8.4 | 5.8 | 4.4 | 5.4 |
| Manufacturing | 5.0 | 3.7 | 5.9 | 5.3 | 33.4 | 21.1 | 17.6 | 20.8 | 17.9 | 15.7 |
| Transport and public utilities | 5.0 | 5.6 | 8.7 | 9.7 | 7.6 | 7.3 | 13.4 | 6.4 | 7.2 | 7.2 |
| Wholesale/retail trade | 13.2 | 11.5 | 13.8 | 14.1 | 8.1 | 6.5 | 6.0 | 6.2 | 21.4 | 21.3 |
| Finance, insurance, and real estate | 9.6 | 9.2 | 1.8 | 2.4 | 7.5 | 6.6 | 6.9 | 4.1 | 6.4 | 6.9 |
| Services | 40.6 | 44.4 | 46.0 | 50.5 | 38.7 | 45.5 | 32.3 | 36.8 | 34.4 | 36.3 |
| Public administration | 0.3 | 0.1 | 3.3 | 5.3 | 1.2 | 0.0 | 12.6 | 11.9 | 5.4 | 4.9 |

followed by manufacturing at 15.7 per cent (down 2.2 per cent from 1995). No other industry category showed a percentage change of more than 1 per cent for workers in traditional arrangements.

Independent contractors were most likely to be employed in the services industry, with a 44.4 per cent share in 2001 (up 3.8 per cent from 1995). The industry with the second-highest proportion of independent contractors was construction, with 19.6 per cent in 2001, down 1.6 per cent from 1995. The distribution of independent contractors among the remaining industry categories remained relatively constant from 1995 to 2001.

On-call and day labourers were predominantly classified in the services industry as well, with 50.5 per cent in 2001. This reflected a 4.5 per cent increase from 1995. Wholesale/retail trade had the second-highest proportion at 14.1 per cent, up 0.3 per cent from 1995. A major percentage change occurred in the construction industry, with a net decrease of 5.1 per cent from 1995 to 2001. Other notable changes occurred in agriculture (down 2.3 per cent) and public administration (up 2 per cent).

Temporary help agency workers were most likely to be working in the services industry, with 45.5 per cent in 2001 (up 6.8 per cent), or in the manufacturing industry, with 21.1 per cent (down 12.3 per cent from 1995). Noticeable percentage decreases over the 1995 to 2001 time period occurred in wholesale/retail trade (down 1.6 per cent) and in public administration, which went from a 1.2 per cent share to virtually zero.

Workers provided by contract firms were much more likely to be employed in the services industry, with 36.8 per cent in 2001, which was up 4.5 per cent from 1995. Manufacturing held the second-highest percentage, 20.8 per cent in 2001 (up 3.2 per cent). Two industries with notable decreases from 1995 to 2001 were construction (down 2.6 per cent) and transport and utilities (down 7 per cent).

## The Supply of Contingent and Alternative Labour

### Gender

Table 7.5 shows the percentage distribution of alternative and traditional workers by selected characteristics. While almost half of traditional workers are female, females are disproportionately underrepresented in independent contracting and contract worker arrangements. Temporary help agency workers are more likely to be female than their traditional counterparts.

### Race

Also as demonstrated in Table 7.5, whites hold the vast majority of traditional positions (83.8 per cent in 2001), while the two most dominant

*Table 7.5 Selected characteristics of alternative workers, 1995 and 2001 (%)*

| Characteristic | Independent contractors | | On-call workers and day labourers | | Temporary help agency workers | | Workers provided by contract firms | | Workers with traditional arrangements | |
|---|---|---|---|---|---|---|---|---|---|---|
| | 1995 | 2001 | 1995 | 2001 | 1995 | 2001 | 1995 | 2001 | 1995 | 2001 |
| Female | 32.7 | 35.5 | 49.9 | 46.9 | 52.8 | 58.9 | 28.5 | 29.4 | 47.2 | 47.8 |
| White | 92.3 | 88.3 | 84.0 | 83.6 | 72.7 | 68.4 | 83.0 | 76.8 | 85.1 | 83.8 |
| Black | 5.0 | 7.0 | 11.0 | 13.3 | 21.8 | 25.4 | 11.7 | 14.9 | 10.9 | 11.4 |
| Hispanic | 5.2 | 7.2 | 12.5 | 11.1 | 11.3 | 17.6 | 8.4 | 10.4 | 8.6 | 11.0 |
| Part-time | 25.6 | 24.8 | 54.6 | 47.4 | 20.5 | 20.8 | 16.0 | 10.3 | 18.3 | 16.8 |

minority groups, blacks and Hispanics, hold about 11 per cent each of traditional employment.[12]

Blacks and Hispanics are disproportionately underrepresented in independent contracting, while they are overrepresented in temporary help agency employment. Blacks especially are more likely to be temps than their traditional counterparts, as 25.4 per cent of temps were black in 2001 (up 3.6 per cent from 1995).

**Part-time status**

Part-time status of alternative and traditional workers is also included in Table 7.5. With the exception of contract workers, those in alternative arrangements tend to work part-time more so than traditional workers. On-call workers are as likely to be employed part-time as full-time, of course because of the nature of on-call work or being called in as needed.

**Age**

Workers in traditional arrangements are most concentrated in the 35–44 age range. In 2001, 27.2 per cent of traditional workers fell into this age category, little changed from 1995. We have observed, however, a slight increase in the age of traditional workers, as the 25–34 age group decreased by 3.5 per cent to 22.9 per cent in 2001, while the 45–54 age group increased by 2.8 per cent over the same time period, to 22 per cent in 2001.

Independent contractors tend to reflect a somewhat higher age distribution than that of traditional workers. In 2001, 29 per cent of independent contractors fell into the 35–44 age group (down 1.8 per cent from 1995), and 28.1 per cent were aged 45–54 (up 2.8 per cent from 1995). On-call workers and day labourers were most likely to be aged 35–44 in 2001, with 25.7 per cent of on-call workers falling into that age group. On-call workers have reflected an increase in age from 1995, when the highest proportion (24.6 per cent) was in the 25–34 age group.

In general, temporary help agency workers tend to be younger than traditional workers. In 2001, the largest proportion, 26.5 per cent, of temps were 25 to 34 years of age. However, this age bracket reflected a decrease of 7.6 per cent from 1995. Interestingly, during the same time period, the combined age groups of 35–64 increased by 10 per cent from 1995 to 2001, reflecting an increase in the number of older temporary workers. In 2001, 28.9 per cent of contract workers were in the 35–44 age bracket, showing an ageing of this alternative category as well. Further reflecting this ageing, in 1995, 39 per cent of contract workers were aged 25–34, compared to 23.3 per cent in this age category in 2001. The proportion of contract workers in the 45–54 age bracket increased a substantial 22.1 per cent from 1995 to 2001, to 23.9 per cent.

**Education**

Regarding the education level of the workforce, traditional workers were slightly more likely to have at least a bachelor's degree (32 per cent) in 2001, up from 28.9 per cent in 1995. This was followed closely by traditional workers with a high school degree (30.6 per cent, down from 32.5 per cent in 1995) and workers with at least some college credit (28.6 per cent, down slightly from 29 per cent in 1995). Compared to traditional workers, a greater relative proportion of independent contractors had college degrees: 34 per cent in 2001 (up 0.3 per cent from 1995). The largest percentage of on-call workers and temporary help agency workers in 2001 had some college credit in 2001 (35 per cent and 36.5 per cent, respectively), reflecting a slightly lower overall education level than traditional workers'. Contract workers reflected the highest average educational attainment, with 41.7 per cent holding a bachelor's degree in 2001, up a substantial 11.1 per cent from 1995.

**Benefits**

Table 7.6 summarizes benefits coverage for alternative workers included in the BLS surveys of 1995 and 2001. The issue of benefits is particularly important from the US perspective. Employer provision of certain benefits is mandatory (for example, workers' compensation for on-the-job injuries, unemployment insurance, social security or Old Age, Survivors and Disability Insurance) but is often based on an 'hours worked' test which can leave out flexible workers. Other benefits, notably health insurance and private pensions, are provided only at the employer's discretion, and almost always explicitly exclude flexible workers. Indeed, the ability to avoid these benefit costs is often cited as one of the major cost advantages of hiring flexible workers.

In 2001, 83.1 per cent of traditional workers had some type of health insurance coverage, little changed from 1995. Independent contractors and contract firm workers had the highest proportion of individuals with benefits coverage of the alternative arrangements in 2001. However, note that independent contractors' benefits are not provided by companies employing their services. Independent contractors are considered by law to be self-employed. Therefore they are not eligible for benefits from client companies because they are not considered to be employees. Some 52 per cent of contract workers received their benefits through their employers in 2001, a percentage similar to that of traditional workers. At the other end of the spectrum, temporary help agency workers have the lowest proportion of benefits coverage, at 48.1 per cent in 2001, and the number being covered by their employers is extremely low (10.7 per cent in 2001). Temporary agencies may offer benefits to their temporary workers, but a relatively high threshold of hours worked precludes many workers from

*Table 7.6 Benefits and pension coverage for alternative workers, 1995 and 2001 (%)*

| Employment arrangement | Per cent eligible for health insurance | | Employer-provided health insurance | | Per cent eligible for pension plan | | Included in pension plan | |
|---|---|---|---|---|---|---|---|---|
| | 1995 | 2001 | 1995 | 2001 | 1995 | 2001 | 1995 | 2001 |
| Independent contractors | 72.6 | 72.5 | NA | NA | * | 3.5 | 2.5 | 2.3 |
| On-call workers and day labourers | 63.5 | 70.0 | 16.9 | 29.8 | 25.3 | 36.9 | 18.6 | 31.3 |
| Temporary help agency workers | 44.9 | 48.1 | 5.7 | 10.7 | 7.0 | 13.3 | 2.5 | 7.6 |
| Workers provided by contract firms | 69.9 | 80.1 | 42.5 | 52.1 | 36.0 | 55.7 | 28.5 | 47.7 |
| Workers with traditional arrangements | 82.7 | 83.1 | 57.2 | 58.3 | 56.0 | 54.5 | 49.0 | 49.5 |

*Notes:*
NA: Not applicable.
* This information was not available. However, it was reported that 35.1 per cent of independent contractors are covered by some kind of retirement, and that 32.6 per cent have an individual IRA (Individual Retirement Account) or Keogh retirement account on their own (Hipple and Stewart, 1996).

taking advantage of such benefits. However, the data do show that temporary help agency workers are increasingly being covered by their employers from 1995 to 2001. On-call workers and contract workers are also increasingly being covered by their employers.

Pension plans are another non-mandatory benefit provided by many employers.[13] As with benefits coverage, flexible workers also have consistently lower proportions of workers covered by pension plans than their traditional counterparts (see Table 7.6).[14] However, it appears that alternative workers are increasingly eligible for inclusion in an employer-provided pension plan. For those alternative workers eligible, it appears from the data that (with the exception of temporary help agency workers) the majority of eligible workers take advantage of the pension benefits. It is interesting to note that an extremely low percentage of independent contractors are eligible for employer-sponsored pension plans (3.5 per cent in 2001). Again, independent contractors are not considered to be employees, as they are self-employed. However, they may sometimes be included in pension plans of organizations.

**Wages**

Table 7.7 reflects the median weekly earnings of alternative workers in 2001, as well as the overall percentage change from 1995 for the various demographic categories of workers.[15] Wage data, as reported in the BLS supplemental surveys, are absolute numbers; that is, they are not adjusted for inflation. As a comparison point, the rate of inflation (using the Consumer Price Index) for the 1995 to 2001 period was 17 per cent. The increase in overall wages for all categories of workers outpaced inflation for the time period.[16]

*Table 7.7 Median weekly wages of full-time alternative workers, by sex and race, 2001, and percentage change from 1995*

| | Independent contractors | | On-call workers and day labourers | | Temporary help agency workers | | Workers provided by contract firms | |
|---|---|---|---|---|---|---|---|---|
| | 2001 ($) | % change from 1995 | 2001 ($) | % change from 1995 | 2001 ($) | % change from 1995 | 2001 ($) | % change from 1995 |
| Overall | 644 | 24.3 | 517 | 33.9 | 396 | 36.6 | 790 | 54.3 |
| Male | 732 | 24.1 | 596 | 37.6 | 435 | 57.0 | 880 | 56.6 |
| Female | 489 | 35.5 | 380 | 42.3 | 367 | 23.6 | 530 | 32.8 |
| White | 659 | 25.0 | 536 | 28.8 | 416 | 39.6 | 801 | 51.1 |
| Black | 519 | 38.4 | 477 | 70.4 | 351 | 34.5 | * | * |
| Hispanic | 473 | 27.8 | 332 | 18.1 | 310 | 30.1 | * | * |

*Note:* * Too few observations to make statistically reliable estimate.

Table 7.7 highlights the disparities among the categories of alternative work arrangements in terms of wages, most likely due to overall differences in education and experience levels. Independent contractors and contract firm workers make more than those workers in on-call and temporary agency arrangements. Temporary help agency workers tend to earn the lowest average wages of all alternative arrangements.

From 1995 to 2001, workers in alternative arrangements realized significant percentage wage gains overall. In particular, workers provided by contract firms realized a remarkable 54.3 per cent gain in wages over the time period. In all alternative categories except for temporary agency work, females enjoyed greater percentage increases in wages as compared to males in the same alternative arrangements. However, females' absolute wage levels remained below their male counterparts' wages.

While whites continued to have higher median wages in 2001 than blacks and Hispanics, blacks and Hispanics made substantial wage gains during the time period. Blacks who classified themselves as independent contractors gained 38.4 per cent in wages. Blacks involved in on-call/day labour realized a 70.4 percentage gain from 1995 to 2001.

**Preference for type of work arrangement**

As shown in Table 7.8, a substantially greater percentage of temporary workers preferred their alternative status in 2001 as compared to 1995. It is evident that the independent contractors overwhelmingly prefer their alternative arrangement. Half of on-call workers preferred their alternative status in 2001, up from 35.8 per cent in 1995.

*Table 7.8 Workers with alternative arrangements who prefer alternative work (%)*

| | Independent contractors | On-call workers and day labourers | Temporary help agency workers |
|---|---|---|---|
| 1995 | 82.5 | 35.8 | 26.6 |
| 2001 | 83.4 | 49.1 | 44.5 |

*Note:* Data were not provided for workers provided by contract firms.

## CONCLUDING REMARKS

What stands out when comparing the USA to other world developed economies is the lack of regulation of the flexible employment arrangement in the USA, as well as the weakly regulated employment relationship in general.

However, increasingly case law that places limitations on 'at-will' employment may be a reason for employers to move towards greater usage of flexible employment arrangements to avoid legal difficulties (Autor, 2000).

The use of contingent and alternative employment has been relatively steady from 1995 on. However, we do not yet have adequate longitudinal data regarding flexible employment relationships to assess any linkages with general economic conditions such as unemployment. We do see some evidence in the BLS contingent and alternative employment data that flexible employment affects various groups differently, however. For example, more highly paid independent contractors tend to be higher education white males, while less well paid temporary agency employment arrangements are dominated by younger minority females. Thus the flexible labour market seems to be segregated and differentially benefits labour market sub-groups. Whether this segregation can be attributed to factors such as education and experience levels, or instead may point to some other less desirable causes such as discrimination, can not yet be determined. Future research will need to address this issue.

The use of contingent labour spans both highly skilled and unskilled labour. In the USA, the fastest growth in agency-managed temporary employment is occurring in professional and technical occupations (American Staffing Association, 1999). Externalization of employment contracts, however, proceeds with varying speed and seems to take different forms not only within the structures of production but through changing legal systems, traditions and institutional frameworks in each country (Appay, 1998; Thaler-Carter, 1999). Thus the use of contingent and alternative labour may be related to long-lasting changes in the functioning of the labour market, which may have considerable consequences for both individuals and organizations.

Research into the causes and consequences of flexible employment is sparse. Many different explanations have been suggested regarding the changing nature of contingent and alternative employment. Changes in the use of contingent labour may be a result of economic cycles (such as fluctuations in staffing needs). Such changes in the use of flexible work may be found in changing employer strategies relating to the permanent workforce, such as the focus on core competencies (Glasgow, 1998; Lepak and Snell, 1999) and the need to reduce labour costs (Clinton, 1997; Houseman, 1999). Use of flexible arrangements may allow organizations to screen workers for permanent positions with reduced liability (Lee, 1996). Its availability may satisfy the needs of individual workers such that there is increasing demand for contingent and alternative employment from employees (Feldman *et al.*, 1994).

The new 'global' economy with its accompanying increased competition has been helped along by increases in technology that facilitate the quick and simple exchange of information (the Internet, e-mail). Firms must increasingly respond to increased global competition within the new economy by becoming 'lean and mean' with 'just-in-time' inventory management and flexible labour forces.

What is most interesting at this point is to examine the vastly different nature of employment that has emerged over the past decade or so in the US labour market (and related global markets). Two examples of a changed labour market are the concepts of the 'portfolio worker' and the 'free agent'. The portfolio worker 'purposely seeks out a variety of assignments to expand skills and knowledge . . . building a valuable portfolio of employment experiences in diverse situations' (Brogan, 1999). Such portfolio workers tend to be independent professionals, often employed within the staffing services sector. The free agent is a 'highly skilled worker who prefers working independently on projects for a variety of clients' (Workplace Visions, 2000). Information technology and the Internet have encouraged many workers to become free agents and portfolio workers. Daniel Pink of Fast Company estimates that more than 16 per cent of the American workforce should be considered free agents. So-called 'free agent agencies' are also proliferating, which may offer on-line databases of job listings, group-rate insurance and retirement plans, back office administrative and benefits services, and even help with pursuing clients who have not paid their bills (Workplace Visions, 2000).

Furthermore, the changing role of electronic commerce and the Internet has affected the ability of individuals to market their skills as independents in the market-place for labour. Improved information and better matching capabilities (of employee to employer) are affecting the manner in which organizations and individuals do business. The proliferation of various contingent and alternative staffing arrangements may serve as a mechanism to improve the efficiency of labour markets within the new global economy.

SkillsVillage.com, for example, is an e-market-place established in 1999 to facilitate the matching of 'enterprise hiring managers and information technology contractors to help match the right candidate with the right projects' (*Business Wire*, 1999). Many free agents work in this type of employment arrangement because they can earn more money working for a number of clients, and can obtain more flexibility in terms of time and work.

In sum, we observe in the USA a healthy economy with very low unemployment accompanied by labour force growth. The percentage of workers considering themselves to be in contingent or alternative employment arrangements has been slightly decreasing in the USA as a percentage of overall employment since 1995. Contingent and alternative work remains a small part of the US labour market, but it may play an important role in allowing organizations to improve their labour force flexibility to meet business or workload fluctuations (Houseman, 1999; *SHRM Alternative Staffing Survey*, 1998). Furthermore, some say the reduction in the unemployment rate below what has historically been considered the 'natural' rate of unemployment (that is, 5 to 6 per cent) is due to the expansion of the staffing services industry in the USA (Katz and Krueger, 1999). Temporary work may even act as a bridge to permanent employment for many workers (Brogan, 2000) and may also reduce labour market bottlenecks and improve labour market efficiency by matching employers and employees (Katz and Krueger, 1999).

So where is the nature of the labour force heading? Will we see a complete marketization of employment contracts in the future? Surely a need will remain for permanent workers in many situations. However, the nature of contingent and alternative employment has changed so rapidly in recent years that we must anticipate further changes.

## NOTES

1. Unless otherwise noted, labour force statistics were obtained from the US Department of Labor, Bureau of Labor Statistics.
2. The employment population ratio is calculated as 100 multiplied by (number employed in demographic group/number in population of corresponding demographic group).
3. These numbers do not add up to 100 per cent, as some Hispanics are also classified as either white or black owing to multi-ethnic origin. Other ethnicities are present in the labour force, but they comprise a small percentage, so they are not reported here.
4. In this section, the term *worker* will include both employees and independent contractors, while the term *employee* will be used to designate only workers categorized as employees.
5. See *Pugh* v. *See's Candies* (1981), cited in Autor (2000).
6. Of course, markets will respond to increased regulation of alternative work arrangements by designing other work arrangements for which workers will also seek regulation. It may occur to legislators and courts that, rather than going through the cycle again, it may be simpler to change what is a major impetus to alternative work arrangements, the legal impediments to employment-at-will.
7. See for example, *Vizcaino* v. *Microsoft, Corp*., 120 F.3d 1006, 1010–13 (9th Cir. 1997) where workers who were classified as independent contractors claimed that, under the Employee Retirement and Income Security Act (ERISA), they were entitled to the same savings and stock option benefits received by employees.
8. According to Houseman (1999), a 1989 Industry Wage Survey estimated that permanent, full-time staff comprised 3.2 per cent of employment in the Help Supply Services Industry.
9. Furthermore, data from the CES may overstate employment in the temporary help supply services sector (Houseman, 1999). The CES counts jobs in the industry. Individuals who are registered with more than one temporary agency would show up more than once in the CES if they worked on two or more jobs for those agencies during the survey week.
10. Wage and salary workers are included even if they have already held the job for more

than one year and expect to hold the job for at least an additional year. The self-employed and independent contractors are included if they expect their employment to last for an additional year or less and they have been self-employed or independent contractors for one year or less.
11. All data in this section, unless otherwise noted, were obtained from the BLS Contingent and Alternative Employment Arrangements surveys for 1995, 1997, 1999 and 2001.
12. The percentage totals for race do not add up to 100 per cent because Hispanics are also included in both the white and black population groups in some cases, most likely owing to the mixed-race background of some respondents.
13. Social Security, a legally mandated benefit, also provides retirement benefits. (This is funded by a tax of equal amount, currently 7.65 per cent, on both the employee and the employer.) However, the level of benefits through this programme is rarely enough for a retiree to live on. Therefore individuals usually supplement their Social Security income, if possible, through employer-sponsored pension plans and tax-deferred individual retirement accounts.
14. Source of 1995 data is Hipple and Stewart (1996).
15. Source of 1995 data is Hipple and Stewart (1996).
16. Earnings data for workers with traditional arrangements were not collected in the 2001 survey. As a reference point, however, traditional workers in 1995 had median weekly earnings of $480, and by 1999 had increased to $540, a percentage increase of 12.5 per cent.

# REFERENCES


American Staffing Association (1999) 'Various statistics' (*http://www.natss.org/staffstats*).

Appay, B. (1998) 'Economic Concentration and the Externalization of Labour', *Economic and Industrial Democracy*, 19, London: Sage, pp. 161–84.

Autor, D.H. (2000) 'Outsourcing at Will: Unjust Dismissal Doctrine and the Growth of Temporary Help Employment', mimeo, MIT.

Barker, K. and K. Christensen (eds) (1998) *Contingent Work: American Employment Relations in Transition*, Ithaca, NY: ILR/Cornell University Press.

Belous, R. (1989) *The Contingent Economy: The Growth of the Temporary, Part-Time and Subcontracted Workforce*, Washington, DC: National Planning Association.

Brogan, T.W. (1999) 'Annual Analysis' (*http://www.staffingtoday.net/staffstats/analysis.00.htm*).

Brogan, T.W. (2000) 'Thriving in a Dwindling Pool of Available Workers', *American Staffing Association's Annual Analysis of the Staffing Industry* (*http://www.staffingtoday.net*).

Bureau of Labor Statistics (2002) (*http://www.bls.gov*).

Clinton, A. (1997) 'Flexible labor: Restructuring the American workforce'. *Monthly Labor Review*, August, 3–27.

Cobble, D.S. and L.F. Vosko (2000) 'Historical Perspectives on Representing Nonstandard Workers', in F. Carre, L.G. Ferber and S.A. Herzenberg (eds), *Nonstandard Work: The Nature and Challenges of Changing Employment Relations*, Champaign, IL: Industrial Relations Research Association, pp. 291–312.

Dertouzos, J.N. and L.A. Karoly (2000) 'Labor-Market Responses to Employer Liability', Rand Corporation Document R-3989-ICJ, cited in Autor (2000).

Feldman, D., H. Doerpinghaus and W. Turnley (1994) 'Managing Temporary Workers: A Permanent HRM Challenge', *Organizational Dynamics*, 23, 46–63.
Freedman, A. (1985) *The New Look in Wage Policy and Employment Relations*, Conference Board Report no. 865, New York: The Conference Board.
Fullerton, H.N. (1999) 'Labor Force Projections to 2008: Steady Growth and Changing Composition', *Monthly Labor Review*, November, 19–32.
Glasgow, K.M. (1998) 'A Strategic Model of Temporary Staffing', doctoral dissertation, Texas A&M University.
Gonos, G. (1998) 'The Interaction between Market Incentives and Government Actions', in K. Barker, and K. Christensen (eds), *Contingent Work: American Employment Relations in Transition*, Ithaca, NY: ILR/Cornell University Press, pp.170–94.
Hatch, J. and A. Clinton (2000) 'Job Growth in the 1990s: A Retrospective'. *Monthly Labor Review*, December, 3–18.
Hipple, S. and J. Stewart (1996) 'Earnings and Benefits of Workers in Alternative Work Arrangements', *Monthly Labor Review*, October (10), 46–54.
Hofstede, G. (1980) 'Motivation, Leadership, and Organization: Do American Theories Apply Abroad?', *Organization Dynamics*, Summer, 50.
Houseman, S.N. (1999) 'Future Work: Trends and Challenges for Work in the 21st Century' (*http://www.dol.gov/dol/asp/public/futurework/conference/staffing/staffing*).
Jung, D.J. (1997) 'Jury Verdicts in Wrongful Termination Cases', mimeo, Public Law Research Institute, University of California Hastings College of the Law.
Katz, L.F. and A.B. Krueger (1999) 'The High-pressure U.S. Labor Market of the 1990s', working paper #416, Princeton University, Industrial Relations Section.
Kochan, T.A. (1999) 'Jump-Starting a New Debate: How to Update Employment and Labor Policies for the 21st Century Workforce and Economy', *Perspectives on Work*, 3(9), 12–17, Industrial Relations Research Association, Madison, WI.
Kunda, G., S.R. Barley and J. Evans (1999) 'Why Do Contractors Contract? The Theory and Reality of High-End Contingent Labor', working paper, Center for Work Technology and Organisation, Department of Industrial Engineering and Engineering Management, Stanford University, April.
Lee, D.R. (1996) 'Why is Flexible Employment Increasing?', *Journal of Labor Research*, XVII(4), Fall, 555–66.
Lepak, D.P. and S.A. Snell (1999) 'The Human Resource Architecture: Toward a Theory of Human Capital Allocation and Development', *Academy of Management Review*, 24, 31–48.
Micco, L. (1999) 'Employment in the 21st Century', *Bulletin to Management*, 25 November, Bureau of National Affairs, Washington, DC, pp. S1–S4.
Polivka, A.E. and T. Nardone (1989) 'On the Definition of Contingent Work', *Monthly Labor Review*, December, 9–16.
*Report on the American Workforce* (1999) US Department of Labor.
*SHRM Alternative Staffing Survey* (1998) Society for Human Resource Management, Alexandria, VA.
'SkillsVillage.com Established to Pioneer First E-Marketplace for IT Contingent Workforce', *Business Wire*, 3 August 1999.
Thaler-Carter, R.E. (1999) 'Euro-temping', *HR Magazine,* June, 122–8.
*Workplace Visions* (2000) 'Free Agents and the HR Profession', 2, 2–3.

# 8. Contingent employment in the Netherlands

**Bas Koene, Ferrie Pot and Jaap Paauwe**

## INTRODUCTION

This chapter examines the development of contingent employment in the Netherlands. Contingent employment is defined as any employment relationship that, within a limited period, can be terminated by the user organization without costs. In this definition, contingent employment includes agency workers, workers with limited duration contracts, on-call workers and self-employed that are hired by the work organization. The development of contingent employment in the Netherlands is interesting for several reasons. First, contingent employment in the Netherlands has a relatively long (legal) history. It was first legalized in 1965 under the Labour Provision Act.[1] Secondly, the legal framework that has developed since then is the product of the cooperative effort of the Dutch government and the social partners and could be seen as the labour contract embodiment of the *polder model.* It has resulted in a quite innovative legislation governing contingent employment relationships in 1999, the Flexibility and Security Act. Thirdly, the market for contingent employment in the Netherlands grew significantly in the 1990s, resulting in a 4.5 per cent share in the Dutch labour market in 1999. Since 1999, this growth has stagnated.

This chapter starts with a general description of developments in the Dutch labour market. The growth of contingent employment appears to be one of the primary trends. Subsequently, we describe the Dutch legal and institutional context. It can be argued that the legal and institutional changes of the recent past have been a response to the growth of contingent employment over the past decade. In 1999, 60 per cent of employment agencies perceived these changes as reflecting a growing acceptance, emancipation and professionalization of the staffing industry in the Netherlands (de Klaver *et al.*, 2000, p. 83). The fourth section analyses the nature of contingent employment in detail by means of statistical evidence, while the final section reviews the developments and discusses the future of contingent employment in the Netherlands.

## GENERAL TRENDS IN THE DUTCH LABOUR MARKET

The development of the Dutch labour market in the last two decades can be characterized by four primary trends: decreasing unemployment, increasing female participation, a growing number of jobs and an increase in the share of atypical jobs. As most of the data are index figures or otherwise converted statistics, it is useful to start with some absolute figures about the size of the Dutch labour market. Table 8.1 shows a labour market with an extremely low unemployment rate.

*Table 8.1 Dutch labour market, 2000, basic statistics*

| | Male | Female | Total |
|---|---|---|---|
| Population 15–64 years (1999) | 5429000 | 5289000 | 10717000 |
| Labour force participation rate | 79% | 55% | 67% |
| Labour force | 4288000 | 2898000 | 7187000 |
| Employed | 4174000 | 2743000 | 6917000 |
| Unemployed | 114000 | 156000 | 270000 |
| Unemployment rate | 3% | 5% | 4% |

*Source:* Statistics Netherlands (CBS), labour force survey, 2002.

Figure 8.1 shows unemployment as a percentage of the Dutch labour force,[2] indicating that unemployment in the Netherlands reached its highest level in the early 1980s. Since then, unemployment has decreased steadily, apart from the brief rise in the 1992–4 period. Unemployment in the Netherlands is much lower than the European average, and near the current rate in the United States (Delsen, 2000).[3]

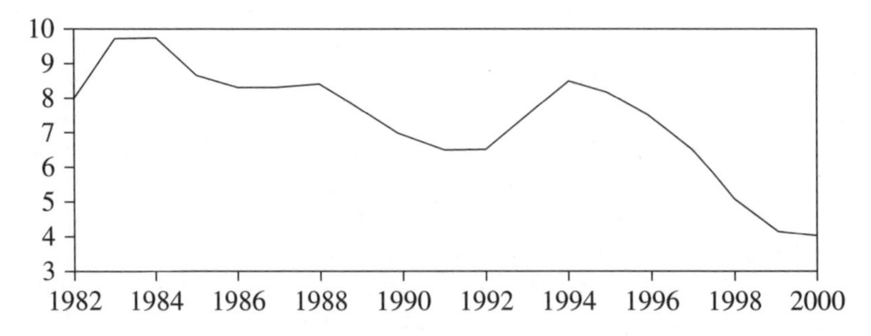


*Source:* Statistics Netherlands (CBS), labour force survey, 2000.

*Figure 8.1 Unemployment as a percentage of the labour force, 1982–2000*

The decrease in the unemployment rate may be due to an increase in employment or a decrease in participation. The increase in participation rates, particularly for women, shows that the fall in unemployment is primarily due to an increase in employment (see Figure 8.2). Altered perceptions on the societal role of women and subsequent changes in the Dutch tax regime and social security seem to be the underlying driving forces for this development. In 1990, the Dutch labour market participation was lower than the European average and far behind that of the USA and Japan. In 2001, labour market participation in the Netherlands had risen to 75 per cent, which is above the present European average (70 per cent) and the rate for Japan (73 per cent). The US rate is still somewhat higher (77 per cent) (Statistics Netherlands, 2001).

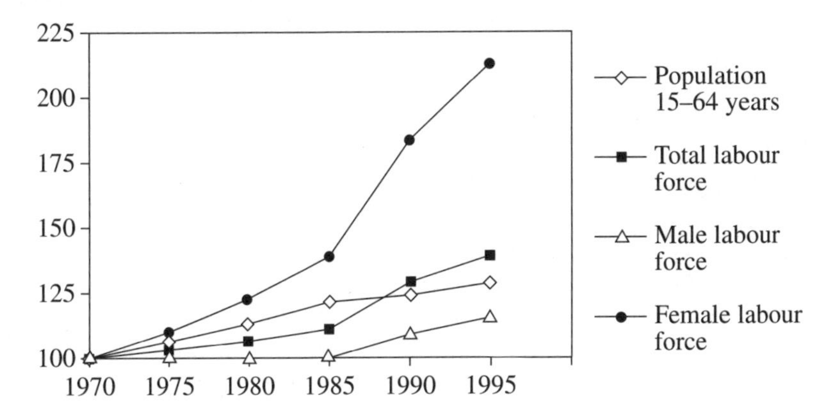


*Source:* Statistics Netherlands (SCP), 1998.

*Figure 8.2 The growth of the labour force, 1970–95*

The decrease in unemployment in times of growing working populations is, thus, explained by the growth of the number of jobs. Job growth in the Netherlands started in 1983 and has consistently been at a relatively high level. Visser and Hemerijck (1997) advance three explanations for this exceptional job growth in the Netherlands. First, based on a national agreement between labour unions and employer associations, the Wassenaar Agreement signed in 1982, wage increases have been moderate in recent decades. Second, the share of labour-intensive services, such as retailing, finance and communication, has grown at the cost of less labour-intensive manufacturing industries. Third, altered attitudes to work by employers and employees have resulted in a sharp increase in the use of part-time and temporary labour.

Job growth in the Netherlands has relied predominantly on the growth of part-time and contingent jobs. Only 15 per cent of the job growth can be attributed to the growth of full-time jobs. In contrast, part-time and contingent employment accounted for, respectively, 57 per cent and 28 per cent of total job growth.

The strong growth rate of part-time and contingent employment has changed the Dutch employment structure. Between 1970 and 1993, there was virtually no growth in full-time jobs in the Netherlands.[4] Over this period the number of part-time jobs almost tripled, from 615000 to 1648000 and the number of flexible jobs rose from 219000 to 533000. Around 12 per cent of current total employment is contingent employment. In 1988, the figure was 8 per cent. Part-time labour's share in total employment increased from 24 per cent in 1988 to 30 per cent in 1999.[5] The share of full-time employment based on an open-ended contract in total employment decreased from 68 per cent to 58 per cent.

## THE INSTITUTIONAL FRAMEWORK AND THE REGULATION OF EMPLOYMENT

The growth of contingent employment in general and agency work in particular evoked a reaction from Dutch policy makers. This section focuses on the way the regulation of contingent employment has changed in response to its growth in the last decade. The major changes in statutory law in the Netherlands were the Flexibility and Security Act (1999) and the WAADI Act (1998). To understand these new pieces of legislation, this section is divided into three parts. First, the regulation of the employment relationship prior to the enactment of both Acts is described. Second, attention is given to the process of change. Third, the outcomes of the change process, including the two new Acts and new collective bargaining agreements, are outlined.

### Regulation of the Employment Relationship before 1999

To understand the use of contingent and open-ended employment contracts, it is important to understand how the legal context influences the relative costs of each of them. The ease, in terms of legal costs and speed, with which contingent employment contracts can be terminated by the user organization differentiates them from open-ended contracts. In the following, we focus first on the costs of terminating open-ended contracts. After that the legal cost advantages of contingent employment arrangements (before 1999) are examined. It should be noted that changes in recent legislation have greatly affected both aspects. These legal changes are examined later in this chapter.

**Termination of the open-ended employment contract**

From an international viewpoint, Dutch law on dismissal protection has some unique features.[6] As a general principle, Dutch law requires that an employer may not dismiss any employee with an open-ended contract without previous permission from the Labour Office.[7] The Labour Office checks whether the employer has just cause for the dismissal.[8] During the authorization procedure, the employee must be paid the normal wages and can demand to be provided with work. In practice, the Labour Office rarely refuses permission. Only a small percentage of employees are successful in challenging the dismissal in the administrative procedure. In cases of collective dismissal, which concerns the dismissal of at least 20 workers within a three-month period, the requested permission was refused in only 1.4 per cent of the cases in the 1974–91 period (Havinga, 1994). In cases of individual dismissal, the threshold for the Labour Office to refuse permission is lower. In cases where individual dismissal was requested for economic reasons, which constituted around half of total requests, 7 per cent were refused in 1991. In cases where the dismissal request is based on other grounds, such as a troubled relationship between employer and employee, 14 per cent were refused (ibid.).

If the Labour Office grants permission for dismissal, the employer is not obliged to pay the employee any kind of compensation. The procedure may, therefore, bring important cost advantages to the employer. However, the procedure has fallen into disuse over the last decade because of the relatively long time that was required to take the procedure to a conclusion. Before 1999, the decision-making process lasted about six weeks in cases which were only formally contested and three to eight months in cases in which the employee opposed the dismissal with substantive legal arguments. Moreover, until the permit was obtained, notice to terminate employment was null and void. The period of notice therefore had to be added to the procedure.[9]

Owing to the lengthy procedure, employers have, since the early 1990s, increasingly evaded the Labour Office procedure and have formalized individual dismissals by means of a lawsuit at a District Court. In such cases, the court establishes a compensation fee in favour of the employee.[10] While in the early 1970s the involvement of the court was exceptional, in the early 1990s the courts passed judgment on more than 30 per cent of individual dismissal cases (OSA, 1995). With regard to collective dismissal, the Labour Office is still involved in almost all cases.

The dismissal procedure involving prior permission of the Labour Office has been extensively discussed in the 55 years of its existence. Nevertheless, the trade unions, the employer associations (especially representatives of the small and medium-sized enterprises) and the state have expressed their wish to retain the public procedure. For the trade unions the procedure provides control over dismissal; to the employers the procedure provides a potential decrease of dismissal costs; and, finally, to the state the procedure provides a check on the inflow of people to social security provisions. However, consensus exists that the procedure needs to be adjusted for certain cost-raising provisions. The recent Flexibility and Security Act (Flexicurity Act for short) which is discussed in detail below, incorporates such adjustments.

**Regulation of contingent employment**

The regulation of contingent employment in the Netherlands has been characterized as liberal, since statutory law contained few restrictions (for example, see Bakkenist Management Consultants, 1998). Before 1999, there were two important aspects of legislation influencing contingent employment relationships. First, there were provisions in the Dutch employment law with regard to limited duration contracts; second, the Temporary Work Act of 1965 regulated contingent employment through employment agencies.

The main provisions in the regulation of limited duration contracts before 1999 were the following. First, no reason was required for using a limited duration contract (could be specified in a collective bargaining agreement); second, no minimum and maximum duration was indicated, although this could be specified in a collective bargaining agreement (changed by the Flexicurity Act); third, by law, the contracts ended on expiry of the fixed term; fourth, conversion to an open-ended contract occurred if the contract was continued beyond the expiry of the fixed term (changed by the Flexicurity Act); fifth, a new contract for a limited duration could be offered after an interruption of one month. Immediate renewal would convert the contract into an open-ended contract, the brief interruption period allowing for unlimited renewal (changed by the Flexicurity Act).[11]

Beyond these provisions, the Temporary Work Act regulated the activities of employment agencies. (1) Temporary Work Agencies were subject to licensing (changed by the WAADI Act). (2) In some industries agency work was forbidden, notably ocean-shipping, professional goods traffic and construction (changed by the WAADI Act). (3) It was forbidden for a temporary work agency to provide services to workplaces hit by strikes. (4) The maximum duration that a hiring organization could employ an agency worker was six months (changed by the Flexibility and Security Act). (5) No objective reason for employing an agency worker needed to be given by the hiring organization. Furthermore (6) agency workers were brought within laws on social security, notably the Unemployment Act and the Sickness and Disability Act. The agency was liable to pay the social security contributions. Finally, (7) regulations written into other Acts, for example, the Equal Treatment Act, the Health and Safety Act or the Working Hours Act, applied equally to agency workers.

## Regulatory Reform: the Change Process

This section provides a description of the process of change that has led to the new regulations. To understand the processes of change, the section starts with a brief introduction of some aspects of the Dutch system of industrial relations, sometimes referred to as the Dutch *polder model*. Then the development of the Flexibility and Security Act is discussed as an example of the way this system of industrial relations produces legislation.

### The Dutch system of industrial relations

The Dutch system of industrial relations is driven by the needs of the same players as in most other countries: employers, employees and the state. The peculiarities of the Dutch system of industrial relations, however, reside in the institutions that govern the interplay between these different actors. The Dutch have created a system of checks and balances that contains socioeconomic policy development at all administrative levels, from central government down to the level of the individual organization with its management and employee representative bodies. Figure 8.3 provides a schematic overview of the formalized institutions at the national, industry and firm levels. Within the Dutch government, there are two ministries involved with labour market issues: the Ministry of Economic Affairs, which is traditionally more concerned about employers' interests, and the Ministry of Social Affairs and Employment, which has traditionally adopted more 'employee-friendly' viewpoints.

At the national level, two independent 'think-tanks' govern the interplay between employers and employees: the Socioeconomic Council (*Sociaal-Economische Raad*, SER) and the Foundation of Labour (*Stichting van de Arbeid*, StAr). Both bodies have an advisory position towards the government in the realm of socioeconomic policies and legislation. The SER emerged in 1950 and is tripartite by nature. The other body, the Foundation of Labour, is a private foundation, founded in 1945, and comprises the major unions and employer associations.

At the industry level, interaction between employers and employees is primarily aimed at formulating collective bargaining agreements. The state is not involved at this level. Some 83 per cent of Dutch workers are covered by

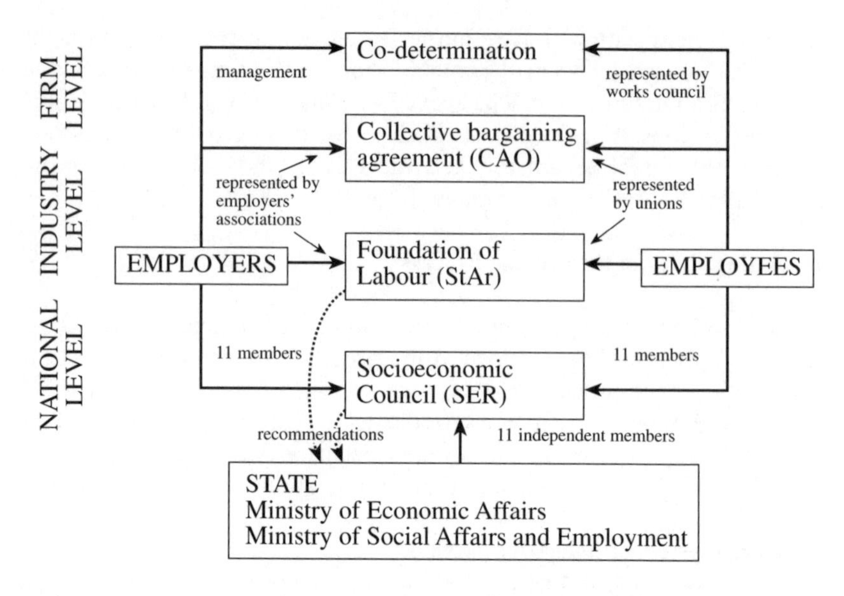


*Figure 8.3 Institutional context governing the Dutch labour market*

a collective agreement (Visser and Hemerijck, 1997). The large majority of firms negotiate these agreements jointly, with the help of an employer association.[12] Under the 1927 Collective Agreement Act, there is no obligation for the employer to negotiate and no recognition rule for unions. However, apart from a few cases, all employers accept the social obligation to bargain in a collective manner with unions.[13] The 1937 Extension and Nullification of Collective Agreement Act supports the high degree of multi-employer bargaining and its extended coverage. This Act allows the government to declare the collective agreement binding upon non-organized employers, if the agreement covers a substantial majority of the industry's employers.

At the company level, interaction between employers and employees is shaped by the Works Council Act of 1950 (amended in 1971 and 1979). This Act installs some form of co-determination between management and works council in Dutch firms with over 35 employees.

**The emergence of the Flexibility and Security Act**

The main recent innovation in the regulation of contingent employment in the Netherlands is the Flexibility and Security Act, which can be seen as a product of the Dutch system of industrial relations. The Act, which came into force on 1 January 1999, aims to strike a balance between the positive sides of contingent labour in terms of increased flexibility for work organizations on the one hand, and the negative sides in terms of less security for contingent workers on the other hand. The emergence of the Act is described below. It must be noted that the Act was not an outcome that was based on a grand design or master plan. It was contingent on developments in the political and economic context on the one hand and on the outcome of the consultation processes between employer associations, unions and the government on the other hand (Wilthagen, 1998). In this respect, however, it can be seen as a true product of the Dutch *polder model.* Government, employers and unions all had their own concerns regarding the development of the institutional context for contingent employment. The final outcome of the negotiations was presented as the 'reasonable compromise' that reflected the needs of all stakeholders.

Until the 1980s, the social partners both had very strong opinions about atypical labour relations. Unions were suspicious of agency work. Agency work was related to bad employment conditions, to illegal black market labour exchanges, and was perceived to take advantage of people with a relatively weak labour market position. Unions were, however, looking for ways to create more flexibility in working time, especially promoting the idea of part-time work. Employers were wary of working time reductions and part-time work, but were looking for ways to increase labour force flexibility. The Dutch employment crisis at the end of the 1970s and a change of government in the early 1980s prepared the ground for a new type of cooperation between employers and collective labour, by now known as *the Dutch model.* A first reflection of this changing attitude emerged in the StAr Agreement[14] of 1982 between employers and collective labour, known as the Wassenaar Agreement. The core of the agreement was a strategy of wage moderation, but it also included a basic understanding that more flexibility in the employment relationship was acceptable if it was combined with increased protection for employees in flexible jobs.

From 1982, the social partners engaged in a constructive dialogue building on the employers' need for increasing labour flexibility and the unions' position that increased flexibility needs to be supported by a social security system that incorporates the needs of flexible workers. Three milestones can be identified in this dialogue: first, the aforementioned 1982 'Wassenaar Agreement'; second, the StAr report, 'A New Course' (StAr, 1993) on the renewal of collective bargaining in the Netherlands, which explicitly notes the need for more flexibility in work patterns, from the perspective of both employees and employers; third, the StAr report, 'Flexibility and Security' (StAr, 1996). In this last report the social partners recognized, on the one hand, a need for more flexible employment contracts for a well-functioning labour market and, on the other hand, the need to bring flexible employment, and especially agency work, under the rules of traditional norms of Dutch industrial relations.

Governmental policy makers, who had also stimulated the debate between the social partners in the early 1980s, started to be concerned with contingent labour in the late 1980s. In this period initial studies on flexible employment were conducted and published on behalf of either the government or the social partners.[15] However, the government's interest in the phenomenon was not uniform. On the one hand, the Ministry of Economic Affairs launched, in the early 1990s, a new programme called 'Markets, Deregulation and Quality of Legislation'. The increase in contingent employment fitted well with their general objective to increase the flexibility of the labour market and, therefore, had to be supported. Other policy options suggested by this ministry concerned the deregulation of dismissal law and the abolition of the Extension and Nullification of Collective Agreement Act. The Ministry of Social Affairs and Employment, however, was more sensitive to the negative consequences of agency employment, such as the insecure situation of the employee, its implications for social security, potential tensions in employment relations and the weakening of the labour movement.

The departmental divide coincided with the contrasting perspectives of employers' associations and unions. Extensive consultation between the three actors in the Socioeconomic Council and the Foundation of Labour enabled a compromise. The first lines of this compromise were visible in a memorandum called 'Flexibility and Security' issued by the Ministry of Social Affairs and Employment in December 1995. This memorandum contained a set of proposals that, on the one hand, would increase the flexibility of the labour market and, on the other hand, would enhance the legal position of contingent workers. The Foundation of Labour was asked for a formal opinion on the memorandum. Their advice was laid down in the aforementioned StAr report, which contained a large number of detailed suggestions, and was released in April 1996. The government included nearly all recommendations in their set of proposals for the new bill. The Flexibility and Security Act came into force in January 1999.

## Recent Changes in the Institutional Context

This section describes three recent changes in the institutional context that govern the employment of contingent labour. First, we provide details of the Flexibility and Security Act, which is considered to be the major reform in the regulation of contingent employment. The new collective bargaining agreement between the temporary work agencies and the unions has complemented this act in an important manner. The second part focuses on this agreement. Third, attention is paid to the Allocation of Workers via Intermediaries Act (WAADI), the second major alteration of statutory law.

**Flexibility and Security Act**

As described above, the Flexibility and Security Act strikes a balance between, on the one hand, labour market flexibility and, on the other hand, social security of the contingent worker. The main measures that aim to enhance labour market *flexibility* concern the duration of temporary employment and the relaxation of statutory dismissal protection.

First, an organization can renew limited duration contracts more easily. Limited duration contracts (LDCs) still end by right and do not provide dismissal protection rights that are linked with open-ended contracts. An LDC converts into an open-ended contract only if (a) the number of repeated LDCs exceeds three (the number used to be one), or if (b) the term of the various LDCs exceeds the duration of three years. In other words, only if a chain of LDCs has exceeded three years or consisted of more than three single contracts does the law convert the LDC into an open-ended contract. (Note that deviation from this regulation by collective bargaining agreement is allowed.[16]) Earlier regulation of the maximum duration for which an agency worker can be hired by an organization from a temporary work agency was abolished. (The maximum term used to be six months.)

Second, the statutory dismissal protection for regular employment contracts has been relaxed. In the first place, the legally required period for giving notice to employees has changed. At present the employee is entitled to a period of notice of four weeks during his/her first five years of employment. After that, the notice period increases by one month for every five years up to a maximum of four months. Employers and employees can agree to lengthen the notice period; shortening of the notice period can only be done in collective bargaining agreements. Secondly, the formal dismissal procedure via the Labour Office has been shortened (from six to four weeks). Furthermore, if the Labour Office grants permission to dismiss, the employer may subtract one month from the notice period to make up for the time lost in the Labour Office procedure (down to a minimum of one month). Finally, the dismissal procedure can be continued for employees on sick leave if sick leave starts after initiation of the dismissal procedure.

The main measures that aim to enhance the *security* of the worker on a limited duration contract are that (a) an LDC is automatically converted into an open-ended contract by law after a chain of three renewals or after a (chain of) contract(s) exceed(s) a duration of three years (see above),[17] and (b) the chain is broken only after an interruption of at least three months (this used to be one month and resulted in the common practice of unlimited renewal). Note that, again, deviation from this rule by a collective bargaining agreement is allowed.

Specific measures that aim to enhance the security of the agency worker are that (a) the contract between the agency worker and the temporary work agency is an employment contract, thus making this contract subject to all provisions of the law on employment contracts (with the exception of the first 26 weeks), and (b) the first 26 weeks of an agency job are not regulated. That is, both parties can terminate the relationship without further obligations. Thereafter, if the agency worker continues to be hired by the temporary work agency, conditions similar to LDCs apply (see above).

Three main measures aim to enhance the security of irregular workers (on-call worker – officially min-max workers – and freelancers). First there is legal establishment of the existence of an employment contract: an employment contract is assumed to be existent once one has worked for an employer in exchange for remuneration for a term of three months and at least 20 hours a month. Determination of the presumed contracted number of hours is based on the average number of hours that are worked during this three-month period. If such a contract is assumed to exist, then, second, the employer bears the risk of continued salary payment even when no services have been delivered. The employer can rule out this risk through a provision in a formal employment contract. However, this provision is only valid during the first six months of the employment contract. (Note that deviations from this legal rule are allowed through a collective bargaining agreement.) Third, an irregular worker has the right to receive a minimum payment of three hours of work for each time they are called upon by the employer (thus even when the actual working time was less than three hours). However, again, this provision is only valid when no clear agreement on working times exists or when agreed working times are less than 15 hours a week and no clear working schedule exists.

**Collective agreement**

From the above discussion of the Flexibility and Security Act it becomes clear that the Act provides a general context for regulating the employment relationship, demonstrating the intention of the Act to increase flexibility, while paying attention to the issue of employee security. The Act also allows for fine-tuning in industry-specific collective bargaining agreements. An investigation of the effect of the Act on such agreements in 1999 showed that many of them already contained provisions to adapt the working of the Flexibility and Security Act to its specific needs. The fine-tuning of the Act in the agency collective bargaining agreements warrants further attention. There are two sector organizations in the agency sector, the ABU and the NBBU, with their membership covering most of the temporary work agencies in the Netherlands.

The ABU, the sector organization for the larger employment agencies, was founded in 1961. It has established collective bargaining agreements with Dutch labour unions since 1971. The NBBU is the sector organization representing the smaller Dutch agencies. It was founded in 1994, foreseeing the abolition of the licensing system for temporary work agencies (TWAs). These two sector organizations (ABU and NBBU) developed collective agreements that worked out the provisions in the Flexibility and Security Act to cope with the specific needs of the agency industry. The collective agreements regulate the agency workers' employment relationship with the agencies through a four-phase system.

With regard to the contractual relationship with the agency worker, the collective bargaining agreement offers the TWA the opportunity to choose between two systems. Either the TWA chooses to employ the agency worker according to the Flexibility and Security Act (that is, to employ the agency worker by means of regular limited duration or open-ended employment contracts) or the TWA chooses to employ the agency worker according to the so-called 'phase system'. The 'phase system', as agreed in the collective bargaining agreement, distinguishes four phases.[18] Phase 1 covers the first 26 weeks. This phase follows the 'agency provision' (*uitzendbeding*) in Dutch labour law. The contract is a contract for the duration of the assignment and can be terminated at will. Both employer and employer are free to discontinue the employment relationship. Note that every week in which the agency worker performs work counts, independent of the number of hours worked. Phase 2 encompasses the subsequent six months. This phase is practically identical to phase 1. In phase 2, however, agency workers are also entitled to a meeting with agency staff to establish their training needs. Furthermore, they start building up pension benefits. In phase 2, weeks in which the agency workers did not perform work also count (with a maximum of 3). Phase 3 starts after one year. In phase 3 the agency worker has to be hired on the basis of three-month contracts. This phase lasts for six months if the agency worker works for only one client organization. It can last up to two years if he or she works for different client organizations. In phase 4, finally, the agency worker is entitled to an open-ended contract with the temporary work agency. The TWA should offer an open-ended contract to the agency worker if he or she has worked 24 months with different users or 18 months with one user. The phase system entails special provisions for agency workers with respect to the continuation of payment in the case of absence and further specifies agency workers' entitlement to a certain salary level, pension benefits, training and employee participation.

In phases 1 and 2 there is no payment in the case of absence from work and no social security sickness compensation. In phases 3 and 4 payments are continued if the assignment is terminated during the (limited duration) employment contract. An agency worker cannot be obliged to accept work that is more than two levels below the work level that is initially agreed. In the case of sickness, payments are continued at 90 per cent until the LDC expires or, in the case of an open-ended contract, for a maximum of 52 weeks.

The agency collective agreements furthermore establish that (1) salary levels that are agreed in the collective bargaining agreements that apply to the user organization prevail; (2) a pension fund for the temporary work agency industry will be established. Every agency worker who works at least 26 weeks is a beneficiary of that fund and this remains the case if he or she continues to be an agency worker without breaks longer than one year; (3) TWAs are obliged to conduct a training interview with the agency worker at the end of phase 1. A percentage of the costs of salary (in 2000, 0.70 per cent) should be devoted to a training fund. A separate foundation will supervise the expenditures of this training fund; (4) in accordance with the Works Council Act, agency workers are given the right to set up a works council at the TWA. Agency workers that are in phases 2, 3 and 4 are provided with voting rights; those in phases 3 and 4 can be elected.

**Allocation of Workers via Intermediaries Act**

The second recent change in regulation of contingent labour is the Allocation of Workers via Intermediaries Act (*Wet Allocatie Arbeidskrachten door Intermediairs*, WAADI). While the aim of the Flexibility and Security Act is more generally to regulate contingent labour, the WAADI is directly concerned with temporary work agencies. Agency work used to be regulated by the Temporary Work Act of 1965. The WAADI Act entered into force in July 1998. The Act distinguishes between a matching function (between a job seeker and a job-offering organization) and the labour provision function (the agency employs the worker and sells his or her services to a user organization).

With regard to the matching function, the Act's main element concerns the permission for commercial agencies to provide this service. Traditionally, this service belonged to the Public Labour Office (*Arbeidsvoorziening*), mostly for fear of abuse of people with a weaker labour market position by commercial agencies. The Public Labour Office is still responsible for granting the permits that are required to perform the matching function, but will only deny permission in the case of grounded fears of abuse. Although commercial agencies are not allowed to demand payment for their services to the job seeker, they can generate income from client organizations and governmental subsidies that are granted when the (long-term) unemployed are successfully helped to find a job.

With regard to the labour provision function, the Act's primary aim is to liberate the market for this service. It does so by abolishing the requirement for a permit, which diminishes the barriers to entry to the industry. This law has resulted in a strong increase in the number of small, specialized temporary work agencies. Moreover, the Act abolishes the ban on agency workers in the construction industry. The construction industry is regarded as a pilot for other industries where a ban on agency workers persists, such as ocean-shipping and professional goods traffic.

## DETAILED DESCRIPTION OF CONTINGENT EMPLOYMENT

This section provides a detailed statistical description of the development of contingent employment in the Netherlands.[19] First, contingent employment is split into various categories. The growth in the use of contingent employment is seen to be mainly due to the increase of agency work, and contingent labour is further analysed in terms of supply and demand. The second subsection concentrates on the users of contingent employment. Finally, the characteristics of the contingent workforce are analysed.

### Breakdown of Contingent Employment

The main forms of contingent employment in the Netherlands are agency work, limited duration contracts, and on-call work.[20] Table 8.2 shows the development of the various categories of contingent employment over time. The data show job growth in all employment categories. The growing numbers of self-employed reflect the trust of individuals in the Dutch economy and to some extent also reflect a flexibilization of labour in the larger organizations who buy the services of these self-employed.[21]

From Table 8.2, it can be concluded that the rise of contingent employment in the Netherlands in the last decade can be attributed primarily to the increase in agency work. This increase (110000) accounts for 64 per cent of the growth in total contingent employment (172000). Table 8.2 also shows that, from 1999, the number of contingent employees has fallen, whilst the total amount of jobs has kept on rising, from 6609000 in 1998 to 6916000 in 2000. Evaluating the growth of contingent employment since 1970 (Figure 8.4) there was a small, but steady, growth of agency work and 'other forms of contingent employment' (comprising on-call and LDCs) during the 1970s and the early 1980s, and a steep growth in the 1990s for all types of contingent employment.[22]

The share of agency work in total contingent employment increased from 25 per cent in 1992 to around 37 per cent in the late 1990s. Since the economic recession in the early 1990s, the volume of agency work has more than doubled, to 180000 full-time job equivalents in 1998.

In 1999, this growth trend was broken. Labour market figures indicate a

*Table 8.2 Breakdown of contingent employment, 1992–2000 (thousands)*

| | 1992 | 1993 | 1994 | 1995 | 1996 | 1997 | 1998 | 1999 | 2000* |
|---|---|---|---|---|---|---|---|---|---|
| Open-ended | 4859 | 4868 | 4797 | 4880 | 4920 | 5077 | 5270 | 5502 | 5588 |
| Self-employed | 627 | 664 | 698 | 706 | 728 | 757 | 734 | 733 | 799 |
| Total contingent | 399 | 392 | 425 | 477 | 538 | 566 | 604 | 571 | 530 |
| Agency work | 100 | 101 | 114 | 150 | 188 | 207 | 223 | 210 | 196 |
| LDC (< 1 year) | 112 | 113 | 126 | 132 | 134 | 135 | 134 | 136 | — |
| On-call work | 118 | 119 | 126 | 137 | 154 | 164 | 187 | 156 | 116 |
| Other | 69 | 59 | 59 | 58 | 62 | 60 | 60 | 69 | 218 |
| Total | 5885 | 5925 | 5920 | 6063 | 6187 | 6400 | 6609 | 6805 | 6916 |

*Note:* * The number for 'other' contingent employment for 2000 includes the number of LDCs (<1).

*Source:* Statistics Netherlands (CBS), enquete beroepsbevolking 1996–2000 (1992–95 in Kleinknecht, 1997).

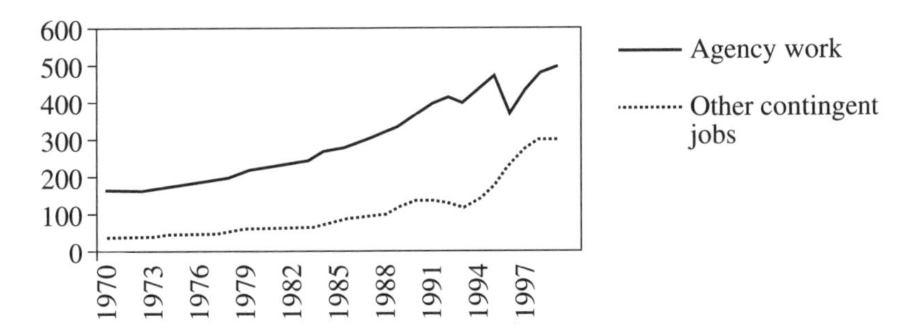


*Source:* Statistics Netherlands (CBS, arbeidsrekeningen), various years.

*Figure 8.4 Number of contingent jobs, 1970–99*

shift from short-term agency employment to employment on the basis of LDCs and open-ended contracts of agency workers by agencies, partly due to the introduction of the Flexibility and Security Act in 1999. In addition, the volume of agency work decreased slightly. The growth in the total number of jobs provided by agencies did come to a halt, but did not fall. In fact, the number of open-ended contracts did grow a little and the number of flexible contracts (including the phase 1 and 2 contracts, but also the phase 3 'three-month LDCs') remained virtually the same in 2000 (Statistics Netherlands, 2001). This indicates that the number of occasions when temporary employees were contracted did not change. The duration of their use, however, must have decreased slightly.

In all, the data show that the strong growth of contingent employment in the Netherlands stagnated at the end of the 1990s. Various explanations for this phenomenon are being proposed. The decrease might be a side-effect of the tight Dutch labour market (job growth continues in the open-ended contracts and self-employed). It might be a consequence of the new Dutch labour market regulation, as the Flexibility and Security Act seems to have increased the price of contingent employment. Finally, to some, the slowdown heralded a general economic downturn, which was otherwise invisible in a labour market as tight as the Dutch one around the turn of the century.

**The Demand for Contingent Employment**

This subsection provides data on organizations that hire contingent workers, in terms of economic sector and the nature of the job. It also presents some survey evidence on the motivations of the hiring company. A breakdown of contingent employment by industry in 1998 (Table 8.3)

*Table 8.3* *Labour force, by employment status per industry, 1998*

| Industry | Employment status (×1000) | | | | | |
|---|---|---|---|---|---|---|
| | Total | Self-employed | Employees | | | |
| | | | Total | Open-ended | Contingent (of which agency work) | |
| A + B Agriculture and fishing | 206 | 120 | 86 | 66 | 21 | (6) |
| C Mining and quarrying | 11 | — | 11 | 10 | — | — |
| D Manufacturing | 1040 | 47 | 993 | 904 | 89 | (62) |
| E Electricity, gas and water | 47 | — | 47 | 45 | — | — |
| F Construction | 441 | 62 | 379 | 357 | 22 | (12) |
| G Wholesale and retail | 1021 | 144 | 876 | 780 | 97 | (25) |
| H Hotels and restaurants | 180 | 36 | 144 | 102 | 42 | (7) |
| I Transport, communication | 410 | 22 | 388 | 347 | 41 | (18) |
| J Financial intermediation | 256 | 10 | 246 | 229 | 18 | (10) |
| K Real estate and business | 749 | 109 | 640 | 586 | 54 | (22) |
| L Public administration | 514 | — | 514 | 490 | 24 | (14) |
| M Education | 438 | 12 | 426 | 398 | 29 | (6) |
| N Health and social work | 899 | 59 | 839 | 743 | 96 | (12) |
| O Other community | 281 | 69 | 212 | 186 | 26 | (6) |
| P Private households | 6 | — | 6 | — | 5 | — |
| Unknown | 104 | 40 | 64 | 27 | 37 | — |
| Total | 6603 | 730 | 5871 | 5270 | 601 | (200) |

*Source:* Statistics Netherlands (CBS), enquete beroepsbevolking 1998.

shows that the absolute numbers of contingent employment in the Netherlands are largest in wholesale and retail, health and social work, manufacturing, and real estate and business. In 1998, manufacturing had the largest number of agency workers.

An analysis of the share of contingent employment in total employees (total employment minus self-employment) and the share of agency work in total contingent employment for each industry for this same period shows that the relative importance of contingent contracts versus open-ended contracts is largest in hotels and restaurants (29 per cent) and agriculture (24 per cent). The high number of limited duration (seasonal) contracts account for this observation. It is largest (more than 50 per cent) in manufacturing, public administration, financial intermediaries and construction. It is lowest in education, health and hotels and restaurants. Other types of contingent employment proliferate in these industries.[23]

The breakdown of contingent labour by industry does not give any indication of the nature of the contingent job. For example, the nature of a contingent job in the manufacturing industry can be administrative or technical. Dutch data on the qualitative aspects of agency work (Statistics Netherlands, 2001) distinguish four categories of jobs: administrative jobs, healthcare, high-skilled technical jobs and low-skilled technical jobs. Around 95 per cent of agency work can be categorized into one of the four categories. It appears that the breakdown of agency employment in terms of job content is relatively stable. The dominant job category is 'low-skilled technical jobs'. Around 49 per cent of the agency jobs are classified as such. The second-largest category is administration with a share of around 31 per cent. Around 11 per cent of agency jobs are highly skilled technical jobs. Finally, healthcare jobs take a minor share of total agency work, fluctuating around 4 per cent. The first data that separate short-term temps from long-term temps (with a three-month contract or an open-ended contract) show a similar spread over the four job categories.

Finally, the motivations of the management of organizations that hire contingent workers have been analysed. In the Netherlands, data were only collected on an incidental basis. However, the outcomes of the various studies have consistent findings. The primary reasons for using contingent workers are temporary replacement of regular workers that are on leave, peaks in business demand and probationary period (see Table 8.4). Recent research of hiring motives of agency workers by innovative firms showed similar results (Timmerhuis and De Lange, 1998). The motivations underlying the hiring of agency workers are the traditional ones: lower search costs of temporary workers, the need for temporary capacity during periods of peak demand and the need for temporary replacement for incumbent employees that are on leave.

*Table 8.4 Motivations underlying the use of contingent workers*

| | Commercial sector | Public sector |
|---|---|---|
| Demand peaks | 44 | 4 |
| Replacement for illness/leave | 21 | 71 |
| Probation | 16 | 13 |
| Temporary nature of job | 6 | 4 |
| Other | 13 | 8 |

*Source:* Organization for Strategic Labour Market Research (OSA), 1995.

**Characteristics of the Contingent Labour Force**

In this subsection we turn to the contingent labour force in the Netherlands and describe it in terms of gender, educational background, age distribution and socioeconomic situation.[24] Finally, the motivations of the contingent labour force are addressed.

In the Netherlands, contingent employment is more frequent among women than among men. However, the differences tend to converge (Table 8.5). In 1992, the share of contingent employment in total employment for female workers was 2.5 times greater than this share for male workers. In 2000, the number had fallen to 1.6.

*Table 8.5 Share of contingent employment in total employment, by gender, 1992–2000*

| | 1992 | 1994 | 1995 | 1996 | 1997 | 1998 | 1999 | 2000 |
|---|---|---|---|---|---|---|---|---|
| Total workforce | 6.8 | 7.2 | 7.9 | 8.7 | 8.8 | 9.1 | 8.4 | 7.7 |
| Male workforce | 4.4 | 5.1 | 5.7 | 6.4 | 6.4 | 6.6 | 6.2 | 6.2 |
| Female workforce | 11.1 | 10.7 | 11.5 | 12.6 | 12.8 | 13.2 | 11.8 | 9.8 |

*Source:* Statistics Netherlands, Statline, 2001.

Considering the relevance of agency work for people with different educational backgrounds, it can be concluded that, among poorly educated workers,[25] the occurrence of contingent employment is higher than among highly educated workers.[26] Some 15 per cent of poorly educated workers were employed in a contingent manner in 1998. Moreover, it can be observed that this divide between poorly and highly educated workers is widening (Figure 8.5). While the share of contingent employment in total employment was stable for highly educated employees at around 8 per cent, the share steadily increased for poorly educated employees.

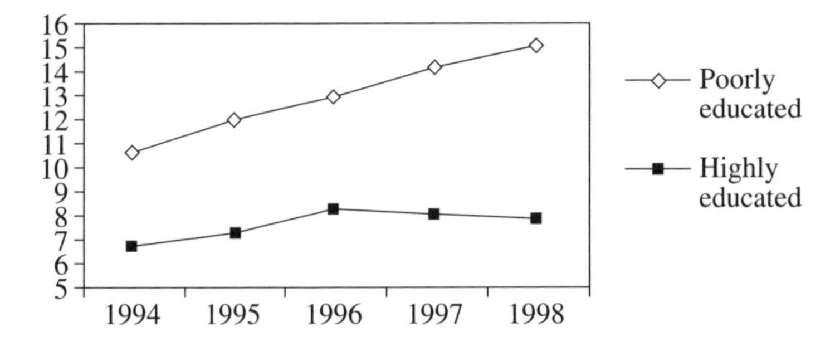


*Source:* Statistics Netherlands (CBS); labour force survey, 1999.

*Figure 8.5 Relative importance of contingent employment for different education levels, 1994–8*

Furthermore, the contingent workforce can be characterized in terms of age. Data are available on the age distribution of agency workers. Table 8.6 shows the share of five age categories in total contingent employment and agency employment specifically. It appears that around 40 per cent of agency workers are younger than 25 years of age. Many of these young agency workers combine their job with education. In 1999, around 40 per cent of agency workers were enrolled in an educational programme (ABU/NEI, 2000). However, the dominance of the 15–24 age group is decreasing.

When considering the socioeconomic position of the contingent workforce, it is interesting to see that a high proportion of agency workers still live in the parental home. This group coincides with the category of young agency workers (15–24 years) who combine agency work with a formal education programme. Furthermore, it can be observed that the category of agency workers whose earnings account for the major household income has increased to 15 per cent. Table 8.7 shows these facts, distinguishing three socioeconomic positions: living in the parental home, living alone, and being married or living as a couple. For the latter category, the importance of the income earned by the agency worker is also established.

An often discussed issue is the true desirability of agency work. Especially private employment agencies in the Netherlands propagate contingent employment through agencies as a true alternative to open-ended contracts. In research the issue is often put in terms of voluntary versus involuntary acceptance of contingent employment. An annual labour market survey provides insight on this issue (OSA, 1999). Table 8.8 shows the results. It appears that in the Netherlands contingent workers in the category 'on-call workers' are to a considerable extent satisfied with their

*Table 8.6 Age distribution of contingent workers, 1992–9 (%)*

| | 1992 | 1993 | 1994 | 1995 | 1996 | 1997 | 1998 | 1999 | 2000 |
|---|---|---|---|---|---|---|---|---|---|
| All contingent employees (including agency workers) | | | | | | | | | |
| 15–24 years | 37 | 39 | 37 | 38 | 36 | 37 | 37 | 38 | 38 |
| 25–34 years | 29 | 28 | 29 | 29 | 30 | 29 | 27 | 25 | 24 |
| 35–44 years | 20 | 19 | 19 | 19 | 19 | 18 | 20 | 20 | 19 |
| 45–54 years | 11 | 11 | 12 | 12 | 12 | 13 | 13 | 13 | 14 |
| 55–64 years | 3 | 3 | 3 | 3 | 3 | 2 | 3 | 4 | 5 |
| Agency workers | | | | | | | | | |
| 15–24 years | 47 | 47 | 46 | 42 | 40 | 41 | 37 | 38 | 38 |
| 25–34 years | 34 | 35 | 35 | 37 | 38 | 35 | 35 | 31 | 31 |
| 35–44 years | 13 | 11 | 13 | 15 | 14 | 16 | 18 | 19 | 20 |
| > 45 years | 6 | 5 | 5 | 6 | 6 | 8 | 9 | 10 | 9 |

*Source:* Statistics Netherlands, Statline, 2001.

*Table 8.7 Socioeconomic position of agency workers, 1993–9 (%)*

| | 1993 | 1995 | 1996 | 1997 | 1998 | 1999 |
|---|---|---|---|---|---|---|
| Parental house | 43 | 47 | 39 | 45 | 44 | 41 |
| Single | 22 | 20 | 22 | 22 | 19 | 20 |
| Married/couple | 34 | 31 | 38 | 32 | 35 | 37 |
| (of which breadwinner) | (5) | (10) | (14) | (10) | (14) | (15) |
| Other | 2 | 2 | — | — | 1 | 2 |

*Source:* Algemene Bond Uitzendondernemingen (ABU)/Nederlands Economisch Instituut (NEI), 2000.

*Table 8.8 Desired state of employment of various types of employees, 1999 (%)*

| | Desired state of employment | | | | |
|---|---|---|---|---|---|
| Existing state of employment | Open-ended | Temporary | Agency work | On-call work | Other |
| Agency worker | 89.0 | 3.3 | 5.6 | 1.1 | — |
| Employee leasing | 97.6 | 1.2 | — | — | 1.2 |
| On-call work | 60.5 | 4.2 | — | 33.8 | 1.4 |
| Open ended | 98.0 | 0.8 | — | 0.5 | 0.7 |
| All employees | 97.1 | 0.9 | 0.2 | 1.2 | 0.7 |

*Source:* Organisatie voor Strategisch Arbeidsmarktonderzoek (OSA), 1999.

current employment status. Other contingent workers demonstrate a clear preference for an open-ended contract.[27]

The high percentage of contingent workers that aspire to an open-ended contract raises the question to what extent they are successful in subsequently securing a permanent position. Data from the association of temporary work agencies (ABU/NEI, 2000) provide insight into this question for the category of agency workers. The data show that 48 per cent of agency workers were actively searching for an open-ended employment contract. Among this group, 45 per cent were successful. Because 21 per cent of those agency workers that were not actively searching for an open-ended contract nevertheless accepted one, an overall percentage of 33 per cent of agency workers became employed in an open-ended manner in 1998, while 38 per cent became employed by the hiring organization.

These findings on the use of agency work as a transitional stage in the

*Table 8.9 Changes in employment status in the 1992–4 period*

| 1992 \ 1994 | Open ended | Contingent | Self-employed | Unemployed | No participant | Total 1992 |
|---|---|---|---|---|---|---|
| Open-ended | 89.0 | 1.8 | 1.0 | 2.2 | 5.9 | 100 |
| Contingent | 47.7 | 30.7 | 2.0 | 7.8 | 11.8 | 100 |
| Self-employed | 6.6 | 0.7 | 86.2 | 0.7 | 5.9 | 100 |
| Unemployed | 19.0 | 19.0 | 2.6 | 34.5 | 25.0 | 100 |
| No participant | 3.8 | 3.3 | 1.0 | 2.0 | 89.9 | 100 |

*Source:* Kleinknecht (1997).

pursuit of open-ended employment are confirmed by Kleinknecht (1997), who analysed changes in employment status in the 1992–4 period. Table 8.9 shows the results. It appears that almost 50 per cent of the workers with a contingent status in 1992 moved into an open-ended contract in 1994.

## DISCUSSION

In the last decade the Dutch labour market has demonstrated an admirable capacity to generate jobs and the unemployment rate has significantly decreased. However, the newly generated jobs are atypical in the sense that they are not like the traditional full-time jobs that are based on open-ended contracts. Instead, the growth of jobs relies primarily on the growth of part-time (based on an open-ended contract) and contingent jobs.

The mechanism underlying the growth of part-time jobs seems to separate it from the growth of contingent jobs. In the Netherlands, the growth of part-time jobs seems to be primarily employee-driven (Visser and Hemerijck, 1997). Employers that aimed to attract the large potential of female workers have been forced to comply with their preferences by offering jobs on a part-time basis. At present, the part-time workforce is still predominantly female, although the number of male part-time workers is increasing (ibid.). The growth of contingent employment, however, seems to be predominantly driven by the desire of employers for more numerical flexibility (OSA, 1999). The majority of contingent workers, excluding student workers, prefer an open-ended contract.

Contingent work in the Netherlands is more and more a phenomenon of agency work. The growth of agency work explains around 60 per cent of the growth of total contingent employment over the last decade. The growth of other appearances of contingent employment, such as limited duration contracts and on-call work, has been significant, but somewhat less pronounced.

Can we draw generalizations on the nature of agency work and the agency worker in the Netherlands? The available statistical data are too broad to draw a fine-grained picture. Nevertheless, with some courage the typical agency job can be characterized as a low-skilled production or administrative job in the manufacturing or wholesale/retail industry. With regard to the agency worker, the data suggest two typical portraits. The first typical agency worker is a young student who still lives in the parental house and combines agency work with a formal educational programme. The second type of agency worker is a poorly educated, middle-aged breadwinner.

The Dutch government, in consultation with employers' associations and unions, has responded to the growth of contingent work in two ways. First, they acknowledged the need of employers to be flexible in their employment of people. Accordingly, measures were taken to speed up dismissal procedures, to facilitate the use of limited duration contracts and to liberalize the industry of temporary work agencies. Second, the Dutch government acknowledged the right of contingent workers to security. Accordingly, measures were taken to prevent agency workers being employed for more than three years without an open-ended contract.

The developments in the Netherlands give rise to a number of questions, which can be distinguished as descriptive, theoretical and practical. First, the description of the development of contingent employment that can be given by means of the available statistics is comprehensive, but still far from perfect. Important gaps in the available statistics lie in the absence of detailed data on various categories of contingent employment, such as workers on limited duration contracts and dependent self-employed workers.

Developments that become apparent from the analysis of descriptive statistics give rise to theoretical questions. The major question that is triggered by the analysis of the Dutch data concerns the explanation of the pronounced upsurge in the use of agency work. Notwithstanding that the development has been at work since the mid-1980s, this explanatory exercise is still due. Many hypotheses have been advanced, but a clear analysis that discriminates between rival explanations still lies ahead. The effects of striving for efficiency, the pursuit of power and the need for social legitimization on the rise of agency work need to be disentangled (for example, Koene *et al.*, 2001). A first attempt to explain the development could run as follows. The use of agency workers economizes on transaction costs and in this way it contributes to higher efficiency. That the use of this resource has only become more widespread in recent decades can be attributed to the effect of legitimization. Agency work has become more accepted by the state, the trade unions and the public only in the last few decades. Further research is necessary to tackle this question. For this exercise, aggregate statistical data will be of little use. Qualitative case study research that confronts the issue in more detail is required.

A final set of questions, which is of special interest to policy makers, concerns the consequences of the new legislation in the Netherlands. First, the new Flexibility and Security Act contains some potential threats to the growth of agency work. It facilitates the termination of open-ended employment contracts and the use of limited duration contracts while it potentially raises the costs of agency work. Furthermore, although the Act aims to improve the security of the contingent labour force, it remains to be seen which agency workers will benefit from this change. Pessimistic voices predict that only highly educated agency workers will be awarded open-ended contracts by the temporary work agency, while the poorly skilled agency worker is forced to shift between assignments of different agencies. Although the first evaluations of the effects of the 'Flexicurity Act' sound reassuring (de Klaver *et al.*, 2000), the issue warrants further attention. Finally, the consequences of the WAADI Act that aimed to liberalize the temporary work industry are of interest. The first observations indicate a sharp increase in the number of small, specialized temporary work agencies increasing competition and signalling the Act's success in lowering the entry barriers to the sector. The recent past has, however, also shown a few high-profile cases of misuse of small agencies. The future shape of this growing industry is certainly an issue that should attract substantial research efforts. For this, the Netherlands offers an interesting research laboratory.

## NOTES

1. Wet Ter Beschikkingstelling Arbeidskrachten, TBA (1965).
2. A person is considered unemployed if he or she is without employment or is employed for fewer than 12 hours a week and has been actively searching for employment for at least 12 hours.
3. However, the structure of Dutch unemployment deviates from the American unemployment structure. While in the United States long-term unemployment makes up only around 8 per cent of total unemployment, in the Netherlands the share of long-term unemployment is significantly higher. Around 50 per cent of total unemployment consists of those who have been unemployed for more than 12 months.
4. In fact, there was a decrease during the 1980s. In 1984, the number of full-time jobs reached an all-time low of 3497000.
5. Part-time work is largely women's work. Women hold nearly 75 per cent of part-time jobs. Around 65 per cent of all employed women have a part-time occupation. Nevertheless, the incidence of part-time work among male workers has increased as well. Around 16 per cent of male workers were employed part-time in 1996 (6.8 per cent in 1983) (Visser and Hemerijck, 1997). Moreover, it appears that part-time work is primarily supply-driven. That is, part-time jobs are created because (potential) workers aspire to them. Survey research shows that part-time workers are in general content with the number of contracted working hours. Only those part-time workers with fewer than 20 working hours desire to work longer hours (OSA, 1999).
6. The main Dutch regulations concerning the employment contract can be found in arts 1637 to 1639 of the Civil Code (Burgerlijk Wetboek).
7. Exempted from the procedure are cases in which the employee has consented to the dismissal. However, the social security system inhibits employees from agreeing with the termination of their employment because their eligibility for unemployment benefits is questioned on account of their being voluntarily unemployed.
8. The Labour Office is advised by a 'dismissal committee', which is composed of representatives of employers' associations, trade unions and the Labour Inspectorate (on health and safety).
9. The Dutch regulation of notice periods is also very unusual. The employee is entitled to a minimum period of notice of four weeks. Before 1999, the notice period increased with the length of service by one week for each year, up to a maximum of 13 weeks. Employees older than 45 years acquired an additional week of notice per year of service, again up to a maximum of 13 weeks.

10. The compensation fee amounts to around a year's salary for every five years of service.
11. It was common practice for employers to send the employee with a limited duration contract away for one month and to offer a new contract for limited duration after their return.
12. Large companies increasingly agree with the trade unions to formulate the collective bargaining agreement at firm level. However, the size and multi-plant character of these firms, such as Philips, Akzo Nobel and Unilever, give these agreements the significance of industry-wide agreements.
13. Examples of firms in the Netherlands that operate without a collective bargaining agreement are Dow Chemicals and Ikea.
14. StAr refers to *Stichting van de Arbeid*, the Dutch labour foundation, which is the platform for negotiations between the social partners in the Netherlands.
15. Three reports were published: *Arbeid op maat*, Ministry of Social Affairs and Employment, December 1986; *Flexibele arbeidsrelaties, Advies inzake flexible arbeidsrelaties*, Socioeconomic Council, 1991; 'Promotion of part-time work and differentiation of working time patterns', Dutch Labour Foundation (StAr), 1993.
16. Examples of collective bargaining agreements (CBAs) that broaden as well as limit the possibilities of employers can be given. However, most collective bargaining agreements conform to statutory law in this respect.
17. In the case of one contract for three years or more, it can only be prolonged by a maximum of three months before it converts into an open-ended contract.
18. Since the enforcement of the Flexibility and Security Act in 1999, it has been possible to distinguish agency workers by the type of contract they have with the TWA. The available statistics distinguish between agency workers in phases 1 and 2 (employed for the duration of the assignment) and agency workers who have either a temporary (phase 3) or an open-ended (phase 4) contract with the TWA. Of the total number of 189000 full-time jobs provided by TWAs in 1999, 156000 belonged to agency workers in phases 1 and 2. The other 33000 were occupied by agency workers in phases 3 and 4.
19. This section makes use of four statistical sources. The official Dutch Central Bureau for Statistics (CBS) provides two kinds of national labour market statistics: first, the 'arbeidsrekeningen' that are based on statistical input from work organizations; second, the 'enquete beroepsbevolking' that is based on an annual survey among employees. Thirdly, the Organization for Strategic Labour Market Research (OSA) provides annual panel data. Finally, the Association of Temporary Work Agencies (ABU) in cooperation with the Dutch Economic Institute (NEI) provides data on the agency industry.
20. Officially labelled 'min-max' contracts in the Netherlands.
21. A prominent form of contingent employment is that of 'dependent self-employed', those workers that are self-employed but depend on one organization for assignments. Dutch statistics provide data on self-employed, but no distinction is made for so-called 'dependent' ones.
22. The discontinuity in the rise of 'other contingent employment' is due to a change in the measurement in 1993.
23. In the education sector, contracts for limited duration are widespread. In health and nursery care, on-call contractual relationships proliferate and in hotels and restaurants seasonal contracts are common (Kleinknecht, 1997).
24. Ethnic background is another feature that is commonly advanced to characterize the contingent labour force. Contingent workers are more likely to be of an ethnic background than regular workers are. However, in the Dutch situation, ethnic origin appears to be of little importance. In 1999, 9 per cent of the Dutch working population was of ethnic origin. The share of ethnic minorities in total agency employment was only slightly higher, 10 per cent (ABU/NEI, 2000).
25. The category of poorly educated employees covers primary education, lower vocational education (vbo), and preparatory general education (mavo, havo and vwo). The category of highly educated employees covers middle and higher vocational education (mbo and hbo) and university education.
26. The relative shares are calculated as follows: total poorly educated workers with contin-

gent jobs/total poorly educated workers and total highly educated workers with contingent jobs/total highly educated workers.

27. It is important to note that the OSA data on contingent employment do not include students who perceive their study as their main activity.

# REFERENCES


ABU/NEI (2000) 'Instroomonderzoek uitzendkrachten 1999', Algemene Bond Uitzendondernemingen, Badhoevedorp/Nederlands Economisch Instituut, Rotterdam.

Bakkenist Management Consultants (1998) 'Temporary Work Businesses in the Countries of the European Union', report submitted to the Confèderation Internationale des Entreprises de Travail Temporaire (CIETT).

CBS, *Arbeidsrekeningen* (*http://www.cbs.nl*) Heerlen: Centraal Bureau voor de Statistiek.

CBS, *Enquete Beroepsbevolking* (*http://www.cbs.nl*) Heerlen: Centraal Bureau voor de Statistiek.

CBS, *Kwartaalbericht Commerciele Dienstverlening* (*http://www.cbs.nl*) Heerlen: Centraal Bureau voor de Statistiek.

Delsen, L. (2000) *Exit poldermodel: Sociaal-economische ontwikkelingen in Nederland*, Assen: Van Gorcum.

Havinga, T. (1994) 'Labour Office and collective dismissal in the Netherlands', in R. Rogowski and T. Wilthagen (eds), *Reflexive Labour Law*, Deventer: Kluwer.

Klaver, P.M. de, D.J. Klein Hesselink, E.P. Miedema and C. Schlangen (2000) *Ervaringen met en effecten van de Wet flexibiliteit en zekerheid*, The Hague: Elsevier bedrijfsinformatie.

Kleinknecht, A. (1997) 'Patronen en economische effecten van flexibiliteit in de Nederlandse arbeidsverhoudingen', Voorstudie Wetenschappelijke Raad voor Regeringsbeleid, SDU Uitgevers, The Hague.

Koene, B.A.S., F. Pot and J. Paauwe (2001) 'Establishment and acceptance of an emerging industry: What factors determine the development and growth of the temporary work industry in Europe?', conference paper, 17th EGOS colloquium, 'The Odysssey of Organizing', Lyons.

OSA (1995) 'Instituties van de arbeidsmarkt', Organisatie voor Strategisch Arbeidsmarktonderzoek/Servicecentrum Uitgevers, The Hague.

OSA (1999) 'Trendrapport: Aanbod van arbeid 1999', Organisatie voor Strategisch Arbeidsmarktonderzoek/Servicecentrum Uitgevers, The Hague.

SCP (1998) 'Sociaal en cultureel rapport 1998: 25 Jaar sociale verandering', Sociaal Cultureel Planbureau/Servicecentrum Uitgevers, The Hague.

Statistics Netherlands (2001) CBS press release PB01–196.

Timmerhuis, V.C.M. and W.A.M. De Lange (1998) *Flexibele arbeid-Quo Vadis? Een toekomstverkenning rond (flexibele) arbeidsinzet en de inzet van uitzendbureaus*, Tilburg: IVA.

Visser, J. and A. Hemerijck (1997) *A Dutch miracle: Job growth, welfare reform and corporatism in the Netherlands*, Amsterdam: Amsterdam University Press.

Wilthagen, T. (1998) 'Flexicurity: A new paradigm for labour market policy reform', discussion paper, Wissenschaftszentrum Berlin für Sozialforschung, Berlin.

# 9. Conclusions: contingent employment in Europe and the flexibility–security trade-off

**Donald Storrie**

## INTRODUCTION

This final chapter is devoted to underlining the main points made in the country chapters and attempting to generalize the developments in the six countries to developments in the other member states of the European Union.

Focus is first placed on the general systems of labour law in the six countries and how they have evolved in the 1990s as regards the regulation of contingent employment. We then explore possible links between the growth of contingent employment (mainly limited duration contracts) and regulation. We also relate the growth of limited duration contracts to the state of the labour market.

However, of the various forms of contingent employment examined in this volume we would argue that temporary agency work is of most interest and worth special attention in this final chapter. There are several reasons for this. It was by far the most rapidly growing form of contingent employment in the 1990s and research on agency work is relatively limited. It is also conceptually a very interesting contractual form, being a hybrid of an employment and commercial contract. From a policy perspective, it was the object of much legislation during the 1990s and as this volume goes to press we await the fate of a directive on agency work currently before the European Parliament.[1] Furthermore, if appropriately regulated, agency work may provide some reconciliation in what is perhaps the major conflict between employer and worker interests in recent years, namely the apparently irreconcilable demand for flexibility for the employers and job security for employees.

## REGULATION OF THE EMPLOYMENT CONTRACT

This section identifies some of the central features of the regulation of employment contracts in the six countries and the changes made during the 1990s. Emphasis is placed on the regulation of limited duration contracts (LDCs) which are the main form of contingent employment in most of the six countries. As mentioned in the introduction, temporary agency work will be the main topic of this chapter and is taken up in later sections.

### Employment Protection in the Six Countries

The countries studied in this volume differ appreciably as regards the regulation of employment protection. The systems of labour law in both the USA and the UK lead to a rather unclear definition of which types of work can be deemed to constitute an employment contract. Furthermore, the obligations placed on the employer when terminating the employment relationship are relatively limited and the grounds under which the employer may terminate are broad. In the OECD (1999) ranking of employment protection, the USA is ranked the most liberal of countries, followed by the UK. However, the UK, not least as a consequence of its membership of the European Union, has undoubtedly a more developed and, for the employer, more restrictive statutory regulation than that in the USA. While collective bargaining is not particularly well developed or widespread in these countries, the near legislative vacuum makes collective agreements of some relative importance. In the USA, workers covered by a collective agreement are clearly viewed as employees, while in the UK, in the sectors where unions still have some presence, the collective agreement is still of considerable importance. In 1993, Richard Hyman stated that, in the UK, 'collective bargaining rather than labor law has been the main source of whatever employment protection exists'. By the end of the decade, even with some labour law reform under the last two Labour governments, the authors of the UK chapter still appear to concur with Hyman's pronouncement.

Given the lack of significant employment protection in these countries, and the uncertainty as to what constitutes an employment relationship, the concept of contingent employment as a distinct legal category is not as clear as in the other countries in this volume. The still rather widespread principle of employment-at-will in the USA, where the employer in principle has the right to terminate the contract unilaterally without cost, and the exclusion of short-term employed in the UK from the few employment protection rights that exist, quite obviously lead to relatively few employees legally defined as being contingent, and appreciably fewer than in the four other EU countries.

Germany, the Netherlands and Sweden are ranked roughly in the middle of the OECD's ranking of employment protection strictness. The concept of an employment contract is, in most cases, clear and the law stipulates that it may only be terminated by the employer if there is 'just cause' or if it is 'socially motivated'. The termination of the contract is coupled with sometimes lengthy and thus costly administrative procedures. In Sweden and Germany, before a permanent layoff may occur the employer is required to try to find an alternative position for the worker. In the Netherlands, the administrative procedures at the Labour Office appear particularly inconvenient to the employer (or costly if the alternative route through the courts is taken). In Sweden, the legal requirement to administer redundancies in accordance with the last in, first out principle is unique. In Germany, the obligations placed on the employer in some cases to compensate the worker for collective redundancy, by means of the so-called 'social plan', are relatively extensive.

In all the three countries there is a well-developed system of collective bargaining on a wide variety of issues, including employment protection and co-determination. Collective agreements have a wide coverage either directly or, as in the case of the Netherlands and Germany, by extension. Legislation can often be viewed as being a framework or a basic floor of worker rights, upon which the collective agreement may add further detail and worker protection.

Regarding trade union influence, it is clear that Sweden is a rather special case. While the coverage of collective agreements is not significantly wider in Sweden, the union presence at the workplace is almost unique in the developed world. Collective agreements both complement and concretize almost every issue in labour law. Sweden is generally placed in the middle of the OECD employment protection rankings, and is less restrictive than Germany but stricter than the Netherlands. However, these rankings have serious limitations as regards the enforcement of regulation, a point made by Bertola *et al.* (2000). There are two issues as regards enforcement: the probability of abuses of the law being detected and processed in the courts and the extent of the ensuing sanctions. As regards the first of these two factors, one could argue that the capacity of the employee to give effective voice to perceived violations of his or her legal rights is vital in ensuring the observance of labour law. One would expect that the exceptionally high rate of union membership and the almost universal union presence at the workplace in Sweden would lead to a high level of awareness of employment protection rights and provide the capabilities and resources to pursue these rights, first at the workplace, and then, if need be, in the Labour Court.[2]

In these three countries the norm is an open-ended contract and only if it is explicitly stated that the contract is not to be open-ended is it of limited duration. Previously, objective reasons, for example, limited employment for a trial period or to replace an absent worker, had to be given. As seen below, this is not now always the case.

The legal regulation of the open-ended contract in Spain has been among the strictest in the OECD. Collective redundancies require administrative approval. The law stipulates payment of up to 12 months' wages if judged fair and up to 42 months' wages if judged unfair. In some circumstances the court may mandate reinstatement. It was in the context of the strict employment protection of workers on open-ended contracts that a number of laws since 1984 provided ample opportunity for the employer to hire on limited duration with low severance payments and without the need of administrative approval. This included the use of LDCs for regular activities; that is, with the requirement of objective reasons.

### Recent Trends in Employment Protection[3]

In the six countries studied there are tendencies to some convergence during the 1990s as there has been some increase in employment protection in both the USA and the UK and decrease in the other European countries.

In the USA, the increase in employment protection has been a continuous process occurring within state courts. Between 1973 and 1995, 46 state courts have passed judgments restricting employers' discretion to dismiss employment-at-will employees. It is becoming ever more clear that the simple characterization of employment relationships as employment-at-will is not an adequate description of employment protection in the USA. Moreover, as pointed out above, the effect of the regulation of employment protection cannot be gauged by the regulation alone, but must also take into account the sanctions applied if it is ruled that the employer is at fault. In the USA, the pecuniary costs to the employer may be enormous. In California, in recent years, the average damage awards have amounted to over half a million dollars (plus legal costs). When, in addition, one considers the uncertainty inherent in case judgments based on non-codified regulation, this may add to the impact of even the relatively modest case law protection in the USA.[4]

In the UK since 1997, the Labour government has introduced an appreciable body of legislation with consequences for contingent labour. The National Minimum Wage Act and the implementation of the EU Working Time Directive provide a floor of rights that can be expected to have an impact on the more marginal members of the labour force. The Employment Relations Act conferred some individual employment rights and increased the maximum financial compensation that can be awarded by an Employment Tribunal. Of most direct impact on contingent labour was the reduction of the length of service threshold to qualify for unfair dismissal, from two years to one. A very important recent innovation is the broadening of the scope of those to which some labour law applies. For example, the minimum wage and working time legislation applies not just to employees but to workers, which is a broader category. It would appear that similar extensions will occur in the future as the Employment Relations Act also conferred powers on the secretary of state to extend coverage to workers as regards other legislation.

In Sweden, there has been some relaxation of the strict seniority rules in cases of collective redundancy. The OECD (1999) views the liberalization in temporary work in Sweden as being the most extensive of all countries during the 1990s. Temporary agency work went from being, in practice, illegal to almost total legal deregulation and the requirement to provide an objective reason when employing for a limited duration was removed.

In the Netherlands, it is not fully clear whether the net outcome of the new legislation on LDCs and agency workers tightens or loosens worker protection. While some of the legislation has tended to clarify and strengthen the contractual status of more marginal workers, with an employment contract after a period of work with an employer, it would appear that the deregulatory forces dominate. Moreover, the lengthy procedures at termination of an open-ended contract have undoubtedly been eased.

Of all the countries studied in this volume, Germany probably experienced the fewest changes in regulation in the 1990s. The important (at least symbolically) removal of the requirement to provide an objective reason for the use of an LDC was enacted in the mid-1980s. Compared to other countries, the extension of the maximum duration of limited duration contracts from 18 to 24 months and the gradual and rather modest deregulation of temporary agency work have not been very significant. However, Germany, like the Netherlands and the UK, has incorporated some of its more marginal workers in the social security system.

Also, in Spain, the recent net regulatory trend is not clear. A new form of open-ended contracts was introduced in 1994, with lower employment protection, and the conditions for the use of LDCs were restricted. What is clear is that these legislative changes *could be expected* to lead to a fall in the proportion of those employed on limited duration contracts in the 1990s.

## ON THE GROWTH OF CONTINGENT EMPLOYMENT IN THE 1990S

The data presented in all the national chapters except that for Sweden show relatively modest growth of LDCs in the 1990s. In the USA, the regular special surveys carried out by the Bureau of Labor Statistics (BLS) show a modest decline in all forms of alternative work arrangements between 1995 and 2001. In the UK, in the early 1990s, aggregate contingent employment increased from 5 to 7 per cent of total employment, flattened out from 1995 onwards, and in the most recent years has declined slightly. In the Netherlands, a similar trend can be observed, though at higher levels. In Germany, the level of most forms of contingent employment was stable up towards the end of the decade, after which it increased somewhat. In Sweden, there was a very rapid increase in LDCs with their share of total employment almost doubling over the period. Spain entered the decade with very high levels of LDCs and this level remained stable throughout the decade.

The individual and job characteristics of contingent work are well known. On average, the young, women and ethnic minorities are overrepresented, most significantly in the service sectors.[5] The US and UK chapters underline the dual nature of contingent employment, in that there are a significant number of workers for whom levels of pay and training are higher than for otherwise comparable workers and they express satisfaction with their contractual status. However, in most countries workers express a clear preference for open-ended contracts.

The potential impact of regulation on the use of contingent employment is related to the regulation differential between contingent and open-ended work. The classic example of this is, of course, the rapid increase of LDCs in Spain in the 1980s. Moreover, it is obvious that it is the liberal regulation of the open-ended contract in the USA and the UK that lead to relatively low levels of contingent employment. However, from the basic features of the changes of legislation in the 1990s and the growth of contingent employment in the 1990s, it is obvious that the relationship is far from clear. In the last decade, Spain has substantially reduced the regulation differential but the level of LDCs has remained stable. In the UK and the Netherlands, it rose until the last two years of the decade and then declined. The only country that appears to reveal a clear relationship between legislation and the use of LDCs is Sweden. However, it is argued in the Swedish chapter that the apparently considerable liberalization of legislation for LDCs, as claimed, for example, in OECD (1999), was largely illusionary.

It is more obvious to consider that the stable level of contingent employment in the USA since 1995 and the decrease in the UK and the Netherlands at the end of the decade were related to the labour market boom during this period. In the Swedish chapter much attention was devoted to the role of unemployment in the increase in LDCs in the 1990s. The most obvious empirical indication that unemployment lies behind the growth of LDCs is that both increased rapidly in the early to mid-1990s. Moreover, the broad evidence from other Nordic countries is also in line with this explanation. (See Holmlund and Storrie, 2002.) Among the other Nordic countries, only Finland has exhibited a similar growth in LDCs. Indeed, the Finnish experience during the 1990s was even more dramatic than the Swedish one, with greater increases both in unemployment and in LDCs. The macroeconomic conditions in Denmark and Norway were much less volatile, with only modest increases in unemployment. It is striking that neither of these two countries experienced any significant rise in LDCs.[6] From flow data, the mechanics of the relationship are clear (Holmlund and Storrie, 2002), as it is simply due to the increase in the number of people in the major source states for flows into LDCs (non-participation and unemployment) with transition rates remaining more or less constant.

There are a number of possible ways in which unemployment can have an impact on the proportion of LDCs in the labour market. In periods of high unemployment, with many job seekers, high screening costs may provide a greater incentive for firms to screen through LDCs, and Holmlund and Storrie (2002) provide some empirical support for this matching hypothesis. On the supply side there may be an increased willingness on the part of workers to accept LDCs when job offers are in short supply. The authors also find tentative evidence of a trend increase in LDCs in the 1990s, irrespective of business cycle conditions. They argue that this may be due to increased product market volatility, but can provide no hard evidence for this.

Also in Spain, the massive increase in LDCs in the 1980s occurred simultaneously with a very rapid increase in unemployment, which rose to over 20 per cent by the end of the decade. Somewhat surprisingly, the literature has not explicitly addressed in any depth the relationship between unemployment and the rise of LDCs. Dolado *et al.* (2002) summarize much of this research. The most interesting aspect of the recent Spanish experience is that, despite falling unemployment, and the narrowing of the regulation differential between limited duration and open-ended contracts, there has been no significant decline in the share of LDCs. Thus the Spanish experience of the 1990s indicates that, even if regulation and unemployment may have combined to increase the number of LDCs, a reversal of these factors does not necessarily lead to a decrease.[7]

Finally, this volume has pointed out the serious empirical limitations of research on contingent employment. There are grounds to believe that labour force surveys seriously underreport the extent, and often incorrectly classify the category, of contingent employment. This point was forcefully made in the UK chapter.[8] Even in the USA, with its ambitious BLS survey, considerable uncertainty remains as to the level of various forms of contingent employment. For example, in the literature one finds many different figures on the number of agency workers (see Autor, 2003; Blank, 1998; and the BLS figures in the US chapter). This is probably at least in part related to the proliferation of new forms of 'non-standard employment relationships' which may be legally rather complicated and thus difficult for respondents to labour force and other surveys to distinguish correctly. Moreover, given the short duration of these jobs, it may be difficult for statistical authorities to capture the dynamics of such a rapidly moving target. Thus, despite the great advances in labour statistics in recent decades, it is a sobering thought that it may well be that our empirical knowledge of one of the basic elements of labour force statistics, that is, contractual status, is poorer today than it was two or three decades ago.

## TEMPORARY AGENCY WORK

As mentioned in the introduction to this chapter, agency work is of particular interest, for a number of reasons. It is by far the most rapidly growing form of contingent employment and in many countries it is a relatively new phenomenon. The 1990s saw great legislative activity in the member states of the European Union and, as this volume goes to press, we await the outcome of the proposed directive from the European Commission. However, perhaps of most interest and importance is its potential to contribute to a resolution of a major conflict in labour markets in the last few decades, namely the security–flexibility trade-off.

### Empirical Background

In the six countries studied in this volume, temporary agency work has been by far the most rapidly growing form of contingent employment. This has also been the case throughout the European Union (Storrie, 2002). Since 1992, agency work has at least doubled in all member states (apart from Greece, where it does not officially exist) and increased at least fivefold in Denmark, Spain, Italy and Sweden and just under fourfold in Austria (see Table 9.1). France, with over 623000, has more agency workers than any other country in the EU and accounts for 30 per cent of the total. The UK is the other major contributor to the EU total. The Netherlands is the most agency work-intensive country, followed by Luxemburg, France, the UK and Belgium. The intensity is low in Austria, Germany and the Scandinavian and southern European countries. While growth has been rapid in all countries throughout the decade, it is noteworthy that in the most agency work-intensive country of all, the Netherlands, the figures for 2000 and 2001 both show a slight decline.

*Table 9.1 Temporary agency work in the European Union, 1999*

| | Number of agency workers | Share of all agency workers in EU (%) | Rate of agency work (%) |
|---|---|---|---|
| Austria | 24277 | 1.2 | 0.7 |
| Belgium | 62661 | 3.0 | 1.6 |
| Denmark | 18639 | 0.9 | 0.7 |
| Finland | 15000 | 0.7 | 0.6 |
| France | 623000 | 29.9 | 2.7 |
| Germany | 243000 | 11.7 | 0.7 |
| Greece | 0 | 0.0 | 0.0 |
| Ireland | 9000 | 0.4 | 0.6 |
| Italy | 31000 | 1.5 | 0.2 |
| Luxemburg | 6065 | 0.3 | 3.5 |
| Netherlands | 305000 | 14.7 | 4.0 |
| Portugal | 45000 | 2.2 | 1.0 |
| Spain | 109000 | 5.2 | 0.8 |
| Sweden | 32000 | 1.5 | 0.8 |
| UK | 557000 | 26.8 | 2.1 |
| EU total | 2080642 | 100.0 | 1.4 |

*Source:* Storrie (2002). This in turn was based on 15 national reports presented to the European Foundation for the Improvement of Living and Working Conditions, Dublin in 2001 and CIETT (2000).

Agency work is highly concentrated among the young in the labour force, with the share of under-25-year-olds ranging between 20 and 50 per cent of all agency workers in the various member states. There is evidence, however, that agency workers are getting older. With the exception of the three Scandinavian member states, the majority of agency workers are men. Male dominance of the sector is most pronounced in Germany and Austria. It is clear that the gender distribution of agency work can largely be explained by the sectors in which the two sexes work.

## The Regulation of Temporary Agency Work

Whatever demand-side explanations may be put forward, it is obvious that the recent increase in agency work could not have occurred in many countries without the deregulationary legislation in the 1990s.

The countries studied in this volume adhere to one of the rather distinct typologies of regulation as defined in Storrie (2002). A definition of temporary agency work, though one that does not apply fully to all countries, is the following: a temporary agency worker is employed by the temporary work agency and is then, via a commercial contact, hired out to perform work assignments at the user firm. While the above definition is a workable definition of the agency worker in most member states, this is not the case in the USA and the UK, where the contractual status of agency workers may be sometimes unclear (see below).

There are two means of regulating agency work, the regulation of the business and the labour law regulation of contracts and assignments. The business is primarily regulated by means of licensing and monitoring procedures, and some countries curtail the scope of an agency's activities by, for example, prohibiting recruitment services. In most countries, labour law regulates, not primarily the contract of employment, but rather the assignment at the user firm. This is typically the case in Continental Europe. Collective agreements also play a role in the regulation of assignments and contracts, in particular in the Netherlands and Sweden and, to a lesser extent, in Belgium and France. The three typologies of regulation are the Continental, the Anglophone and the Scandinavian.

**The Continental countries**

Belgium, France, Italy, Luxemburg, Portugal, Spain and Germany have a detailed regulation of temporary agency work. In both labour and company law, agency work is seen as a distinct activity. Companies must obtain a licence to set up business and are monitored by special institutions. Labour law restricts the type and duration of assignment at the user firm. The legal objective grounds for assignments are similar to those for LDCs (but not in Germany). The extensive legislation must be seen as being amongst the most interventionist in the Union. While the regulation is extensive and detailed, there is evidence of non-observance of the law. Collective bargaining is most prevalent and most developed in Belgium and France, and is beginning to emerge in Spain, Germany and Italy, while in Portugal it remains negligible.

While sharing some of the extensive regulation of the other countries in this group, Germany is a special case. The objective reasons in the other countries in the Continental model do not apply in Germany. Regulation focuses instead on the duration of the contract, which may not be only for the duration of a single assignment (the synchronization ban).

**The Anglophone countries: USA, UK and Ireland**

The UK and Ireland have a common law system of labour law and this has led to a rather different concept of agency work than in other countries. For example, in the UK those engaged in what is commonly referred to as agency work may be viewed as employed at the user firm or the agency, or even self-employed. Despite modest specific legislation of agency work, several laws do make special provisions for agency workers: for example, regarding working time in the UK and unfair dismissals in Ireland. However, as the specific legislation is limited and, above all, because of liberal general labour law, for example as regards employment security, agency workers are awarded relatively limited legal protection. A distinctive feature of agency work in Ireland is that the user firm adopts many of the obligations of the employer and may even be liable for unfair dismissal.

In the UK, there are only a few minor sector collective agreements, most notably in the audio-visual sector. The big companies, such as Manpower and Adecco, have company-wide agreements but, as they constitute only a small share of the business in the UK market, coverage is limited.

**The Scandinavian countries**

Denmark, Finland and Sweden have practically no special regulation of the temporary agency business and assignments, and the legal treatment of agency work per se is probably the most non-interventionist in the European Union.[9] However, this does not mean that less employment protection is awarded to agency workers than, for example, in the UK, the USA or Ireland. The lack of specific legislation means agency work is not a distinct form of employment and must conform to mainstream labour law. In Finland and Sweden, statutory law provides significant protection to all workers and thus even to agency workers. Moreover, in Sweden, collective agreements cover the entire sector and, most notably, award workers guaranteed pay corresponding to at least 80 per cent of the monthly wage, regardless of the availability of assignments. Labour law in Denmark, particularly as regards employment protection, is appreciably less strict. However, several collective agreements have specifically addressed agency work and include special calculations of seniority to accommodate agency work.

As, prior to the legislation of the 1990s, agency work could best be described as illegal, the current legal status of the sector in Scandinavia represents a remarkable degree of deregulation and marks without doubt the most radical shift of all member states during the 1990s.

Three EU countries fit poorly into the classifications above. The Netherlands is a distinctive model with little regulation of the business but with detailed and specific law pertaining to the contract at the agency, with job security increasing with time spent at the agency. The regulation resulted from a long process of negotiation between the social partners and collective agreements play an important role in regulation. Austria shares the liberal regulation of the sector in Scandinavia and the Anglophone countries. However, specific legislation establishes temporary agency work (TAW) as a specific form of employment. Agency work is prohibited in Greece.

In the Continental countries (with the partial exceptions of Austria and the Netherlands) and as exemplified by Spain in Chapter 5 of this volume, TAW is seen as a distinct phenomenon, as regards both labour (assignments) law and company (licensing and monitoring) law. At the other extreme, as perhaps best represented by Sweden and, to a lesser extent, the UK, agency work is treated as any other form of business and the employment contractual status is regulated no differently from other forms of employment. The Dutch model is somewhere between these two: only after a period of time at the agency does the worker receive the protection that labour law may provide to all other workers. See the Dutch chapter for more details.

Thus, in the non-Continental countries, the legal status and degree of employment protection of agency workers is totally dependent on the general system of labour law. For example, the specific legal regulation of temporary agency workers in the UK and Sweden is similar but, owing to very different general systems of labour law, the legal status of agency workers in both countries is very different. Thus it is obviously not possible to pronounce judgement on a particular legal model solely by examining legal aspects of agency work alone. In the Continental countries, with their detailed specific regulation of agency work, the impact of the general system of labour is of somewhat less importance.

**On the Increase of Temporary Agency Work**

At the upper end of the wage distribution some workers express a preference for agency work. However, most of the country chapters in this book show that they are a minority (see also Cohany, 1998). The deregulation of agency work, as outlined above, has obviously been an important factor behind the growth of agency work. Citing Autor (2003), the US country chapter suggests that it is not only the regulation of agency work but the tightening of the regulation of employment contracts generally in case law that may lie behind the rise of agency work in the 1990s in the USA. Moreover, it is also clear that the position taken by various institutional actors has affected the growth of agency work and the contrasting position taken by the German and Swedish trade unions (see the country chapters) is a case in point. However, regulation is hardly exogenous and we would prefer to view the rise of agency work in terms of the demand from user firms for this type of labour and the temporary work agencies' capability to supply it.

There are a number of reasons why the firm may hire labour on a temporary basis, such as for a specific task that is limited in duration, to replace an absent permanent employee and so on. Whatever the reason, severance costs may make frequent open-ended employment contracts for a short duration unprofitable for the firm. As this volume has demonstrated, one of the most prominent trends in labour law in the last two decades in Europe has been the proliferation of the circumstances in which the employer may hire labour under conditions other than those under open-ended contracts. The employment protection literature explaining the rise and consequences of 'flexible' employment contracts takes relatively lower severance costs as a theoretical point of departure. See Dolado *et al.* (2002) for a recent review of the interesting Spanish research. Here we do not address the issue of why establishments in most OECD countries over the last two decades have, to an increasing degree, used various forms of temporary employment contracts, but take it as a stylized fact. However, it is relevant here to demonstrate that agency work may be a more appropriate means of performing the same functions as temporary employment contracts.

The truly distinguishing feature of agency work in this context is that all adjustment costs are directly borne by the agency. Of course, the client firm pays for this service, and this is a source of agency profits. However, the specialization of such functions in agencies with the potential for economies of scale, together with the potential for agencies to spread employment termination risks between various firms and sectors of the economy, may lead to lower costs through an outsourcing of these functions to the agency, rather than for the client firms performing them in-house.

The outsourcing of some functions of the personnel department at the client firm is most obviously apparent when viewing recruitment. Matching is the key issue in an equilibrium unemployment model of agency work developed in Neugart and Storrie (2002). The model argues that the emergence and growth of temporary agency work is due to an upward shift in the matching efficiency parameter. The question is, why may this have occurred?

As was mentioned above, in many European countries one of the key factors is almost certainly deregulation. The impact of deregulation in Sweden, in particular must be viewed as indisputably a necessary condition for the rapid growth there in the latter part of the decade. Deregulation was also extensive in Spain and this has been the general trend throughout the European Union. As deregulation increases the opportunity for agencies to perform matching activities, it is certainly one of the obvious candidates to enable the emergence and growth of agency work in the 1990s in the OECD.

We may say that the characteristic feature of agency work is the outsourcing of the labour adjustment function to the intermediary, and in particular the performance of the matching function for the user firm.

Matching on the labour market is one of the classic examples of exchange under asymmetric information (see Spence, 1973), and is often expressed in terms of job seekers having more information on their capabilities and effort levels than the firm. In this situation an intermediary can reduce the uncertainty facing the firm as the agency will have the incentive to report accurately the quality of their workers to the client firm in order to build and maintain their reputation. The agency will be more concerned with reputation than a single job seeker, as the agency has a greater number of possible future transactions. Furthermore, as the agency specializes in recruitment, that is, search, screening and possibly training, this specialization will probably imply that an agency will recruit more workers than a typical client firm and thus may exploit economies of scale. In the case of a temporary work agency, the uncertainty of the client firm is further diminished by the fact that, unlike a recruitment agency, the client firm does not need to accept any employment risk and, indeed, a guarantee of quality may even be stipulated explicitly in the commercial contract between the agency and the client firm for the duration of the assignment.

As was seen from some of the country chapters, the issue of reputation has obviously been of great importance to agencies. The improvement of reputation has been a very prominent strategy of many agency companies in the last decade, with several companies, such as Manpower and Randstad, having now become recognizable brand names. This is almost certainly related to the two factors mentioned above: the information role played by agencies and the recent legal history of agency work. Prior to deregulation, when agencies often operated in a legal grey zone, reputation was in many cases very low and many agencies were associated with shady practices. They have sought to build reputation with both potential employees and client firms by means of ethical codes of practice, advertising campaigns and the signing of collective agreements (see Storrie, 2002). Reputation building is costly and the knowledge that such investment has been made may further convince client firms of agencies' commitment to quality. Furthermore, the agency sector has undergone considerable market consolidation during the 1990s. According to CIETT (2000), by 1998 the top five temporary work agencies accounted for over 50 per cent of turnover in 11 of the 14 member states where agency work exists. This process may have further served to push out some of the smaller and less reputable agencies. Improved reputation has presumably served to improve the matching efficiency of temporary work agencies, in that they are able to attract better job applicants and to gain acceptance of agency workers by the personnel departments and the trade unions at the client firm.

Petrongolo and Pissarides (2001) note that technological advances can shift the matching parameter upwards. The rapid growth of agency work since the beginning of the 1990s coincided with the widespread introduction of information and communication technology (ICT). Internet job sites are able to contain appreciably more vacancy and job seeker information at much lower cost than, for example, newspapers. However, the availability of this technology by no means necessarily implies that there will be an increase in the direct contact between firms and job seekers without going through a matching intermediary. The fact that the technology significantly lowers the cost for the job seeker to apply for jobs may lead to employers being inundated with applications. Thus, as argued in Autor (2001a), intermediaries such as temporary work agencies will be required in order that employers may reap the benefits of the computerized matching technologies. Furthermore, the role of intermediaries in providing high-quality information is a much-researched issue in the e-commerce literature; see Malone *et al.* (1987) and Sarkar *et al.* (1995), who stress economies of scale and scope and the reputation issue mentioned above. Thus the idea here is that ICT has the potential to increase matching efficiency. However, this potential can only be fully realized if it is exploited by matching intermediaries such as temporary work agencies.

Coordination failures, that is, the uncoordinated action of firms and workers, are according to Petrongolo and Pissarides (2001), potentially a major source of matching inefficiency. Just as the business and industrial organization literature has observed how supply and client firms coordinate their activities, there is evidence of increased coordination between agency and client firms. Indeed, Belkacem (1998), in a comparative study of France and Germany, compared the agency–client firm relationship with other subcontractors of the client firm. Macaire and Michon (2001) found that agency work is becoming more integrated into management systems of the client undertakings and is thus much more than a one-off measure to cope with unexpected situations. Thus, as temporary work agencies build up business relationships with their client firms and better understand their labour requirements, they may be more able to avoid coordination failure. This is a process that takes time and may be related to learning-by-doing. The learning process of agencies may also be related to sectors or regions, as empirically illustrated for France in Lefevre *et al.* (2001).

Thus the explanation for increased matching efficiency in temporary work agencies is that, with deregulation, agencies were able to devote themselves to these activities, in some countries, for the first time and in others more easily. After deregulation the agencies were able to build upon their reputation in order to attract workers and client firms. Reputation is also a vital factor in convincing the client firm that the agency will provide it with correct information on worker capabilities. As the agency becomes more like a supply firm, the closer relations between the agency and the client firm serve to reduce coordination failure. The learning-by-doing process also may apply to sectors and locations. There are thus a number of reasons why matching efficiency in agencies may have increased in the 1990s and, of course, we cannot distinguish between these various possibilities.

Finally, the comparison with LDCs highlights one of the most important *potential* social advantages of temporary agency work, in that it can provide an open-ended contract for the worker while contributing to numerical flexibility for the user firm. Any type of LDC is by definition associated with job insecurity and with negative consequences for the employees.[10] However, in contractual terms, employment at a temporary work agency does not necessarily mean employment insecurity, and there are some agency workers with open-ended employment contracts. Thus temporary agency work has the potential to contribute to the solution of one of the major conflicts in European labour markets in recent decades, namely to reconcile the firm's preference for flexibility and the worker's preference for job security. While of course there are problems specific to agency work (see below) it does, in principle, provide one means of attaining a positive sum solution to this basic conflict of interests for the types of economic activity for which it is suitable. As such the 'flexicurity' perspective may provide the basis for a compromise with mutual benefits to the social partners. Indeed, it was the exploitation of this opportunity that contributed to the Dutch social partners reaching their compromise.

However, it must be underlined that a major concern about agency work *is* related to the precarious nature of agency work: in terms of job security, in practice and in most countries most agency work is not typically performed with an open-ended contract. Moreover, even when agency work is with an open-ended contract, the sector's extreme sensitivity to the business cycle results in considerable de facto precariousness (see Storrie, 2002).[11]

## Some Problems Associated with Agency Work

We should also emphasize that there are a number of other problems related to agency work, as shown in the country chapters in this volume, and in Storrie (2002). A major problem is the difficulty of finding an appropriate means of financing investment in human capital. The skills required for agency work are obviously not firm-specific. According to human capital theory, firms will not be prepared to finance non-firm-specific human capital fully, as they may not be able to reap the return on their investment if the worker should quit (see Autor, 2001b). Moreover, the propensity to quit may be high, as the agency worker may be poached while on an assignment at the user firm. There is ample evidence of low training levels for agency workers in the country chapters (see also Paoli and Merllié, 2001).

There are two features specific to agency work that may be expected to lead to poor working conditions. These are the frequent change of workplace at user firms and the duality of employer responsibility. This means that all matters that require some form of dialogue between employers and employees are likely to be difficult to deal with. Indeed, there is evidence (Storrie, 2002) that testifies to the problems in setting up the institutions of social dialogue at the workplace for agency workers.

Nowhere does the combination of dual employer responsibility and rapid workplace turnover combine to such potentially problematic effect as in health and safety at the workplace. These matters have been regulated in Directive 91/383/EEC, which aims to ensure equal treatment. The main thrust of the legislation is to place primary responsibility with the user firm and to require the TWA to inform the worker of the risks specific to each assignment. The directive does require that the worker be given sufficient training to deal with health and safety matters, but does not specify who is responsible for the provision of this training. It is far from obvious where the responsibility should lie. For example, what does the user firm know about an agency worker's previous training and what does the agency know about the particular form of training required for a particular user firm? When one also considers the very short duration of a typical assignment, it is far from obvious how these problems can be solved and one should expect some problems with health and safety in agency work.

There is much anecdotal evidence of poor working conditions in agency work (Storrie, 2002) but much less hard evidence. Moreover, most research cannot differentiate between the factors related to the agency work per se (the contractual form) and factors related to the job or the worker. However, Storrie shows that, in some countries, agency work is associated with appreciably worse working conditions (accidents and health hazards) than other employment forms. The most detailed evidence is to be found in the *Third European Survey on Working Conditions* (Paoli and Merllié, 2001). Compared to all other employment contractual forms, including LDCs, temporary agency work has the worst record as regards a number of indicators of working conditions, including information about risks in using materials, products and instruments and repetitive work.

Finally, it is obvious that the commercial contract between the agency and the user firm has the potential to undermine the pay and working conditions determined by law, collective agreements or norm for workers directly employed at the user firm. Storrie (2002) provides some empirical evidence of this and it is discussed in more detail in the next section.

## REGULATION, EQUAL TREATMENT AND THE FLEXIBILITY–SECURITY TRADE-OFF

One of the major sources of conflict between the employers and employees has always been the employer demands for greater numerical flexibility and the employees' preference for employment security. These two aims appear irreconcilable and more of one appears to imply less of the other. However, as mentioned above, temporary agency work has the potential to provide both security, by means of an employment contract at the agency, and flexibility, by means of assignments at various user firms.[12] Thus the final section of this volume explores how, in principle, the regulation of agency work could develop to meet this dual aim.

The regulation of assignments, in terms of duration or objective reasons, is currently the main means of regulating agency work in labour law, particularly in the Continental countries. It is far from obvious that such regulation of the assignment is in the interests of the agency worker. As regards employment security for the agency worker, the regulation of the assignment per se is not the critical issue, but rather the security of the employment contract which, in most member states, is with the temporary work agency. The regulation of the assignment at the user firm appears primarily to serve to ensure that agency work does not become widespread in terms of job category and duration at the user firm and thus undermine standards. The regulation of assignments is thus primarily related to the interests of the workers in the user firm. This, while perhaps obvious, should be made explicit. If one is to regulate working conditions and pay to the benefit of agency workers, the regulation of the assignment, in terms of duration and objective reasons, is not the relevant issue.[13]

However, in no way is it implied that the interests of the workers at the user firm are not valid interests. There is clearly potential for agency work to undermine the collective agreement, at the user firm, as it may be circumvented by a commercial contract. This explains why the main issue for the unions in the European Social Dialogue was equal treatment for agency and user firm workers. It may also explain why Swedish unions were able to accept the radical statutory deregulation, as they believed (correctly as it turned out – see the chapter on Sweden) that they could maintain the integrity of the user firm collective bargain.

If the maintenance of standards of pay and working conditions at the user firm is the major concern, this can be achieved in a number of ways. Legislation can limit the extent of agency work at the user firm, through the regulation of assignments, as typically is the case in the Continental countries. If agency work does not become widespread, poorer working conditions for agency workers may not affect the user firm. However, the growth and current level of agency work in these countries suggest that this is not a successful strategy.

Another option is to legislate directly on equal treatment, as exemplified by the recent wage equalization law in Spain. However, it is far from obvious what equal treatment should entail and the experience of several member states is that legislation may not be effective. As was pointed out in Storrie (2002) and the Spanish chapter, the intrinsically fuzzy and somewhat complicated nature of the *ménage à trois* that is agency work makes the day-to-day implementation of the law rather difficult. In this context, clarity on what equal treatment is supposed to achieve, that is, the maintenance of standards at the user firm, may be helpful. If it is possible to legislate equal treatment directly and effectively, this should have most impact in member states which lack other means to ensure equal treatment, such as the UK. However, in the UK, the recent tendency in labour law to use the broad term 'worker' as opposed to 'employee' could also be seen as a means of obtaining equal treatment; see the UK chapter.

Another means of achieving equal treatment is through the trade unions at the user firm. In Sweden, trade unions have the right to veto the placement of agency workers at the user firm, if they have reason to believe that it may undermine the collective agreement. In addition, practically the entire temporary agency sector is covered by collective agreements. The lack of such widespread coverage of collective agreements and trade union presence at the workplace hardly makes this an option in most other member states.

As mentioned above, perhaps the major issue in all forms of temporary work is the apparent trade-off between flexibility for employers and employment security for the workers. However, agency work has the *potential* to resolve this conflict by providing an employment contract at the agency and flexible assignments at the user firm. Policy makers should pursue the potential of agency work to resolve this seemingly intractable issue.

## A Positive Sum Policy Proposal

How, then, can legislative initiatives be conducive to providing this best of both worlds? As noted above, the regulation of the assignment does not serve the job security interests of the agency worker. Indeed, limitations on the duration of assignment, in particular, may obviously limit job tenure. It is the regulation of the contract at the temporary work agency that should be the focus of attention. Different countries have different levels of protection for employment contracts and it is hardly appropriate to recommend specific proposals for all countries. Nevertheless, it appears reasonable to suggest that agency workers should have the same employment protection as other employees. Thus the presumption should be that employment is with an open-ended contract, unless there are objective grounds to contract otherwise.[14] In some countries repeated use of LDCs is limited and, if abused the contract may be transferred to an open-ended contract. This is the situation in Sweden, the Netherlands and Germany. The current Dutch regulation is a half-way house, moving away from the previous regulation of assignments at the user firm to regulation of the employment contract at the temporary work agency, in that the first period at the agency resembles 'employment-at-will', followed by an LDC and finally an open-ended contract. Longer-term employment contracts may also serve to award agency workers more seniority rights at the agency.

Employment protection for agency workers cannot be achieved by statutory law alone, as Swedish and Dutch experience indicates. In both these countries there appears to have been a fundamental acceptance of the phenomenon of agency work and a willingness to seek regulation that is not exclusively focused on the risk of agency work undermining the integrity of the collective agreement at the user firm. In other Continental European countries, for example Germany and Spain, this acceptance has been both reluctant and late. Given that employment protection of agency workers is a valid aim, there is a need for unions to relinquish any remaining reluctance to organize at agencies and to act to provide for employment protection.

It was argued above that there may be appreciable economic benefits of agency work for user firms and profits to agencies *without having to circumvent the standards of employment at the user firm*. There are potentially economies of scale and scope to be reaped for some types of economic activity. Moreover, the risk-pooling function of the labour market intermediary may promote employment creation. Agency work also provides more numerically flexible labour than LDCs and there are reasons to believe that job matching through agency work may be particularly efficient and thus serve to reduce frictional unemployment.[15] From this perspective there may be much to gain from deregulation of the sector along the lines of the Netherlands and Sweden. The removal of the barriers to entry and monitoring procedures, limitations in scope of the activities of temporary work agencies and, above all, the removal of objective reasons for assignments would almost certainly be of benefit to the sector, the user firms and perhaps the entire economy.

There are thus three principal regulatory issues: to allow temporary work agencies to pursue profitable business activities, to ensure the integrity of the collective bargain at the user firm, and finally to ensure some degree of job security for agency workers. An ideal solution would be one that truly awarded equal treatment to all. *Equal treatment for the temporary agency sector*, in terms of company law, might be of benefit not only to the sector itself, but also to user firms and the economy as a whole. *Equal treatment for agency workers in terms of employment status in labour law* would provide the same level of employment protection as for other employees, that is, an open-ended contract or, if objective grounds exist, a contract of limited duration. More secure contracts, together with increased employment levels from deregulation, could promote the opportunity for agency workers to have careers and to benefit from seniority rights. The final piece of this integrated ideal policy package is ensuring the integrity of standards at the user firm by providing *equal treatment as regards pay and working conditions for agency workers at the user firm.* These three aspects of equal treatment cannot be implemented piecemeal. It would appear that, of the three, the most difficult to achieve, especially through legislation alone, is equal treatment for agency and user firm workers as regards pay and working conditions.

The regulatory programme broadly sketched above is of course far from fully developed and is written in general, not country-specific, terms and, to be successfully implemented, would require detailed national adoptions. Some recent comments of Michael Piore, perhaps the leading economist of work organization of the last three decades, appear to concur with the general thrust of this broad policy programme:

> In the old system, employment continuity and career development depended heavily upon the personnel policies of the productive enterprise as modified and amended in collective bargaining. As these enterprises have become less stable, and the structure of employment within them subject to more frequent and more radical changes, a variety of intermediary institutions have emerged to guide workers through the labor market and convert irregular jobs into more continuous employment. But these institutions are extremely various in character, ranging from temporary help services and executive search firms to identity-based networks formed around the social affiliations that structure social mobilization, and alternatively networks of alumni of educational institutions or former employees of prominent corporations. The role these institutions play is similar to that played by craft unions and professional associations in labor markets when these were the dominant form of work organization. This suggests that we are moving toward an organization based on crafts and professions, and that one could impose upon the emergent intermediaries the obligations previously assumed by the productive enterprise itself. (Piore, 2002, p. 20)

While we argue that agency work is a potential means of ensuring employment security and career development, there is ample evidence to suggest that it is not yet performing this role, and indeed in many countries it is associated with considerable employment insecurity, poor wages and low human capital investment. However, as succinctly put by Deakin (2002), 'The labour law of yesterday issued not from the heads of experts but from engagement, conflict and collective negotiation. There is no reason to think it will be any different in the future.' The role of policy is to provide an enabling legislative framework, in terms not only of labour but also of social security law, upon which the involved parties may hammer out the appropriate institutional arrangements. In terms of labour law, the first step should be to provide agency workers with the same employment contract status as other employees.

## NOTES

1. The main aim of the directive is to establish the *general principle of non-discrimination*, in terms of basic working conditions, of agency workers compared to workers in the *user* firm doing the same or similar work There are, however, several important exceptions: where a temporary worker has a *permanent contract* and is paid between assignments, where social partners can conclude *collective agreements* derogating from the principle by providing for alternative means to secure adequate protection and where an assignment or series of assignments with one user firm will *not exceed six weeks*.
2. This may be expected to be even of some importance in the Netherlands and Germany, which also have greater worker representation and influence at the workplace than, for example, the USA and the UK.
3. Temporary work agencies are only briefly mentioned in this subsection. They are dealt with in detail below.
4. One should also note that, in 1988, the WARN Act introduced legislation, for the first time on a federal basis, that required procedures to be observed by employers in cases of collective redundancies.
5. However, it should be noted that temporary agency work differs somewhat, in that it is more prevalent among men and most intense in industry. This is particularly the case in Germany.
6. Sweden, Norway and Finland have similar regulation of employment contracts. Denmark is more similar to the more liberal regimes as in, for example, the UK.
7. It should, however, be pointed out that, at least, the 1990s saw a levelling out of the number of LDCs, and they have in fact declined in the private sector.
8. See in particular Burchell *et al.* (1999).
9. We note, however, that this is not the case in Norway, which can be seen as adhering to the Continental model.
10. See Benavides and Benach (1999) and Paoli and Merllié ( 2001).
11. But note that, owing to the risk diversification argument stated above, one could argue that TAW may still provide more employment security when business cycle shocks hit the economy asymmetrically.
12. Once again it should be underlined that, in practice, agency work is usually still very strongly associated with extreme precariousness in the labour market.
13. The exception is the prohibition of agency workers performing an assignment that may be detrimental to their health. We should also note that a longer duration of assignments would serve to diminish the rapid assignment turnover that could be detrimental for agency workers.
14. Of course the terminology does not apply to the UK and the USA. In the UK, the corresponding presumption would be that agency workers are granted status as employees at the agency in all aspects of labour law and not just in terms of the specific legislation, as mentioned in the UK chapter of this volume.
15. There is some empirical indication of this in Katz and Krueger (1999).

## REFERENCES

Addison, John T. (1989) 'The Controversy Over Advance Notice Legislation in the United States', *British Journal of Industrial Relations*, 27(2).

Autor, D. (2001a) 'Wiring the labor market', *Journal of Economic Perspectives*, 15, 25–40.

Autor, D. (2001b) 'Why do Temporary Firms Provide Free General Skills Training?', *Quarterly Journal of Economics*, 116(4), November, 1409–48.

Autor, D. (2003) 'Outsourcing at Will: The Contribution of Unjust Dismissal Doctrine to the Growth of Employment Outsourcing', *Journal of Labor Economics*, January.

Belkacem, R. (1998) *L'institutionalisation du travail intérimaire en France et en Allemagne. Une étude empirique et théorique*, Collection Logiques Economiques, Paris: L'Harmattan.

Benavides, F. and J. Benach (1999) *Precarious Employment and Health-related Outcomes in the European Union*, European Foundation for the Improvement of Living and Working Conditions, Luxemburg: Office for Official Publications of the European Commission.

Bertola, G. (1990) 'Job Security, Employment and Wages', *European Economic Review*, 34, 851–79.

Bertola, G., T. Boeri and S. Cazes (2000) 'Employment Protection in Industrialized Countries. The Case for New Indicators', *International Labour Review*, 139(1), 57–72.

Blank, R. (1998) 'Contingent work in a changing labour market', in R. Freeman and P. Gottschalk (eds), *Generating Jobs: How to Increase Demand for Less-Skilled Workers*, New York: Russell Sage Foundation.

Burchell, B., S. Deakin and S. Honey (1999) *The Employment Status of Workers in Non-standard Employment*, EMAR Research Series No. 6, London: DTI.

CIETT (2000) *Orchestrating the Evolution of Private Employment Agencies Towards a Stronger Society*, Paris: International Confederation of Private Employment Agencies.

Cohany, S. (1998) 'Workers in alternative employment arrangements: a second look', *Monthly Labour Review*, 121, 3–21.

Deakin, S. (2002) 'The Evolution of the Employment Relationship', paper presented to France-ILO Symposium on The Future of Work Employment and Social Protection, 17–18 January, Lyons, France.

Dolado, J., C. Garcia-Serrano and J. Jimeno (2002) 'Drawing Lessons from the Boom of Temporary Jobs in Spain', *Economic Journal*, 112, June, F1–F25.

Holmlund, B. and D. Storrie (2002) 'Temporary Work in Turbulent Times: The Swedish Experience' *Economic Journal*, 112, June, F1–F25.

Hyman, Richard (1993) 'Labor Law, the Labor Market, and the State: British Industrial Relations under the Conservatives', in C. Buechtemann (ed.), *Employment Security and Labor Market Behavior*, Ithaca, NY: ILR Press.

Katz, L.F. and A.B. Krueger (1999) 'The high-pressure U.S. labor market of the 1990s', *Brookings Papers on Economic Activity*, Washington, 1, 1–87.

Knight, F. (1921) *Risk, Uncertainty and Profit*, Boston: Houghton, Mifflin.

Lefevre, G., F. Michon and M. Viprey (2001) 'Zeitarbeit in Frankreich – Der Markt, der Wirtschaftssektor, die neuen Entwicklungen', in J. Gabriel and M. Neugart (eds), *Ökonomie als Grundlage wirtschaftspolitischer Entscheidungen – Essays on*

*Growth, Labor Markets, and European Integration in Honor of Michael Bolle*, Berlin: Leske & Budrich, pp. 135–50.

Macaire, S. and F. Michon (2001) *Temporary placement in France*, Dublin: European Foundation for the Improvement of Working Life and Living Conditions.

Malone, T., J. Yates and R. Benjamin (1987) 'The logic of electronic markets', *Harvard Business Review*, 166–71.

Milgrom, P. and J. Roberts (1992) *Economics, Organisation and Management*, Englewood Cliffs, NJ: Prentice-Hall International.

Neugart M. and D. Storrie (2002) 'Temporary Agency Work and Equilibrium Unemployment', Discussion Paper FS I 02-203, Social Science Research Centre, Berlin.

OECD (1999) *Employment Outlook 1999*, Paris: OECD Publications.

Paoli, P. and D. Merllié (2001) *Third European Survey on Working Conditions*, European Foundation for the Improvement of Living and Working Conditions, Luxemburg: Office for Official Publications of the European Commission.

Petrongolo, B. and C. Pissarides (2001) 'Looking into the black box: a survey of the matching function', *Journal of Economic Literature*, 39, 390–431.

Piore, M. (2002) 'The Reconfiguration of Work and Employment Relations in the United States at the Turn of the Century', paper presented to France-ILO Symposium on The Future of Work Employment and Social Protection, 17–18 January, Lyons, France.

Rudolph, H. and E. Schröder (1997) 'Arbeitnehmerüberlassung: Trends und Einsatzlogik', *Mitteilungen aus der Arbeitsmarkt- und Berufsforschung*, 102–27.

Sarkar, M., B. Butler and C. Steinfeld (1995) 'Intermediaries and cybermediaries: a continuing role for mediating players in the electronic marketplace', *Journal of Computer-Mediated Communication*, special issue on electronic commerce, 1.

Schmid, G. and D. Storrie (2001) 'Employment Relationships in the New Economy', in L.-H. Röller and C. Wey (eds), *Die Soziale Marktwirtschaft in der neuen Weltwirtschaft*, Yearbook of the Social Science Research Berlin (WZB) Centre, Berlin: Sigma.

Spence, M. (1973) 'Job Market Signalling', *Quarterly Journal of Economics*, 87, 355–74.

Storrie, D. (2002) *Temporary Agency Work in the European Union*, consolidated report, Dublin: European Foundation for the Improvement of Working Life and Living Conditions.

# Index